D1501685

Petrine Ministry and the Unity of the Church
"Toward a Patient and Fraternal Dialogue"

*A Symposium Celebrating the 100th Anniversary
of the Foundation of the Society of the Atonement*

Rome, December 4–6, 1997

James F. Puglisi, Editor

A Michael Glazier Book
THE LITURGICAL PRESS
Collegeville, Minnesota

A Michael Glazier Book published by The Liturgical Press

Cover design by David Manahan, O.S.B.

1   2   3   4   5   6   7   8

Library of Congress Cataloging-in-Publication Data

Petrine ministry and the unity of the Church : toward a patient and fraternal
    dialogue : a symposium celebrating the 100th anniversary of the foundation of
    the Society of the Atonement, Rome, December 4–6, 1997 / James F. Puglisi,
    editor.
        p.   cm.
    "A Michael Glazier book."
    Includes bibliographical references and index.
    ISBN 0-8146-5936-5 (alk. paper)
    1. Papacy and Christian union–Congresses.   2. Popes–Primacy-
-Congresses.   3. Petrine office–Congresses.   I. Puglisi, J. F.
BX9.5.P29P48   1999
262'.13–dc21   98-33867
                                                                CIP

Contents

Contributors

Bishop Pierre Duprey, M. AFR., secretary, Pontifical Council for Promoting Christian Unity

Prof. Dr. Erich Geldbach, professor of Theology, Evangelical Theological Faculty of the Ruhr University, Bochum, Germany

Bishop John Hind, Anglican bishop of Europe and chairman of the Faith and Order Advisory Group

Archbishop Dr. Mesrob K. Krikorian, patriarchal delegate of the Apostolic Armenian Church for Middle Europe and Sweden

Prof. Nicolas Lossky, professor of English Intellectual History, University of Paris-Nanterre, of Church History, Orthodox Theological Institute of St. Sergius, Paris, former director of the Institut supérieur d'études œcuméniques, Catholic Institute of Paris and board member of the Faith and Order Commission of the World Council of Churches

Dr. Harding Meyer, former director of the Institute for Ecumenical Research, Strasbourg and former member of the Lutheran-Roman Catholic Study Commission

Prof. Dr. Dumitru Popescu, professor of theology, Orthodox Theological Faculty, Bucharest

Prof. James F. Puglisi, S.A., director, Centro Pro Unione, Rome, professor of ecumenical theology, Pontifical University of St. Thomas Aquinas-Angelicum, Pontifical Atheneum "Antonianum," Pontifical Atheneum San Anselmo, Rome and the Institute of Ecumenical Studies "San Bernardino," Venice

Prof. Klaus Schatz, S.J., professor of Church history, St. George School of Philosophy and Theology, Frankfurt

Prof. Jean-Marie R. Tillard, O.P., professor of theology, Dominican Faculty of Theology of Ottawa, University of Fribourg, Switzerland, member of the Joint International Commission for the Theological Dialogue between the Roman Catholic Church and the Orthodox Church, of the Anglican-Roman Catholic International Commission, of the International Commission for Dialogue between the Catholic Church and the Disciples of Christ, and vice-moderator of the Faith and Order Commission of the World Council of Churches

Dr. Lukas Vischer, former director of the Faith and Order Commission of the World Council of Churches

Prof. Miroslav Volf, professor of systematic theology, Fuller Theological Seminary, Pasadena, California; University of Tübingen, Germany, Evangelical Theological Faculty, Osijek, Croatia; and member of the International Pentecostal-Catholic Dialogue Commission

Prof. Geoffrey Wainwright, Cushman Professor of Christian Theology, Duke University (U.S.A.), chair of the World Methodist Council's Committee on Ecumenism and Dialogue and co-chair of the Joint Commission between the Roman Catholic Church and the World Methodist Council

Metropolitan John (Zizioulas) of Pergamon, ecumenical patriarchate, professor at King's College, London, and at the Faculty of Theology, University of Thessalonica, member of the Academy of Sciences in Athens and member of the Joint International Commission for the Theological Dialogue between the Roman Catholic Church and the Orthodox Church

Introduction

Bishop Pierre Duprey, M. Afr.

In the context of the ecumenical dialogues which have taken place after the Second Vatican Council, few topics have generated discussion and reflection as that of the papacy. In the past, what has been the pattern of functioning of this service of unity? What are the foundations of its existence? What are its unrelinquishable elements which cannot change? What can be renewed in the manner in which the office is carried out? These topics and many more were examined by numerous theologians, in great part Catholic, during a meeting in 1996.

We could then ask what was the reason for convoking another symposium on THE PETRINE MINISTRY AND AUTHORITY IN THE CHURCH? The answer is to be found in the encyclical letter of John Paul the II "On Commitment to Ecumenism," *Ut unum sint*. In this letter the Bishop of Rome recognizes not only the difficulty that the Petrine office holds for many on the ecumenical journey, but he also goes further. He exhorts Church leaders and theologians "to engage [him] in a patient and fraternal dialogue" on this ministry.[1] This symposium which begins today is a first attempt to begin this dialogue in Rome with theologians from the other Christian traditions: the Oriental and Orthodox tradition, the Anglican, Lutheran, Reformed, Methodist, Baptist and Free church traditions.

After an historical overview of some of the critical issues involved in the Petrine ministry, its foundation and its mode of functioning, our

---

[1] Cf. John Paul II, *Ut unum sint. That They May Be One: On Commitment to Ecumenism* (Washington, D.C.: United States Catholic Conference, 1995) §96 (hereafter cited *Ut unum sint*).

speakers will present from their ecclesial traditions some of the theological, canonical and biblical elements which they feel are important and indeed necessary for a dialogue on the Petrine ministry and the unity of the Church. The speakers are all theologians and historians who have been involved in the official dialogues of their Churches and/or with the dialogue process of the Faith and Order Commission of the World Council of Churches. They will allow us to profit from their knowledge of the historical and theological dossiers of such issues as ministry, authority and this service of unity. Furthermore the organizers of the symposium have asked each of the speakers to faithfully represent their Church's tradition on the issues and problems involved and to speak openly and frankly to the Catholic Church "leaving useless controversies of the past behind." To conclude the three days of study and reflection, Fr. Jean-Marie-Roger Tillard has been given the difficult task of listening attentively and of bringing together the different positions, issues, and suggestions which will have been exposed. He will also attempt to suggest a way forward for this dialogue.

A word needs to be said about the places where this symposium is being held. For the first and third day we are being graciously hosted by the University of St. Thomas Aquinas, John Paul II's *alma mater*. The Angelicum, as it is commonly known here in Rome, is one of the few Roman Universities that offers a specialization in ecumenical studies. For this reason this symposium feels "at home" in this ecumenical context of the Angelicum.

The Pontifical Oriental Institute will host us on Friday, the day dedicated to reflections from the Oriental and Orthodox churches. This setting is quite natural since the Oriental Institute has a long tradition of preparing many Westerners, pastors, theologians, historians, liturgists, and canonists in the oriental traditions.

Last but not least, the occasion of this symposium marks the beginning of the centenary celebrations of the foundation of the Franciscan Friars and Sisters of the Atonement. These two congregations were founded by Fr. Paul Wattson and Mother Lurana White in 1898 within the Episcopal Church of the United States. Their purpose is to work and pray for the unity of the Church of Christ.

The anniversary celebration of the religious family of the Atonement encourages me to pose a question to you.

Before beginning the symposium, I ask us all to renew our gratitude before the Lord for so many witnesses that have courageously taken up the long road of the search for the unity of christians; who have put themselves in a position of listening to the Spirit of the Lord who teaches us how to read the "signs of the times"; who have tirelessly worked so that the very noble aim[2] of their unity might grow on the path towards full communion; who have contributed to putting the accent "on love as the sole and unquestionable criterion" not to be neglected.[3]

I wish the criterion of love be present during these days in the awareness that it must guide, sustain and nourish the theological dialogue and the search for truth to lead the problems that we have inherited from the past to their just proportions and to flood the path to unity with never fading light.[4]

---

[2] Cf. *Ut unum sint*, 3.

[3] I refer to the conference of Metropolitan Damaskinos Papandreou given at Rome, November 5, 1997, on the occasion of the presentation of the book of Valeria Martano, [*Athenagoras, il Patriarca (1886–1972). Un cristiano fra crisi della coabitazione e utopia ecumenica*, Testi e ricerche di scienze religiose, nuova serie 17 (Bologna: Il Mulino, 1996)] which called to mind this "criterion" of Patriarch Athenagoras.

[4] *Ibid.*

1

Historical Considerations Concerning the Problem of the Primacy

Klaus Schatz, S.J.

Isti (sc. Petrus et Paulus) sunt qui te (Roma) ad hanc gloriam provexerunt, ut gens sancta, populus electus, civitas sacerdotalis et regia, per sacram beati Petri sedem caput orbis effecta, latius praesideres religione divina quam dominatione terrena.[1]

In these words of Leo the Great for the Feast of Peter and Paul in 441, there seems to be an inextricable confusion of apostolic Rome and imperial Rome. Rome even becomes the new *populus electus*, almost the Israel of the new covenant. It is true that, on this and other occasions, Leo stresses the radical difference in the foundation and the very nature of this prerogative: political Rome being founded on fratricide, that is, on violence and murder, whereas Christian Rome is founded on the martyrdom of the new couple of founders, Peter and Paul, and so is opposed to imperial Rome as the *civitas Dei* of Augustine to the *civitas terrena*. However, it cannot be denied that here Christian Rome is not only an antithesis, but also completes and perfects imperial Rome, while it is itself transformed by the latter with its mentality and historic heritage. Peter as prince of the apostles is sent to Rome "ut lux veritatis quae in omnium gentium revelabatur salutem, efficacius se ab ipso capite per totum mundi corpus effunderet."[2] Peter as *head* of the college of apostles is united to Rome as *caput mundi*, Christian universalism to Roman universalism. What is reflected here is the historical process of the primacy

[1] Leo the Great (PL 54, 422D–423A).
[2] *Ibid.*, 424A.

in the fourth and fifth centuries: Rome as place of the witness brought by the privileged apostolic tradition is transformed into Rome *caput mundi,* handing on to the world its laws (Peter as the new Moses, as *legislator* of the new covenant).[3] Few texts bring into such clear relief as that quoted above the historical reality and the historical problems of the primacy: on the one hand, its claim to represent and guard a unity and universality that are not political, that are of another nature; on the other hand, its involvement in the concrete human history of the struggles for power.

The historical problem of the primacy consists in the constant amalgamation—from the beginning and throughout all its further development—of these two factors that can never be clearly separated: concern for Christian unity and, at the same time, a conception of this unity in contingent forms of cultural unity, of better self-defense against ideologies or political systems, and even an expression of the primacy in political or quasi-political forms. And these factors cannot be distributed between two different periods—as has been several times attempted, beginning with Febronius and Döllinger: a first period of healthy, organic development, when the Bishop of Rome exercises his function of *centrum unitatis* in a subsidiary fashion; and a second period of cancerous, metastatic growth, the original sin of the primacy being situated in the Pseudo-Isidorian falsifications of the eighth century, in the "Gregorian turning-point" of the eleventh century, or already in the fourth and fifth centuries, when the Roman nobility became Christianized and juridical concepts altered the original concept of Petrine *parádosis.* It must rather be said that the problem of *continuity* or *rupture* arises whenever the primacy, in response to new historical challenges, takes on a new historical form. As a general rule we can say that a right or a new idea is never invented without roots in the earlier tradition. At least the thought processes, the terms and concepts, the images are old; but in a new situation and in the context of a specific challenge, they are brought together into a new whole, in an overall image and a reality of the primacy that are a break with the past. This can be shown, for instance, in what was certainly the most incisive "revolution" in the history of the primacy, in the "reform" or "Gregorian turning-point" of the eleventh century.[4] The

---

[3] Cf. C. Pietri, *Roma christiana. Recherches sur l'église de Rome, son organisation, sa politique, son idéologie de Miltiade à Sixte III (311–440)* 2 vols. Bibliothèque des Écoles Françaises d'Athènes et de Rome, 1ˢᵗ series, 224–25 (Paris: Boccard, 1976).

[4] Cf. Y. Congar, "Der Platz des Papsttums in der Kirchenfrömmigkeit der Reformer des 11. Jahrhunderts," in J. Daniélou and H. Vorgrimler, eds., *Sentire ecclesiam.* Festschrift for Hugo Rahner (Freiburg: Herder, 1961) 196–217; idem., *Die Lehre von der Kirche von*

individual elements are traditional: Rome as *caput, fons, mater omnium ec-clesiarum*, as having the *sollicitudo omnium ecclesiarum*.

What, instead, is new is the gathering up, the collecting of all these individual elements into a coherent synthesis, in which Rome is no longer only the center but the source of unity, the head on which depends the health of the whole body. Each time a new historical reality is created, a form of primacy which did not previously exist, but which gives tradition as its reference, although in a form that is critically open to question (as, for instance, in the case of the arguments put forward in Vatican I in favor of papal infallibility) but which, in spite of the doubtful value of the individual arguments, is not without any foundation, because its fundamental line can be traced back almost to the beginning. This is the case, for instance, for papal infallibility: the idea developed slowly, but "the beginnings disappear"; it is not possible to fix a precise historical situation, a precise century in which it appears.[5] We find its roots in the first millennium: the privileged tradition of the Roman Church, founded on the twofold apostolicity of Peter and Paul, testified already by Irenaeus of Lyons;[6] then, from the fifth century, we find the idea, professed at times also by Eastern authors, that "the Roman Church has never been in error, nor can be in error, in the faith." This idea is certainly not identical with the dogma of Vatican I, both because it is directed more to the Roman tradition as such, and because it is more global and less focused on individual new decisions as such and on the person of the Pontiff. Even Gregory VII, in his *Dictatus papae*, does not go beyond this old idea.[7] From the twelfth century, we have in the West the formula that it is for the pope to decide in matters of faith—stressing in this way the active aspect of new decision and not only preservation of the faith, but leaving still in obscurity the relation between pope and *consensus ecclesiae*.

Augustinus bis zum Abendländischen Schisma, Handbuch der Dogmengeschichte. Christologie, Soteriologie (Freiburg: Herder, 1971) 53–68.

[5] Cf. K. Schatz, *Papal Primacy: From Its Origins to the Present*, trans. from German [*Der Päpstliche Primat: Seine Geschichte von den Ursprungen bis zur Gegenwart*] by J. A. Otto and L. M. Maloney (Collegeville: The Liturgical Press, 1996) 117–23.

[6] *Adversus haereses* III/3, 1–2.

[7] No. 22: *Quod Romana ecclesia nunquam erravit, nec in perpetuum, Scriptura testante, errabit* (cf. no. 26). Cf. L.F.J. Meulenberg, *Der Primat der römischen Kirche im Denken und Handeln Gregors VII* (s'Gravenhage: Staatsdrukkerijen Uitgeverijbedrif, 1965) 38–48; idem., "Une question toujours ouverte: Grégoire VII et l'infaillibilité du Pape," in H. Mordek, ed., *Aus Kirche und Reich. Studien zu Theologie, Politik und Recht im Mittelalter*. Festschrift for Friedrich Kempf (Sigmaringen: J. Thorbecke, 1983) 159–71.

It is only from the fifteenth century, after the traumatic experience of the separation between the pope and the Council of Basel, that infallibility was placed decidedly in the pope by the anti-conciliarist authors; and this was done more unconditionally only in the Counter-Reformation. Finally, only after the French Revolution do many people begin to think of infallibility almost as the kernel and inner essence of the primacy. The *regimen supremum* is no longer the main question as in the *societas christiana* (and therefore the *plenitudo potestatis*) but rather, *certitudo* and therefore infallibility.[8]

One more ancient example of this link between tradition and a new historical challenge: the Council of Sardica in 342 decides that a bishop deposed by the provincial synod can apply to the see of Rome for revision of the sentence (not as an appeal in the strict sense!), initiating in this way a new synodal procedure.[9] The problem is new. The deep divisions in the episcopate as the Arian crisis begins create a situation with which the regional synods are no longer capable of dealing: a bishop deposed by a synod and defended by another bishop. The right conferred on the see of Rome was new, and no one even claimed that it was long-established. But neither was it merely a practical and pragmatic measure. The reason why Rome has to exercise this function is: *Petri memoriam honoremus*. In other words: it is the authority, not yet juridical, but religious, of the Roman Church, as Church of Peter and Paul, that qualifies it to exercise a juridical function that has become necessary in a new historical situation.

We can identify five of these new steps in the development of the primacy; each time traditional elements are gathered into a new synthesis, determined by a new historical challenge. Before the fourth century we cannot speak of a primacy of the Roman Church in juridical terms. But this does not mean that there did not exist any prerogative whatever of Rome. On the contrary, we can speak, right from the beginning, of a pre-juridical authority of a religious nature, a spiritual nimbus of the Roman Church, due to its twofold apostolicity. From the end of the second century, this qualifies the Roman *parádosis* with a normative character that is not absolute or sufficient in itself: a greater *auctoritas*, but not *potestas*. This authority, that is more religious, pre-juridical, still applies

---

[8] K. Schatz, *Vaticanum I 1869–1870*, vol. 1: *Vor der Eröffnung* (Paderborn/Munich/Vienna/Zurich: Ferdinand Schöningh, 1992) 5f.

[9] C. III-V: J. D. Mansi, *Sacrorum conciliorum nova et amplissima collectio*, new ed., L. Petit and J.-B. Martin. Reprint [1ˢᵗ ed. 1759–1798] (Graz, 1960–1961) vol. 3, 7–10 (hereafter cited Mansi).

for the Church of Carthage in Augustine's day; and it is often still the role that the see of Rome has in relation to the Churches of the East in the first millennium, in the context of the pentarchy of the five patriarchs—although there is no unambiguous evidence of this. This does not mean, however, that it is a mere symbol of no practical importance. As a religious authority it is almost a super-juridical reference, which is invoked as refuge in emergency situations, when the normal juridical structures can no longer be of any help, as, for instance, after the so-called "Latrocinium" or "gangster synod" in Ephesus in 449 by Flavian of Constantinople, Eusebius of Dorylaeum, and Theodoret of Cyrus.[10]

1. The first new epoch-making step is therefore, in the fourth and fifth centuries, the process already mentioned, beginning with Damasus (366–384) and culminating with Leo the Great (440-461): the translation in *juridical terms* of the apostolic *parádosis* as ultimate reference for the *communio* of the Church. From the Church qualified by the martyrdom and tomb of the two *coryphei*, Peter and Paul, the emphasis is transferred to the Bishop of Rome as "vicar" (not yet successor) of Peter and heir to his prerogatives. The historical background to this "rereading" is, on the one hand, we might say, "Roman inculturation," that is, the Christian transformation of the city and of its *forma mentis*; on the other hand, the grave trinitarian and christological crises in the Church, that threaten her unity and that the normal structures, even the synods, are no-longer capable of dealing with by themselves—we need only think of Seleucia/Rimini and Ephesus II. This new form of primacy—it is important to bear in mind—is only partially accepted in the East, by certain authors and at certain moments, especially of crisis, but not in general. More than ever, the further steps will be only Western.

2. The second step is the rank that Rome acquires in the conversion of the Germanic peoples in the seventh and eighth centuries; that is, Rome as *norm and guarantee of "correct" religious practice,* not only in matters of faith, but also in liturgy and law. The historical background is, on the one hand, Rome's new function for the unity and the common consciousness of the new peoples, especially for the Carolingian Empire; on the other hand, an "archaic" form of religiosity: to make contact with the divinity and take possession of the divine force, you have to practice

[10] See E. Schwartz et al, eds., *Acta Conciliorum Oecumenicorum* (1941ff) II.II.1 (II) 77–81; Theodoret of Cyrus, *Lettres,* Sources Chrétiennes 3 (Paris: Cerf, 1955) 56–58. Cf. S.O. Horn, *Petrou Kathedra. Der Bischof von Rom und die Synoden von Ephesus (449) und Chalcedon (451),* Konfessionskundliche und Kontroverstheologische Studien 45 (Paderborn: Bonifatius-Druckerei, 1982) 76–99.

"correct" rites, pronounce "correct" words; a wrong word, a rite in the wrong place or time, can ruin everything.[11] Rome, personified in St. Peter, the powerful holder of the keys of heaven, offers this guarantee more than anyone else.[12] So King Oswiu of Northumbria decides at Whitby in 664 to follow the Roman date of Easter; he is afraid that, otherwise, arriving one day at heaven's gate, he will find no one to open it for him because he has incurred the wrath of Peter.[13]

3. The third epoch is from the eleventh to the thirteenth century, beginning with the Gregorian reform and culminating with the popes of the thirteenth century from Innocent III to Boniface VIII. From now on it is Rome *as head of the Church* upon whom the whole life of the body depends and all its functions; and the pope is "Vicar of Christ" (no longer of Peter).[14] The historical background is the functional link of the papacy in a West that is entering upon a new phase of its history. After the "archaic" period of undifferentiated unity of kingdom and priesthood in the three centuries between the kingly anointing of Pippin (751) and the Synod of Sutri (1046)—a period characterized, moreover, by the scarcity of super-regional contacts—the West is now entering a period of increased super-local contacts and, at the same time, of institutional differentiation. Many of these developments—from the struggle for the *libertas Ecclesiae* in the Gregorian period to the new religious orders no

---

[11] P.E. Schramm, "Karl der Große. Denkart und Grundauffassungen—die von ihm bewirkte Correctio," *Historische Zeitschrift* 198 (1964) 306–45; idem., *Kaiser, Könige und Päpste. Beiträge zur allgemeinen Geschichte*, vol. I, *Von der Spätantike bis zum Tode Karls des Großen* (Stuttgart: Hiersemann, 1968) 302–41.

[12] R. Schieffer, "'Redeamus ad fontem', Rom als Ort authentischer Überlieferung im frühen Mittelalter," in A. Angenendt and R. Schieffer, *Roma–Caput et Fons. Zwei Vorträge über das päpstliche Rom zwischen Altertum und Mittelalter*, Gerda Henkel Vorlesung (Opladen: Westdeutscher Verlag, 1989) 45–70; K. Schatz, "Königliche Kirchenregierung und römische Petrusüberlieferung im Kreise Karls des Großen," in R. Berndt, ed., *Das Frankfurter Konzil von 794–Kristallisationspunkt karolingischer Kultur*, vol. 1: *Politik und Kirche*, Quellen unde Abhanlungen zur mittelrheinischen Kirchengeschichte 80/1 (Mainz: Selbstverlag der Gesellschaft für Mittelrheinische Kirchengeschichte, 1997) 357–71.

[13] Bede [the Venerable], *The Ecclesiastical History of the English People*, ed. J. McClure and R. Collins (Oxford/New York: Oxford University Press, 1997) 3.25. A similar text of Alcuin from 798, recommends Roman baptismal practice, "ut, unde catholicae fidei initia accipimus, inde exemplaria salutis nostrae semper habeamus; ne membra a capite separentur suo; ne claviger regni caelestis abiciat quos a suis deviasse intelligit doctrinis": in *Monumenta Germaniae Historica*, Ep. IV, No. 137, p. 215, r. 10–15.

[14] K. Schatz, "Papsttum und partikularkirchliche Gewalt bei Innocenz III (1198–1216)," *Archivum Historiae Pontificiae* 8 (1970) 61–111; K. Pennington, *Pope and Bishops: The Papal Monarchy in the 12th and 13th Centuries*, The Middle Ages (Philadelphia: University of Pennsylvania Press, 1984).

longer held to the *stabilitas loci*, and even to the universities–would not even be comprehensible without the decisive role of the primacy. On the other hand, this period marks also the definitive separation from the Oriental Church.

4. The fourth step is taken against the background of the ecclesiastical splits and divisions from the fourteenth to the sixteenth century; both those that were finally overcome, like the great papal schism of 1378 to 1417, and the later one between the papacy and the Council of Basel (1439–1449); and the schism that remained from the Reformation of the sixteenth century. The pope is now the *point of confessional identity*[15] or the criterion of the true Church. Understandably, the magisterium and infallibility now take on an importance they did not have as yet in the thirteenth century when it was still possible to find, in the same authors, a decisive affirmation of the *plenitudo potestatis*, together with a rudimentary concept of the papal magisterium or an affirmation of the council as ultimate reference in matters of faith.

5. The fifth step (so far the last, but who knows?) supposes, as historical background, the French Revolution, Western liberalism, the separation of State and Church and the dissolution of the *societas christiana*, culminating in the definitions of Vatican I. There is a stronger affirmation of the aspect of primacy as point of identity; not, however, only as center and reference point for the Catholic world against a Protestant world, but as the *"stable rock" of the Church against the tempest of the times*.[16] Understandably, the emphasis is moved still further in the direction of the magisterium, of the security that the primacy is called to communicate in a world where nothing is secure. To this are added the historical possibilities the papacy comes to enjoy through modern means of transport and communication; already in the time of Pius IX, and more still, with the "travelling papacy" of Paul VI and John Paul II. This brings about, among other things, a "personalization" of the primacy: more and more the person of the pope takes the place that was formerly

---

[15] U. Horst, *Papst–Konzil–Unfehlbarkeit. Die Ekklesiologie der Summenkommentare von Cajetan bis Billuart*, Walberger Studeien. Theologische Reihe 10 (Mainz: Matthias-Grünewald-Verlag, 1978); idem., *Unfehlbarkeit und Geschichte. Studien zur Unfehlbarkeitsdiskussion von Melchior Cano bis zum 1. Vatikanischen Konzil*, Walberger Studeien. Theologische Reihe 12 (Mainz: Matthias-Grünewald-Verlag, 1982).

[16] Y. Congar, "L'ecclésiologie de la Révolution française au concile du Vatican sous le signe de l'affirmation de l'autorité," in R. Aubert et alii. *L'ecclésiologie au XIX siècle,* [Unam Sanctam] 34 (Paris: Cerf, 1960) 77–114; H.J. Pottmeyer, *Unfehlbarkeit und Souveränität. Die päpstliche Unfehlbarkeit im System der ultramontanen Ekklesiologie des 19. Jahrhunderts*, Tübinger theologische Studien 5 (Mainz: Matthias-Grünewald-Verlag, 1975).

occupied as object of veneration by the tombs of the apostles and the martyrs.

As I have said, for all these new developments the question arises of continuity or rupture, and therefore of legitimacy. The new steps must become legitimate through a substantial continuity, a substantial fidelity to tradition. Furthermore, I would say that there are two positions that are not possible, because both are an immunization against history and cannot advance the ecumenical dialogue. One would be a traditionalism that would deny a priori the legitimacy of the new steps and for which, if a primacy was ever recognized, it would have to be reduced to the dimensions of the first three centuries. The other would be the "Catholic" danger, that is, the equally aprioristic defense of the historical developments as being brought about under the guidance of the Holy Spirit. We have to accept the possibility of developments that are against the Gospel, if not in the judgement of a whole era, which as a whole is always very vast, ambiguous, and heterogeneous, at least as regards particular aspects.

I would say now that this dialogue about the historical processes that, throughout history, have created the primacy in the Catholic sense, cannot take place only in systematic fashion by comparing each time the evidence from before and from after the process. To speak about the primacy, we have to enter into the history that created or at least developed it. There is now a certain consensus that the "divine right" of the primacy and its "institution by Jesus Christ" cannot be understood statically and unhistorically. To grasp the implications of this "institution," that is, of the Petrine passages in the New Testament, we need the experiences from history and we have to wait until the fourth century for these to appear with sufficient clarity. So, for any judgement about the primacy, we need to discuss the Christian importance of the historical challenges to which it tried to respond; we need also to speak about the value of the responses that were given from the viewpoint of the Gospel—and, of course, also about the experiences of the Churches that lived without the primacy. The fundamental question as to how the unity of the Church can be maintained as visible, that is, as a unity of faith and sacraments in mutual recognition, cannot be solved a priori, without recourse to the experiences of the actual history. The judgement about the primacy is therefore intimately bound up with a theological concept of the history of the Church. This does not, of course, mean imposing a priori categories of "salvation history" on a reality that is always multiform, but rather, taking the sources as basis and trying to understand them in the context of their time, and then interpreting them in the light of the Gospel, but of the Gospel situated in the context of the time.

With this in view, there are some more remarks to make:

1. It is certainly clear that the primacy did not develop only as a result of theological factors and ecclesiastical necessities, but also *through political factors and interests,* these moreover being closely inter-related in pre-modern times. More than political factors in the strict sense, which can usually change in a short space of time, it was often a matter of long-lasting models of political thought. We need only think of the influence of reflection about the best form of state constitution on ecclesiological thinking from the thirteenth to the nineteenth century: e.g., the idea of *princeps legibus solutus* coming from Roman law and its repercussion in the concept of the pope as being above positive law.[17] The conciliarists, on the contrary, take as reference corporativist concepts of society, or at least, the *regimen mistum* as the best constitution according to Aristotle. However, papal authors of the fifteenth century, starting with Torquemada, also use the argument of monarchy as the best form of government;[18] so does Bellarmine, for whom it goes without saying that Christ must have given his Church the constitution that is naturally the best.[19] On the contrary, it is a Gallican like Tournely who affirms: for the State the absolute monarchy may be the best form of government, but a different law is right for the Church.[20] Paradoxically, after the French Revolution, Gallicans and Ultramontanes move in opposite directions. In the "Civil Constitution" of the Revolution we have the consequent attempt to introduce democratic principles into the Church, while the Ultramontanism that will triumph in Vatican I stresses contrast with the political trends of civil society: the dogma of infallibility even as antithesis and "counter-dogma" against the principles of 1789. These factors certainly contribute at least to the relativising of particular forms of primacy. This is true also for all the functions closely linked to the role of Rome as factor of unity in Western civilization from the time of

---

[17] L. Buisson, *Potestas und Caritas. Die päpstliche Gewalt im Spätmittelalter,* Forschungen zur kirchlichen Rechtsgeschichte und zum Kirchenrecht 2 (Cologne: Böhlau, 1958) 82–86; W. Ullmann, *Principles of Government and Politics in the Middle Ages* (London: Methuen, 1961); M. Wilks, *The Problem of Sovereignty in the Later Middle Ages. The Papal Monarchy with Augustinus Triumphus and the Publicists,* Cambridge Studies in Medieval Life and Thought. New Series 9 (Cambridge: Cambridge University Press, 1963).

[18] J.A. Black, "Politische Grundgedanken des Konziliarismus und Papalismus zwischen 1430 und 1450," in R. Bäumer, ed., *Die Entwicklung des Konziliarismus: Werden und Nachwirken der konziliaren Idee,* Wege der Forschung 279 (Darmstadt: Wissenschaftliche Buchgesellschaft, 1976) 295–328.

[19] *De Summo Pontifice* lib. I, c. 3.

[20] H. Tournely, *Praelectiones theologicae de Ecclesia Christi,* vol. I (Paris: R. Mazieres, 1749) q.3, a.6. "Quale sit a Christo institutum regimen Ecclesiae," 535–72.

Charlemagne. If these remarks are necessary, we also need to consider two aspects of these "political factors":

a) Certain political factors consist rather in the collapse of earlier political supports; for example, the fall of the empire in the West during the barbarian invasions, and the secularization of the State after the French Revolution. These developments show more clearly the need for a *centrum unitatis* in the Church, an authentically ecclesiastical need that was formerly obscured.

b) On the other hand, we have to ask ourselves which political factors were an obstacle for the function and importance of the primacy. Could we not say, for instance, that, already in the first millennium, the role of the emperor and the empire made the primacy superfluous, at least in normal times: because Eastern Christianity lived more by the unity between Church and empire, because the emperor could decide differences between the patriarchs, the need for an *ecclesiastical centrum unitatis* was not felt so urgently? So it seems to me that the crucial and exceptional moments when this unity was broken, as for instance, in the Iconoclastic conflict of the eighth century, are especially important in trying to define the common tradition. The formula that is often used: "return to the unity that prevailed in the first millennium before the separation," is historically vague and ambiguous. Especially as regards the role of Rome in the pentarchy (first in a series of equals or a special service of unity?), interpretations differ greatly, according to periods and persons, not only between Rome and the Orient, but also between Oriental authors. What we need to ask is rather: how and with what criteria did the Orient find unity within itself and with the West in moments of crisis, for example, in the Nicene II of 787?[21]

2. An aspect that is often forgotten: the effective exercise of the primacy is closely dependent on the *historical possibilities of communication:* travel, exchange of letters, cultural interchanges. Where there is little communication, as between Western countries after the barbarian invasion, primacy remains a dead letter. The growth of the function of primacy in the West from the eleventh century is closely related to the

---

[21] An important testimony is that of Mansi 13, 208 ff. Cf. V. Peri, "La synergie entre le Pape et le Concile œcuménique. Note d'histoire sur l'ecclésiologie traditionnelle de l'Église indivise," *Irénikon* 56, 2 (1983) 163–93. Other parallel texts: Mansi 12, 1134; PG 100, 597 A/B. We can recall Teodoro d'Abu Qurra (around 800) as example of an author for whom the pope becomes the decisive authority, since the emperor is not important: H.J. Sieben, *Die Konzilsidee der Alten Kirche*, Konziliengeschichte Reihe B, Untersuchungen (Paderborn: Schöningh, 1979) 169–91, esp. 177.

general phenomenon of the increase at this time of communication and supra-local contacts, which was consciously fostered by the papacy through pilgrimages, councils, and new religious orders. Vice-versa, we can ask if some Churches outside the Roman Empire became separate, not for theological reasons, not by decision, but simply for lack of contact. There were models of unity in the first millennium that suppose very sporadic communication and for particular countries (Gallia, Spain) an isolation such that, for instance, an event of primary historical importance like the conversion of King Reccared of the Wisigoths from Arianism to Catholicism in 587 became known in Rome only four years later. These models, therefore, make no sense for our time. From this point of view also a "return to the unity of the first millennium" is a utopian dream, although some elements and structures of this unity (e.g., the polycentrism of the pentarchy) are still of importance today.

3. Closely related to the problem of communications is the *distinction between claim and reality* (whether the claim is made by Rome or by official recognition in the periphery). Officially recognizing the see of Rome as the norm not only for faith, but also for rites and customs, can go together with persistently going one's own way when Roman decisions are not agreeable. This applies, for instance, for the Carolingian period, e.g. in the question of the Filioque and in the non-recognition of Nicene I: Only printing in the sixteenth century and, still more, modern communications in the nineteenth and twentieth centuries, made possible in practice a centralism that formerly existed only in theory.

4. A history of the primacy would be incomplete and a mere "history of the victors" if it abstracted from *the resistance and the obstacles* that the increasing affirmation of the primacy met with throughout its history. The resistance runs like a guiding thread through the history, from the controversy over the date of Easter and over the baptism of heretics to the opposition in Vatican I, and, still to modern contestation of Roman centralism. We have to say, moreover, that these episcopalist, conciliarist, and Gallican trends also belong to Catholic tradition. It is true that they are not systematically structured before the late Middle Ages, but they have paleochristian roots. Above all, the concrete development of the primacy itself points to two structural limitations that were interior moments without which the primacy could not have developed.

a) The primacy developed within a *polycentrism*, in which not all the episcopal Churches (apart from Rome) were on the same level. The *Sedes apostolicae* enjoyed a special authority. The Church of Rome was only the most outstanding example of a general principle: that the

Churches historically closer to the apostles were on a higher level than the others. This concept became, from the third century, that of the (three) principal Churches (later considered by Rome to be the three *Sedes Petrinae*): Rome, Alexandria, Antioch; and from Chalcedon, that of the patriarchal pentarchy.[22] It seems to me that the concept according to which all the Churches outside Rome are on the same level and only Rome enjoys a primacy of divine right, is clearly expressed for the first time in the *Libri Carolini* about 791.[23]

From Pseudo-Isidore the prevailing theory in the West is that, for other Churches, a special rank can only be founded on a concession from the Church of Rome, which calls other Churches in *partem sollicitudinis*, while always retaining the *plenitudo potestatis*.[24] This can be found also in the formula for union of Lyon II;[25] but Florence marks the return to the polycentric model of the pentarchy, although in a somewhat artificial confrontation with the monarchical primacy.[26] Theologically the question of polycentrism remains open even after Vatican II. On the one hand, it is clear that the special position of the "Apostolic Churches," and more still of the five patriarchs (considered at times as the true "successors of the Apostles"[27] or as the "five senses of the body of the Church")[28] is based on conceptions that are historically outdated. But, on the other hand, should we not affirm the ecclesiological rank (not merely the administrative rank as a purely practical necessity) of inter-

---

[22] Cf. F. R. Gahbauer, *Die Pentarchietheorie. Untersuchung zu einem Modell der Kirchenleitung von den Anfängen bis zur Gegenwart*, Frankfurter theologische Studien 42 (Frankfurt: Knecht, 1993).

[23] *Libri Carolini* III.11: *Monumenta Germaniae Historica* Concilia Suppl. 123.

[24] P. Hinschius, ed., *Decretales Pseudo-Isidorianae et capitula Angilramni* (Leipzig: Bernhardi Tauchnitz, 1863) 712. Then in a Salzburg falsification, about 970/980: *Monumenta Germaniae Historica Scriptores* VII.404.

[25] In the confession of the Greek Emperor Michael Palaeologus: ". . . Ad hanc (sc. Romanam ecclesiam) sic potestatis plenitudo consistit, quod ecclesias ceteras ad sollicitudinis partem admittit; quarum multas et patriarchales praecipue diversis privilegiis eadem Romana ecclesia honoravit . . ." in H. Denzinger and A. Schönmetzer, eds., *Enchiridion Symbolorum. Definitionum et declarationum de rebus et fidei et morum*, 36th ed. (Freiburg/Rome/Barcelona: Herder, 1976) no. 861, hereafter cited *DS* followed by number of paragraph.

[26] In the decree of union "Laetentur coeli": the order of the five patriarchs is recognized and their privileges and rights are safeguarded, without being derived from the *plenitudo potestatis* of the Roman Church (*DS* 1308).

[27] Cf. Teodoro Studita (PG 99, 1417).

[28] Anastasio the Librarian (Mansi 16,7). At the same time, the imperial commissar Baanes applies Matt 16:18 to the five patriarchs, who can never be in error, all at the same time, in matters of faith (Mansi 16, 140).

mediate structures between Rome and the individual episcopal Churches, in consideration of the fact that without these structures the primacy could not have developed?

b) The relation between *pope and council* is at times one of conflict. Historically, we have, on the one hand, to recognize, already in the first millennium, the important role played by Rome for a clear line of continuity and legitimacy of the councils: councils once recognized will be defended at all costs, councils condemned by Rome cannot be given authority. But this is only one side of the medal; solving these conflicts by a total and absolute subordination of the council to the pope means not taking seriously enough the experience of history. Above all, the history of the primacy cannot overlook the fact that the very unity of the primatial summit was once restored, not through the primacy itself, but by a council and through the theory that (at least in such an emergency situation) the council is above the papacy. This was the case of the papal schism that was terminated by the Council of Costanza and through the decree *Haec Sancta* of 1415. I cannot here go into the details of this complicated affair. To be sure, the discussions about the content and value of this decree that were provoked and stimulated by Vatican II have shown with certainty that *Haec Sancta* was not and did not intend to be a dogmatic definition. But this does not mean that the decree has no significance at all for the Church of the future. I think Brian Tierney is right in affirming that we cannot deny all value to this decree, since in the situation of the time it was the only means of safeguarding the unity of the Church and the continuation of the papacy.[29] To consider illegitimate *Haec Sancta* and the procedure of the Fathers of Costanza is to "saw off one's own branch," by contesting the very means without which the unity of the primatial summit could not be restored. So we can say that this procedure keeps its character of "model" for cases of extreme emergency, such as schism and a heretical pope: in these cases a council, without prior papal authorization, could consider itself to be a "supra-juridical" authority, just as the Bishop of Rome was in certain cases arising in the fourth and fifth centuries.

[29] B. Tierney, "Hermeneutics and History. The Problem of *Haec Sancta*," in idem., *Church Law and Constitutional Thought in the Middle Ages*, Collected Studies Series 90 (London: Variorum Reprints, 1979) 354–70, here 362.

2

"Suprema auctoritas ideo ab omne errore immunis": The Lutheran Approach to Primacy

Harding Meyer

I. A short historical view on the Lutheran understanding and critique of papal primacy

It is fairly well known that the Lutheran Reformation did not set out with a critique of the papacy of its time but rather with the concern for the "pure" preaching and teaching of the Gospel of Christ. It is also well known that soon—in view of the impending and then definitive formal rejection of the Reformation concerns by the Roman hierarchy (Bull threatening excommunication, June 1522)—the pope and the Roman doctrine of the papacy were included in Luther's critique. It is, finally, well known that Luther's critique—first hesitatingly and hypothetically[1]

---

[1] We are rather well informed on how the idea that the pope is the "Antichrist" successively took shape in Luther's mind (see e.g., the studies of E. Bizer, *Luther und der Papst*, Theologische Existenz heute. Neue Folge 69 (München: Kaiser, 1958); R. Bäumer, *Martin Luther und der Papst*, 2nd ed., Katholisches Leben und Kämpfen im Zeitalter der Glaubensspaltung 30 (München: Aschendorff, 1971); S. H. Hendrix, *Luther and the Papacy. Stages in a Reformation Conflict* (Philadelphia: Fortress Press, 1981). What is important is that in the beginning this idea is only a question, a suspicion, a concern, a hypothesis which always refers to 2 Thess 2:4 (and to Dan 11:36). This is evident from Luther's private letters from December 1518 to February 1520, from his "Resolutiones" (September 1519) following the Leipzig dispute, from his writing against Eck, also of September 1519, or from his "Operationes in Psalmos" (1519/20) where he takes up the question of "Antichrist." His argument is always: *If* the pope considers himself to be above the word of God, *then* he carries—according to 2 Thess 2:4—the marks of the "Antichrist." For more

but then, since the middle of 1520, very outspokenly—culminated in the verdict that the pope was the "Antichrist," a radically polemical view which he maintained until the end of his life.

This "Antichrist" verdict was not simply a curse word, an expression of a "profound hate against the pope," as it is has been said occasionally. In the last analysis this verdict was the biblical abbreviation or cipher for both a fundamental and a precise theological critique of the papacy of that time. It aimed at three things:[2]

1. The pope "claims for himself the exclusive right to interpret the Scriptures." He has been made in Rome "judge over the Scriptures" who "does not let himself be judged by the Scriptures" since he thinks that "he cannot err."
2. The pope establishes "new articles of faith" claiming that it is "necessary for salvation to accept them and to place our trust in them."
3. The pope insists that "Christians cannot be saved without his power" and without their "being obedient to him."

The kernel, the "nucleus" of the "anti-Christian" papacy is for Luther the righteousness earned by works and the denial of the evangelical conviction "sola fide in Christum sine operibus nos pronuntiari justos et salvari."[3]

Melanchthon's view is very similar.[4] He, too, makes these three reproaches against papal primacy.

1. Its being exempt from any criticism, even from critique by the Holy Scriptures.
2. Its power to establish new doctrine and laws binding faith.
3. Its claim that obedience to it is necessary for salvation.

---

details and references see my article "Das Papsttum bei Luther und in den lutherischen Bekenntnisschriften," in W. Pannenberg, ed., *Lehrverurteilungen—kirchentrennend?* vol. 3: *Materialen zur Lehre von den Sakramenten und vom kirchlichen Amt*, Dialog der Kirchen 6 (Freiburg/Göttingen: Herder/Vandenhoeck und Ruprecht, 1990) 306–28.

[2] For details and references, see my "Das Papsttum . . ." 320f.

[3] Weimar Edition of Luther's Works: Weimarer Ausgabe, *D. Martin Luthers Werke. Kritische Gesamtausgabe* (Weimar: Hermann Böhlaus Nachfolger, 1883ff) 40/I, 357 and 355, hereafter cited *WA*.

[4] I am referring particularly to Melanchthon's "Treatise on the Power and Primacy of the Pope," in T. G. Tappert, ed., *The Book of Concord. The Confessions of the Evangelical Lutheran Church* (Philadelphia: Fortress Press, 1959) 319–35, hereafter cited *BC*.

Somewhat differently from Luther, Melanchthon sees the roots of all that in the claim, or more exactly in the exaggerated claim of papal primacy to be *iure divino*.[5]

Each of these three reproaches which, at that time, by no means were mere inventions indicate exactly what in the mind of the Reformation was "anti-Christian" about the papacy of that time. However, they also clearly indicate that these "anti-Christian" aspects do not reside in papal primacy as such but rather in the manner it is being understood and exercised at that time.

This distinction between, on the one hand, papal primacy as something given which was not the object of criticism and, on the other, the manner in which it is understood and exercised which was rejected is important and has to be kept in mind. This distinction becomes particularly apparent and operative in what one can call the "conditional recognition" of primacy which one encounters in Luther even after 1520, i.e., even after he had came to the conclusion that the pope was "Antichrist." While during the years before the mid 1520s, his equation of pope and "Antichrist" was only "conditional."[6] This "conditional equation" is now, as it were, reversed. While until summer 1520 Luther argued: If it were really true that the pope considers himself above the word of God, *then*–according to 2 Thess 2:4– he would carry the marks of "Antichrist." Now he argues if "the pope would keep the Gospel free and pure," *then* "I would let him be what he claims to be."[7]

Looking back at the Diet of Augsburg (1533) Luther can affirm what he also affirms in his *Commentary on Galatians* (1531–35):[8] "until now we always and particularly at the Diet of Augsburg humbly offered the pope and the bishops not to dissolve their canon law and their power but to willingly be ordained and governed by them if only they would not force us to accept un-Christian articles (*scilicet* of faith)."[9]

The most famous affirmation of this kind one finds in a passage of Luther's *Commentary on Galatians* which later on he repeats again.[10] "All we aim for is that the glory of God be preserved and that the

---

[5] Luther, too, speaks critically of the *iure divino* claim ("The Smalcald Articles" in *BC* 287ff).

[6] See references cited in note 1.

[7] In his letter to the preachers in Soest (October 1535) Luther writes: "Ich will noch sagen und zugeben, wil der Bapst das Evangelion frey und reine lassen gehen, wie er schuldig ist zu thun, so wil ich meiner person jn lassen sein, was er selber wil. . ." (*WA* 38, 195).

[8] *WA* 40/I, 358.

[9] *WA* 30, 195.

[10] *WA* 40/I, 357.

righteousness of faith remain pure and sound. Once this has been established, namely that God alone justifies us solely by His grace through Christ, we are willing not only to bear the pope aloft on our hands but to kiss his feet."[11]

Even in his last and sharpest writing against the papacy the title of which comes very close to a categorical rejection of the papal office as such ("Against the Papacy in Rome, instituted by the Devil," 1545), Luther nevertheless affirms that the pope might have a primacy "of honor and superiority" and "of oversight over teaching and heresy in the Church."[12]

For Luther it is true that it appears most unlikely that the pope would fulfil the requirements of the Reformation. Nevertheless, those affirmations are an important commentary which in a crucial way qualify Luther's critique. They clearly show that in the last analysis his rejection of the papal office, in spite of all its harshness, is an empirical judgement rather than a judgement in principle.[13] It says: The state of things in my time and already long since is such that I can carry only a radically negative judgement; it may be conceivable that the state of things could change so that my judgement no longer applies, but I consider this only as a merely hypothetical not as a real possibility.[14]

In Melanchthon, too, one encounters this idea of a "conditional recognition" of papal primacy. But for him the possibility of a papacy renewed in the sense of the Reformation does not appear so gloomy.

---

[11] *WA* 40/I, 181.

[12] *WA* 54, 231: ". . . das der Bapst der Oberst were, nicht allein der ehren und des fürgangs (Vorrangs) halben (welchs jm wol gegönnet werde), auch nicht allein der Superattendentz halben, das er ein Aufseher were auff die Lere und Ketzerey in den Kirchen (welches doch eim einigen Bischoff viel zu viel und unmüglich ist in aller Welt zu thun). . . ."

[13] This is also the opinion of W. Pannenberg, "Das Papsttum und die Zukuft der Ökumene. Anmerkungen aus lutherischer Sicht" in V. von Aristi et alii., eds., *Das Papstamt. Dienst oder Hindernis für die Ökumene?* (Regensburg: F. Pustet, 1985) 141 and G. Wenz, "Papsttum und kirchlicher Einheitsdienst nach Maßgabe evangelisch-lutherischer Bekenntnistradition" in Johann-Adam-Möhler-Institut, ed., *Das Papstamt. Anspruch und Widerspruch. Zum Stand des ökumenischen Dialogs über das Papstamt* (Münster: Aschendorff, 1996) 72 [=*Catholica* 50, 2 (1996)]. Cardinal J. Ratzinger holds a different view: "After the definitive rupture Luther categorically rejected the papacy . . . ," see J. Ratzinger, "Luther und die Einheit der Kirchen," *Internationale Katholische Zeitschrift* (1983) 571. The conviction that primacy and primatial church structures are in principle "opposed to the Scriptures" and "incompatible with the gospel," for example as Paolo Ricca says, is, indeed very common in Protestantism, read "Ende des Papsttums?" *Materialdienst des Konfessionskundlichen Instituts Bensheim* 30, 6 (1979) 109.

[14] *WA* 50, 270f: "Denn er [der Papst] will ungereformiert sein, wirds auch wol bleiben ewiglich."

Against Luther's critical assertions in his "Smalcald Articles," which were not only utterly pessimistic about a possible renewal of papacy but which came close to a rejection in principle,[15] Melanchthon formulated his famous reserve:

> I, PHILIP MELANCHTHON, regard the above articles as right and Christian. However, concerning the pope I hold that, if he would allow the Gospel, we, too, may concede to him that superiority over the bishops which he possesses by human right, making this concession for the sake of peace and general unity among the Christians who are now under him and who may be in the future.[16]

Martin Bucer, the Reformer of Strasbourg, should be mentioned along with Luther and Melanchthon. Like them he "does not attack the office (of the pope) itself, but rather its abuses and its bearers who are bringing discredit on the office." Bucer declares himself "ready to recognize papal primacy provided that it becomes again a ministry for the edification of the Church, exercised in episcopal collegiality and under the condition that the great principles of the Reformation be permitted—salvation by grace alone, rejection of the free will."[17]

---

[15] Although less consistently than Melanchthon, in his "Treatise on the Power and Primacy of the Pope" Luther, too, can argue that all false claims of the papacy are rooted in its *iure divino* claim. Could papal primacy give up this claim? Hypothetically Luther can say that this might happen, but immediately he returns to his pessimistic view: this "is impossible, . . . he [the pope] cannot do this." Luther even contests the "avail" and the "necessity" of such a papacy "for the unity of Christendom." He argues that it would even increase disunity. In short: "The holy Christian church can exist very well without such a head, and it would have remained much better if such a head had not been raised up . . ." (*BC* 299). Also the idea that papal primacy has been "raised up by the devil," an idea which one encounters in this context and which Luther takes up in his last writing about the papacy in *Vom Papsttum zu Rom, vom Teufel gestiftet* 1545 (*WA* 54, 206ff) comes very close to a categorical rejection of papal primacy as such.

[16] *BC* 316f. Already three years earlier Melanchthon could say in his statement to King François I in *De potestate ecclesiastica*: "Prodesset iudicio meo illa monarachia Romani Pontificis ad hoc, ut doctrinae consensus retineretur in multis nationibus. Quare facile potest constitui concordia in hoc articulo de superioritate Pontificia, si caeteris articulis conveniri potest," Ph. Melanchthon, *Opera quae supersint omnia*, Corpus Reformatorum 2, 746 August 1534. Melanchthon re-affirms this in his "Treatise on the Power and Primacy of the Pope" (1537), which is part of the Lutheran confessional writings.

[17] G. Hammann, *Entre la secte et la cité. Le projet d'Église du Réformateur Martin Bucer (1491–1551)*, Histoire et société 3 (Geneva: Labor et Fides, 1984) 292. Hammann quotes Bucer: "A nobis itaque nihil prorsus fuerit, quod plane Ecclesiarum concordiae restituendae ullo pacto obstet. Per nos licet pontifex Romanus et coeteri episcopi omnem suam potestatem, imo et ditiones retineant, tantum potestate sua utantur ad aedificationem Ecclesiae, non certam destructionem." If one follows J.-J. von Allmen something similar is

In summary, despite the harshness of their criticism the issue of papal primacy remains for the Lutheran Reformers, in a somewhat surprising and peculiar manner, an "open question." Indeed, all three major reproaches addressed to the pope, which I mentioned above, are identical with the main reproaches the Reformers addressed to their contemporary theology and church at large, quite independently from the issue of primacy. What according to their conviction was at stake were (1) the Holy Scriptures as the supreme norm of the Church's life and teaching (*sola scriptura*), (2) the gratuity of salvation (*sola gratia/sola fide*) and (3) the unique mediatorship of Christ (*solus Christus*). This triple criticism was, as it were, "pinned" to the papacy, but it did not grow out of its essence. With positive Roman response to this criticism for which the Reformers hoped, although in vain, their criticism of the papacy by implication would have become without object and would have vanished.

Despite the dangerous self-dynamics that the "Antichrist" verdict displayed and which, in the general opinion of later Protestant generations, made the papal office appear as something evil in itself, this conditional "openness" for the primacy never was lost completely.[18]

Without any doubt, Vatican I with its dogmatic constitution *Pastor aeternus* presented a serious crisis for those who still had maintained that hope. As recently as 1967 a Lutheran theologian, P. Brunner, wrote that until Vatican I the question of papal primacy had remained "dogmatically open," but with the decisions of 1870 "the door has been definitely closed."[19] This was the general Protestant judgment.

---

true of the Calvinistic wing of the Reformation. He writes: "Les textes du XVIe siècle . . . ne sont pas aussi radicalement négatifs . . . *Si* le papa faisait vraiment office d'évêque, *si* le papa prêchait l'Evangile et aidait à le faire connaître et respecter, *alors* on pourrait envisager de reconnaître la primauté de cette Église" in *La primauté de l'Église de Pierre et Paul: remarques d'un protestant*, Ökumenische Beihefte-Cahiers œcuméniques 10 (Fribourg/Paris: Éditions universitaires/Cerf, 1977) 40.

[18] The Lutheran theologian Balthasar Meisner (1587–1616) could allow that in the New Testament Peter had a role of leadership among the Twelve, and Johann Gerhard's extensive and careful treatment of the papacy in his "Confessio Catholica" (1634–1637) are some examples. At the turning from the 17th to the 18th century Lutheran Abbot G. Molanus (1633–1722) and the German philosopher G.W. Leibniz (1646–1716) must be mentioned. In the conversations with the Roman Catholic bishops Bossuet and Spinola, Molanus was willing to concede that by positive ecclesiastical law the Bishop of Rome is the first patriarch, the first bishop of the Church, and as such entitled to obedience in spiritual matters, and Leibniz could suggest to the Lutheran theological faculty at Helmstedt to grant to the pope even a certain degree of *ius divinum*.

[19] P. Brunner wrote: While during the time of the Reformation and afterwards the question of papacy had remained "dogmatically open" and even the Council of Trent "did not decide anything nor pronounced any condemnations in this matter, . . . Pius IX, the

Today, however, this judgment no longer seems to be generally shared by Protestants. For some time, the question of papal primacy is at least as "open" as it was in the Reformation era, perhaps even more. The reason is not the teaching of Vatican II on papal primacy. Rather on the contrary, I would say that *Lumen gentium,* although putting papal primacy in a broader ecclesiological setting, had basically restated the teaching of Vatican I. What was much more influential was the general ecumenical opening of the Roman Catholic Church operated by Vatican II and its declared readiness for ecumenical dialogue which initiated immediately after the council and did not avoid the issue of primacy.[20] Other factors contributed: the manner in which the popes of our time were and are exercising their ministry, their awareness of the ecumenical problematic of their office (Paul VI, John Paul II), and most recently the pronouncements of John Paul II concerning his ministry and his invitation to the non-Roman Catholic Churches to engage with him in "a fraternal, patient dialogue" about the papal ministry,[21] an invitation which is one of the motives for our symposium.

II. The present and future dialogue on papal primacy in the light of its Lutheran understanding and critique

It goes without saying that the "conditional openness" for papal primacy the Lutheran Reformation had preserved is a strong asset and a most favorable presupposition for the Roman Catholic-Lutheran dialogue. This has often been observed and affirmed. It allows us to deal with the issue of primacy not as if it were a totally controversial issue. Rather there is a positive historical starting point. Not only the polemi-

---

First Vatican Council and also the papal mariological definitions, in the meantime, definitely have closed the door in this matter," in "Reform–Reformation, Einst–Heute. Elemente eines ökumenischen Dialoges im 450. Gedächtnisjahr von Luthers Ablaßthesen," *Kerygma und Dogma* 13, 3 (1967) 182.

[20] Only two years after P. Brunner had written that, with Vatican I, the question of papacy has lost its dogmatic openness the international Lutheran-Roman Catholic dialogue, already in its third session (1969), came to quite different conclusions. See "Report of the Joint Lutheran-Roman Catholic Study Commission on 'The Gospel and the Church,' 1972" in H. Meyer and L. Vischer, eds., *Growth in Agreement. Reports and Agreed Statements of Ecumenical Conversations on a World Level,* Faith and Order Paper 108 (New York/Geneva: Paulist Press/World Council of Churches, 1984) §66, hereafter cited "The Malta Report."

[21] John Paul II, *Ut unum sint. That They May Be One: On Commitment to Ecumenism* (Washington, D.C.: United States Catholic Conference, 1995) §§88–96, hereafter cited *Ut unum sint.*

cal equation of pope and "Antichrist," also the idea of a rightly exercised primacy are part of the Lutheran theological legacy. This positive starting point is that according to the Lutheran theological tradition, papal primacy—to use once again the words of Melanchthon—can serve "the peace and general unity among Christians."

Especially today this is exactly what is so strongly emphasized on the Roman Catholic side to be the meaning and mission of papal primacy and what, at the same time, constitutes the overarching perspective under which papal primacy is viewed in large circles of the ecumenical movement today.

It suffices to point to the encyclical letter *Ut unum sint* of John Paul II where he sees his office entirely under this perspective, i.e., as a "ministry of unity," as "visible sign and foundation of unity."[22] We should not forget that this was the perspective also of Vatican I,[23] whatever one thinks of its further teaching. Is it not John 17:20f—the biblical leitmotif of the ecumenical movement—which is referred to in the very first sentences of the dogmatic constitution *Pastor aeternus?*[24]

This emphasis on papal primacy as a "ministry of unity" is shared by those who in the present ecumenical movement, especially in the Commission on Faith and Order, try to re-think what visible unity of the church means in the light of the communion/koinonia concept. The concern is how this unity—understood also as *communio*—could become visible on the universal level. The question is raised if whether a personal "service to the universal Church" could be envisaged. The World Conference in Santiago de Compostela (1993) therefore suggested that the question of a "presidency of the communion of churches," of a "service to the universal unity of the Church" be "taken up once again" in ecumenical dialogues.[25] And *Ut unum sint* refers to that suggestion.[26]

[22] *Ibid.*

[23] Vatican I, First Dogmatic Constitution on the Church of Christ *Pastor aeternus,* in N. P. Tanner, ed., *Decrees of the Ecumenical Councils,* vol. II: *Trent to Vatican II* (London/Washington, D.C.: Sheed & Ward/Georgetown University Press, 1990) 812, lines 4f, hereafter cited Tanner followed by page and line number [=H. Denzinger and A. Schönmetzer, eds., *Enchiridion Symbolorum, definitionum et declarationum de rebus et fidei et morum,* 36th ed. (Freiburg/Rome/Barcelona: Herder, 1976) no. 3051, hereafter cited *DS* followed by number of paragraph]. Here Peter is seen as *"unitatis principium ac visibile fundamentum."*

[24] Tanner 811, 29f [=*DS* 3050].

[25] See Report of Section II §§28–30 in T. F. Best and G. Gaßmann, eds., *On the Way to Fuller Koinonia. Official Report of the Fifth World Conference on Faith and Order,* Faith and Order Paper 166 (Geneva: W.C.C. Publications, 1990) 243.

[26] *Ut unum sint,* 89.

It is in the same perspective that all Lutheran/Roman Catholic dialogues as far as they speak about the papal office—and there are only few which do not speak about it—see the meaning and the mission of papal primacy.[27] They at the same time emphasize the "importance of a ministerial service of the communion of churches,"[28] even the "need for a ministry serving the unity of the church universal."[29] The North American Lutheran-Roman Catholic dialogue on "Papal Primacy and the Universal Church" describing such a ministry uses the term "Petrine function,"[30] thus adopting a term very similar to expressions like "Petrine office" *(Petrusamt)* or "Petrine service" *(Petrusdienst)* already used a few of years before.[31]

The crucial question is: How do these recent Lutheran affirmations relate to the Reformers' harsh criticism of papal primacy which equally—and perhaps even more than their "conditional openness"—is part of the Lutheran theological tradition and which during the centuries following the Reformation has even increased and hardened?

In the present dialogues Lutherans do what also the Reformers repeatedly had done: They take the critical reproaches up and turn them into "expectations," if not to say into "requirements" with regard to papal primacy.

Of course, this is done by taking into account the historical difference between now and then. Thus, for example, the Reformation reproach that the pope exercises secular power—a reproach which I did not even mention in the first part of my lecture—is no longer voiced, neither the third reproach I had mentioned, i.e., that obedience to the pope is claimed to be "necessary for salvation."

In two of the Lutheran-Roman Catholic dialogues these Lutheran "expectations" or "requirements" with regard to papal primacy have been summarized in a somewhat general but, nevertheless, rather precise manner and with reference to the criticism and the requirements of the Reformation. First I quote "The Malta-Report" of 1972:

---

[27] See B. Neumann, "Das Papstamt in den offiziellen ökumenischen Dialogen," in *Das Papstamt. Anspruch . . .* , 12–26 [=*Catholica* 50, 2 (1996) 87–120] who lists the Lutheran-Roman Catholic dialogues and what they say about primacy.

[28] "The Malta Report," §66.

[29] U.S.-Dialogue on papal primacy: P. C. Empie and T. A. Murphy, eds., *Papal Primacy and the Universal Church* (Minneapolis: Augsburg Publishing House, 1974) §28, hereafter cited *Papal Primacy.*

[30] *Ibid.*, §4.

[31] See the studies of O. Karrer in the 1950's for example, *Peter and the Church: An Examination of O. Cullmann's Thesis*, Quaestiones disputatae 8 (Freiburg/Edinburg-London: Herder/Nelson, 1963).

> The office of the papacy as a visible sign of the unity of the
> Churches was . . . not excluded insofar as it is subordinated to the
> primacy of the Gospel by theological reinterpretation and practical
> restructuring.[32]

And this statement is immediately followed by a reference to an important controversial question the clarification of which is expected or required, too:

> The question . . . whether the primacy of the pope is necessary for
> the church, or whether it represents only a fundamentally possible
> function.

In the North American dialogue on papal primacy something very similar is said:

> The one thing necessary, from the Lutheran point of view, is that
> papal primacy be so structured and interpreted that it clearly serve
> the gospel and the unity of the church of Christ, and that its exer-
> cise of power not subvert Christian freedom.[33]

If one takes both dialogue statements together—and I am convinced that
they do reflect Lutheran thinking—they delineate something like a
Lutheran "agenda" for a dialogue on papal primacy understood as a
ministry for the unity of Christendom which would be acceptable also
for Lutherans.

This "agenda" more or less would look like the following:

1) *The great and overarching expectation is that papal primacy, in turn, be placed
    "under" the "primacy of the gospel" and "serve" it, "clearly."*

Serve it as the North American dialogue emphasizes means: it is not
sufficient that the subordination of papal primacy to the primacy of the
gospel be merely asserted and affirmed, rather it must be made evident
and recognizable. And "gospel" means here for Lutheran thinking the
Holy Scriptures, the center of which is the message of unmerited gratuity of salvation for Christ's sake as unfolded in the Reformation doctrine
of justification.

2) *It is expected that this subordination to the Gospel be made clearly evident and
    recognizable in two respects:*

—on the one hand with a view to the theological understanding of
papal primacy, particularly with regard to its *teaching authority,* i.e., its

---

[32] "The Malta Report," §66.
[33] *Papal Primacy,* §28.

claim for infallibility or indefectibility of its *ex cathedra* decisions, and with regard to its claim of being *"necessary for the church"* or—which amounts to the same— of being *iure divino*;

—on the other hand with a view to the *ecclesiological (both structural and juridical) aspects of papal primacy,* i.e., with regard to its *authority and exercise of leadership* because here, too, the primacy of the gospel can be at stake particularly where the relationship of papal primacy to the whole people of God is concerned.

To put it simply and with a view to the twofold dogma of papal primacy of Vatican I: on the one hand it is mainly the problem of *magisterial primacy,* on the other it is principally the problem of *jurisdictional primacy.*

As to the expected or required clarification of the problem whether papal primacy is *"necessary"* for the church (Malta Report) and to the expected or required safeguard of *Christian freedom* (U.S. dialogue), both concerns are substantially implied in those expectations or requirements which have already been mentioned: the question of *"ecclesial necessity"* of papal primacy bound up with its theological understanding, particularly with the *iure divino* problematic, and *Christian freedom*—i.e., the liberation from the law's constraint—can be subverted both by a specific theological understanding of primacy and by certain juridical and structural forms of primacy and its exercise.

These are the basic lines of an "agenda" for a Lutheran-Roman Catholic dialogue on papal primacy.

However, this "fraternal, patient dialogue" to which John Paul II has invited the non-Roman Catholic churches is for Lutherans not something which still needs to be initiated. It has already begun over the last decades and it continues.[34] It takes place even where papal primacy is not explicitly addressed, e.g., where questions such as ministry in the Church, the relationship between Scripture and tradition, ecclesiology and, not least, the doctrine of justification are being dealt with. As I explained already, all these questions are for Lutherans closely connected with the problem of papal primacy. It is here, in the realm of papal primacy where all these questions reappear in a very concrete manner. As a matter of fact, for the Reformation the notions "pope" and "papacy" were frequently employed

---

[34] See the Malta dialogue and its report (1972), the U.S. dialogues on papal primacy and infallibility (1974 and 1978) already mentioned. In addition, the Lutheran-Roman Catholic dialogue in Germany ("The Church as Communion of Saints") which is about to conclude will have in its final report a section on primacy and also the agenda of the continuing international dialogue on "Apostolicity of the Church" includes the issue of papal primacy.

as equivalents for Roman theology and the Church in general. "Pope" and "Roman Church" were used almost as synonyms.

Therefore, wherever in the dialogues issues such as justification, church, Scripture and tradition or ministry are being dealt with and clarified, by implication, also the problem of papal primacy is touched and brought closer to solution.[35]

This more and more leads me to what–although with some hesitations–I would call the "specific Lutheran" concern with regard to papal primacy.

III. The theological understanding of primacy as center of its problematic

As I survey the present debate on papal primacy both the inner Roman Catholic and the wider ecumenical debate–and I confess that I know only a segment of it–it appears as if *the questions of its structural and juridical aspects* are very much in the foreground.

What is being debated, for example, are the relationships between primacy and episcopacy or between the pope and the college of bishops, the importance of the principles of conciliarity, collegiality and subsidiarity, the relation between universal Church and particular churches, the scope and the actual execution of the different "offices" of the pope (as Bishop of Rome, as patriarch of the West, as pastor of the universal Church), the interrelation of the personal, the collegial, and the communal/synodical elements in the concept of primacy and its exercise, and the like. To put it roughly: what seems to be in the foreground of the debate are mostly questions related to the primacy of jurisdiction.

It is, therefore, mostly on this level that questions, expectations and requirements are being addressed to papal primacy. For instance:

> –One expects "voluntary limitations by the pope of his exercise of jurisdiction" made possible by "a canonical distinction between the highest authority and the limited exercise of the corresponding power."[36]

[35] This "indirect" approach to the problem of papal primacy is illustrated by Luther's word which I already quoted: "Once this has been established, namely that God alone justifies us solely by His grace through Christ, we are willing not only to bear the pope aloft on our hands but to kiss his feet" (*WA* 40/I, 181; cf. *WA* 40/I, 357).

[36] The Roman Catholic participants in the Lutheran-Roman Catholic U.S. dialogue on *Papal primacy . . .* §27. See also K. Rahner and H. Fries, *Unity of the Churches. An Actual Possibility*, trans. from German [*Einigung der Kirchen-reale Möglichkeit*] by R.C.C. Gritsch and E.W. Gritsch (Philadelphia/N.Y.: Fortress/Paulist Press, 1985) 72f. In this context also the affirmation of Cardinal Ratzinger should be mentioned: "Rome must not require more

—One expects from the exercise of primacy a clearer differentiation between the particular papal "offices." With respect to the Reformation churches this would mean their "formal dismissal from the jurisdictional power of the Latin patriarch," i.e., from the "office" of the pope as "patriarch of the West," although not "from the universal responsibility in the sense of a Petrine ministry for the unity of Christendom claimed by the bishop of Rome."[37]

—One expects from papal primacy in its "personal" exercise by the bishop of Rome an explicit integration of the "collegial" and the "communal/synodical" elements or dimensions. The universal Petrine ministry should be formally embedded in "structures of collegial responsibility exercised by the ordained clergy" as well as of "communal/synodical responsibility exercised by non-ordained and ordained representatives of the people of God."[38]

These considerations and expectations with regard to a primacy which in its ecclesial structures and juridical form could be acceptable as a genuine "Petrine ministry" and "service of unity" also for other Churches are, without any doubt, of great importance for many Churches and Christians, even of decisive importance. Lutherans share and support such considerations and expectations which indeed describe a way towards a common mind concerning papal primacy.

---

from the East with respect to the doctrine of primacy than had been formulated and was lived in the first millennium," from a lecture on "Prognosen für die Zukunft des Ökumenismus," 1976, reprinted in J. Ratzinger, *Principles of Catholic Theology. Building Stones for a Fundamental Theology*, trans. from German *[Theologische Prinzipienlehre]* (San Francisco: Ignatius Press, 1987) 199.

[37] W. Pannenberg, "Petrusdienst im Dienst an der Einheit" in *Zur Debatte* Katholische Akademie in Bayern, March–April 1997, 5.

[38] U. Kühn, "Papsttum und Petrusdienst–Evangelische Kritik und Möglichkeiten aus der Sicht reformatorischer Theologie" in Johann-Adam-Möhler-Institut, *Das Papstamt . . .* 114 [=*Catholica* 50, 2 (1996) 190]. See also the World Conference on Faith and Order at Santiago de Compostela, Section II, §28 in T. F. Best and G. Gaßmann, eds., *On the Way . . .* (cf. Commission on Faith and Order, "Baptism, Eucharist, Ministry. Report of the Faith and Order Commission, World Council of Churches, Lima, Peru 1982" section on "Ministry" §26 and §27 with "Commentary." The document of the Groupe des Dombes, *Le ministère de communion dans l'Église universelle* (Paris: Le Centurion, 1986) should be mentioned for its statement that the three dimensions of a ministry of communion are of central importance: ". . . que le ministère de communion s'exerce selon une triple dimension personnelle, collégiale et communautaire" (§9). This general ecumenical expectation comes very close to what, within an ecclesiology of communion, has often been said on the Roman Catholic side requesting papal primacy to clearly take into account the principles of conciliarity, collegiality, and subsidiarity.

Nevertheless, I should repeat that such considerations may touch but do not yet address sufficiently *the real center* of Lutheran criticism as well as expectation, i.e., *the problem of theological understanding and "reinterpretation" of papal primacy.* For Lutherans this problem requires an answer even if and after the ecclesiological, structural and juridical problematic of papal primacy has found a satisfactory response.

What is meant by "theological understanding" and by "theological reinterpretation" of papal primacy as required by Lutherans?[39]

In the Lutheran mind—and referring back to the Reformation—theological understanding and reinterpretation of papal primacy embraces in particular two things. On the one hand (a) the theological claim of papal primacy to be *iure divino,*[40] on the other (b) the theological claim of papal primacy that its doctrinal decisions or definitions *ex cathedra* are "infallible" and "irreformable"[41] and, hence, exempt from criticism.

A. The *iure divino* claim of papal primacy

Today not only Roman Catholics but Lutherans, too, are aware of the ambiguity and the restricted usefulness of the categories *ius divinum—ius humanum.*[42] Nevertheless, for the Reformers as well as for Lutherans today two important questions were and still are involved: first the question whether papal primacy is "necessary," second whether certain doctrinal decisions of the pope are irreformable and irrefragable. Both questions require a satisfactory answer.

Today one can discern at least some starting points for a possible answer and thus for a "theological reinterpretation" of papal primacy. Let me very briefly sketch them:

---

[39] "The Malta Report" and U.S. dialogue, see above.

[40] Tanner 813, 21f [=*DS* 3058]: ". . . ex ipsius Christi domini institutione seu iure divino. . . ."

[41] Tanner 815, 5ff [=*DS* 3065ff]: Caput IV "De Romani pontificis infallibili magisterio" and Tanner 816, 26-37 [=*DS* 3074] with canons: Tanner 812, 37–41 and 816, 38f [=*DS* 3055 and 3075].

[42] See "The Malta Report" §31 and U.S. dialogue *Papal Primacy* . . . §§30 and 35 (pp. 30f) with footnote 32. Compare also e.g., Y.-M. Congar who said about primacy: "Il n'y a en elle que le 'ministère de Pierre.' Jean 21, 15–17 en donne une formule très substantielle, mais dont la forme de réalisation a connu bien des variations et peut en connaître encore. Cela ne signifie pas qu'il n'y ait aucun 'droit divin' dans la primauté papale, mais qu'à la prendre en sa réalité concrète, c'est-à-dire dans l'histoire, son âme de droit divin n'existe que dans un corps humain . . . ," "Jus divinum," *Revue de droit canonique* 28, 2–4 (1978) 121.

a) As for the first, the question of *necessity* of papal primacy is concerned, it definitely is no longer a question of its "necessity for salvation" as it was at the time of the Reformers. Today it is "only"–I dare say–a question of its "*ecclesial* necessity," i.e., whether papal primacy is indispensable for the church and for being a church. But even under such a moderated form this claim of papal primacy raises for Lutherans great difficulties and certainly it can not be answered in a way which questions the former and the present ecclesial status of the Lutheran churches.

Could, perhaps, a distinction between "necessary for being a church" and "necessary for *the unity of the church*" move us closer to an answer? I am fully aware of the difficulties which such a distinction raises. But is it not true that–as we all know–the present ecumenical openness for primacy is grounded in an understanding of primacy as a "ministry *of unity*" and in the hope that it might serve the "*communion* of churches?" What is affirmed about primacy and what is expected from it, what can even be considered as "needed" is exactly this "Petrine function" or "Petrine ministry" for the unity of the church universal. In short, the entire non-Roman Catholic expectation with regard to papal primacy, it seems to me, ultimately drives us towards such a distinction between "church" and "unity of the church" and focuses on the latter.

b) Concerning the second aspect or implication of the *iure divino* claim of papal primacy, i.e, the claim for *infallibility and irrefragability of its doctrinal decisions,* the Reformers thought this, too, was rooted in the *iure divino* claim. This may not be true although the reasoning of Vatican I, reflected in the Latin title of my lecture, may come close to that. Be this as it may Melanchthon seems to indicate a way to answer the Reformation requirement for a fundamental reformability of papal decisions and their openness to criticism despite the *iure divino* claim and without surrendering that claim.

In his "Treatise on the Power and Primacy of the Pope" (1537) for which the *ius divinum* of papacy was the crucial problem, Melanchthon, in the last analysis, did not radically deny such a *ius divinum.* Two almost identical statements are important and very illuminating. I quote one of them:

> Even if *(etiamsi)* the bishop of Rome did possess the primacy by divine right *(iure divino),* he should not be obeyed inasmuch as he defends impious forms of worship and doctrines which are in conflict with the Gospel. On the contrary, it is necessary to resist him as Antichrist *(tamquam Antichristo).*[43]

[43] *BC* 330. The other statement is on page 326: "Even if *(etiamsi)* the bishop of Rome should possess primacy and superiority by divine right *(iure divino),* obedience would still

Melanchthon refers not only to Gal 1:8 but also to canonical law according to which no obedience is owed to heretical pope. He illustrates this idea by referring to the high priests of the Old Testament who did exercise their priesthood *de iure divino* but to whom obedience was denied inasmuch as they turned to be godless high priests, as the example of Jeremiah and other prophets shows.[44]

Thus one could say what Melanchthon in his "Treatise on the Power and Primacy of the Pope" is repudiating is an exaggerated understanding of the pope's *iure divino* status. In this perspective the Reformation insistence on the *ius humanum* character of papal primacy basically, and in its main intention, is not the categorical denial of the *ius divinum* but the correction of its maximalistic interpretation. This also could open an avenue for a promising dialogue on a "theological reinterpretation" of papal primacy.

This brings us directly to the second large question about the theological understanding or "reinterpretation" of primacy and also to the last part of my paper.

B. Infallibility and irreformability of papal doctrinal decisions

Here, finally, I must refer to the Latin title of my lecture. I had chosen this title a long time before I started working on my text. In retrospective I might have chosen a somewhat different title. But even so the present title still has its meaning. I used this quotation from the conciliar debates at Vatican I—and it reappears there several times although under slightly different forms[45]—in order to illustrate how closely the primacy of jurisdiction or the authority of leadership is connected with the

---

not be owing to those pontiffs who defend godless forms of worship, idolatry, and doctrines which conflict with the Gospel. On the contrary, such pontiffs and such government ought to be regarded as accursed (*tamquam anathema*)."

[44] *Ibid.*, 326f.

[45] G. Schneemann and T. Granderath, eds., *Acta et Decreta Sacrorum Conciliorum Recentiorum, Collectio Lacensis* (Freiburg: Herder, 1890) VII.924. See the article of H. J. Pottmeyer which carries a title similar to that of my lecture: "Auctoritas suprema ideoque infallibilis" in G. Schwaiger, ed., *Konzil und Papst: historische Beiträge zur Frage der höchsten Gewalt in der Kirche*, Festgabe für Hermann Tüchle (München/Paderborn/Viena: F. Schöningh, 1975) 518. See also A.W.J. Houtepen, *Onfeilbaarheid en Hermeneutiek: de betekenis van het infallibilitas-concept op Vaticanum I* (Brugge: Uitgeverij Emmaüs, 1973) and A.B. Hasler, *Pius IX (1846–1878), päpstliche Unfehlbarkeit und I. Vatikanisches Konzil: Dogmatisierung und Durchsetzung einer Ideologie*, Päpste und Papsttum 12/1-2 (Stuttgart: Hiersemann, 1977) especially 319–23.

claim for infallibility.[46] It has rightly been said that for Vatican I papal infallibility is "the necessary qualification of the primacy of jurisdiction."[47] This means that one cannot isolate the question of papal infallibility just as one cannot isolate the question of papal jurisdiction, and, therefore, both questions have to be dealt with also in a dialogue on papal primacy.

For Lutheran theology, where does the unanswered problematic of the dogma on papal infallibility lie? I can only attempt to sketch two main aspects which converge in a kind of fundamental critique and expectation.

1. Papal doctrinal definitions and the people of God

It is common Christian belief that the church as a whole has been given the divine assurance that she will remain in the truth and that, in spite of temptations and dangers, she will never definitely fall from truth and ". . . *portae inferi non praevalebunt adversus eam*."[48] In this sense the conviction *ecclesia non potest errare* is fundamental for our churches as is the conviction that this gift, at the same time, implies for the Church the task and the responsibility to watch over the truth and to preserve it from error.

Equally—and despite certain differences—there is no controversy between our churches that the divinely instituted ministry in the Church has a particular responsibility in this respect.

The real difference between Roman Catholic thought and that of the Reformation is seen only where, according to the Reformers, the responsibility for perseverance in the truth is transferred to and concentrated in the hierarchical office—the bishops and the pope. Ultimately it is taken away from the Church as a whole although it is precisely the whole Church which has been given the divine assurance of and the responsibility for remaining in the truth. According to the Reformers this occurred in the Church of their time and long before. This they severely criticized and denied. Clearly in the background there was, of course, the historical experience of the Reformers that the truth of the Gospel as they perceived it was rejected by the hierarchy.

Therefore, the basic principle of the Reformation with regard to the divine assurance of and the responsibility for perseverance in the truth

---

[46] Bishop Gasser's statement in his *Relatio* at the end of the conciliar debates on papal infallibility (July 11, 1870): "We derive the highest teaching authority from primacy as one derives the species from the gender" (Mansi 52, 1221).

[47] H. J. Pottmeyer, *Unfehlbarkeit und Souveränität. Die päpstliche Unfehlbarkeit im System der ultramontanen Ekklesiologie des 19. Jahrhunderts*, Tübinger theologische Studien 5 (Mainz: Matthias-Grünewald-Verlag, 1975) 352.

[48] Matt 16:18.

was: *"Nec est ad pontifices transferendum, quod ad veram ecclesiam pertinet, quod videlicet sint columnae veritatis, quod non errent."*[49] This "transference" of responsibility from the Church to the hierarchy, for Protestants, found its final conclusion in the dogma on papal infallibility of Vatican I: the Bishop of Rome, so the definition runs, "possesses . . . the infallibility with which the divine redeemer willed His Church to be endowed." His doctrinal definitions have validity *"ex sese, non autem ex consensu Ecclesiae."*[50]

2. Papal doctrinal definitions and Holy Scriptures

The Church's remaining in the truth is her remaining in the truth testified to by the apostles. The Church is *ecclesia apostolica* or she is not the Church. This, too, is the common Christian conviction and confession of faith.

Equally it is a common conviction that, in the course of history, this apostolic truth has been witnessed to in many ways and also in binding form, but that the apostolic scriptures of the biblical canon are and remain the supreme norm. All endeavors for perseverance in the truth, also those of the magisterium, are bound to this norm. In the judgement of the Reformation this binding of the papal magisterium to that supreme norm was no longer evident, as a matter of fact, it seemed to have been surrendered.[51]

In the following centuries this remained the Lutheran opinion. This opinion seemed to be confirmed by Vatican I and its teaching on papal infallibility that certainly spoke of the binding of the papal magisterium to the apostolic Scriptures but did so only in the indicative,[52] excluding the possibility of its being tested and judged by reference to the Scriptures.

These are the two main aspects or lines of Lutheran and, of course, general Protestant criticism addressed to the Roman Catholic theological understanding of papal primacy in its magisterial function.

Both lines of criticism converge in the requirement that the claim of papal primacy to teach with authority be always put under a fundamental reserve and remain open for the possibility of being judged by

[49] In the Latin version of the Apology of the Augsburg Confession (1531) VII, 27 in *Die Bekenntnisschriften der evangelisch-lutherischen Kirche* (Göttingen: Vandenhoeck und Ruprecht, 1967) 6th ed.

[50] Tanner 816, 36 [=*DS* 3074].

[51] I refer back to Luther who said that the pope has been made "a judge over the Scriptures," who does "not let himself be judged" by them (*WA* 6, 322).

[52] Tanner 815, 32–816, 5 [=*DS* 3069].

the Church at large and according to the norm of Scriptures. The Reformation and subsequent Lutheran theology do not require papal primacy to give up its claim for authoritative teaching. However, they require, or better, they expect papal primacy to acknowledge or to respect in its teaching what has been called the "dialectical tension between the claim of its binding nature and the reservation relating to that binding nature."[53]

How far is such a "theological reinterpretation" of papal primacy which would answer the Lutheran criticism and expectations possible for Roman Catholics?

There are certain attempts which seem to go in that direction and I would like very briefly to mention two of them.

First, the new emphasis in Roman Catholic theology on *reception* also with regard to papal doctrinal definitions seems to be important. This reception by the whole people of God is, as Y.-M. Congar said, an "ecclesiological reality"[54] and it has to take place. Although such a reception would not decide the formal "validity" of papal doctrinal definitions once pronounced, it, nevertheless, would decide their "living power and spiritual fruitfulness in the church"[55] in the sense of "an increase in force *(surcroît de puissance)* which the consent . . . adds to a (doctrinal) decision once taken."[56] This emphasis on reception would not dispel the Lutheran concerns completely, but it would shed a new light on the problem of "papal doctrinal definitions and the people of God."

Second, even more important, it seems to me, is the attempt of some Roman Catholic theologians to understand what Vatican I said about the *binding of the papal magisterium to the "depositum fidei" contained in Scripture and tradition*[57] not only as "indicative," i.e., as something always given but as something *normative*, i.e., as necessary precondition for the legitimacy of papal teaching. If this is a legitimate interpretation of the dogma on papal infallibility—as e.g., K. Schatz and H. J. Pottmeyer argued[58]—it would be an important advance towards that "theological rein-

<hr/>

[53] Lutheran-Roman Catholic Joint Commission, *Church and Justification. Understanding the Church in the Light of the Doctrine of Justification* (Geneva: Lutheran World Federation, 1994) §214. In the original German text: ". . . dialektische Spannung zwischen Verbindlichkeitsanspruch und Verbindlichkeitsvorbehalt. . . ."

[54] Y.-M. Congar, "La 'réception' comme réalité ecclésiologique," *Revue des sciences philosophiques et théologiques* 56, 3 (1972) 369–403.

[55] *Church and Justification* . . . §218.

[56] Y.-M. Congar, "La réception . . ." 401.

[57] Tanner 815, 22-816, 14 [=*DS* 3069 and 3070].

[58] Both do not refer to the Lutheran criticism, however, they refer to the opinion of the minority bishops at Vatican I. Schatz writes "that . . . the complementary perspec-

terpretation" of papal primacy Lutherans are requiring. Both theologians, in this context, referred to what Cardinal Ratzinger wrote in 1969: ". . . criticism of papal pronouncements is possible and necessary inasmuch as they lack congruence with Scripture and creed, or with the faith of the universal Church. Where there is neither unanimity in the universal church nor a clear testimony of the sources a binding decision is not possible. If (nevertheless) it formally would be made it would lack its preconditions so that the question of its legitimacy would have to be raised."[59]

---

tive of the minority also today cannot be considered as outdated but that it preserves its significance and its legitimacy;" he wonders whether "at least today in subsequent interpretation of the dogma an understanding is beginning to impose itself which to a large degree corresponds to the fundamental conviction of the minority of Vatican I" in *Kirchenbild und päpstliche Unfehlbarkeit bei den deutschsprachigen Minoritätsbischöfen auf dem I. Vatikanum. Zur Geschichte ihrer Konzilsopposition im Lichte der theologisch-kirchlichen Ideenwelt* (Rome: private publication, 1975) 492f. Pottmeyer says: "Their (the minority bishops') fundamental concern is the organic linkage between pope and church. This linkage does not consist only in the obedient linkage of the Church to the pope and his decisions but no less in the binding of the pope to the entire church which precedes a decision. The pope must ground himself in Scripture and tradition and in the consensus of the Church in faith in such a manner that this can be proven and tested (*in feststellbarer und nachprüfbarer Weise*). . . . In short: an important minority of bishops has agreed to the dogma of infallibility only with the understanding described above. This understanding was tolerated and indirectly even approved by Rome. The wording of the dogma on infallibility itself is certainly open to this interpretation" in his "Das Unfehlbarkeitsdogma im Streit der Interpretationen," in K. Lehmann, ed., *Das Petrusamt. Geschichtliche Stationen seines Verständnisses und gegenwärtige Positionen* (München, 1982) 98f.

[59] J. Ratzinger, *Das neue Volk Gottes. Entwürfe zur Ekklesiologie*, 2nd ed. (Düsseldorf: Patmos Verlag, 1970) 144.

3

Primacy and Unity:
An Anglican Contribution to a Patient
and Fraternal Dialogue

Bishop John Hind

Introduction

In this lecture I offer an Anglican contribution to the "patient and fraternal dialogue" on the subject of the universal primacy for which Pope John Paul II has asked in his encyclical *Ut unum sint*.

Although I am chairman of the Church of England's Faith and Order Advisory Group as well as being a diocesan bishop, I want to stress that I am not speaking on behalf of the Church of England or the Anglican Communion. Mine is an Anglican contribution and my presentation only has my own authority. I shall of course do my best both to be fair in describing some of the different ways in which Anglicans understand the matter, as well as clear about my own position.

I must at this point give a health warning! The Church of England is not the Anglican Communion. Nevertheless there is a real sense in which the Church of England as the mother church of the Communion continues to exercise a role of leadership. This is clearly inseparable from the personal ministry of the archbishop of Canterbury as head of the Communion and there is an ongoing debate about the relationship between the legal, moral, personal and honorific aspects of primacy. I shall be discussing universal primacy in relation to primacy at other levels, and shall argue that all forms of primacy, including the ministry of the Bishop of Rome, are forms of episcopal ministry.

I. Background

An Anglican reflection on the Petrine ministry might well take its starting point from Resolution 8 of the 1988 Lambeth Conference. According to paragraph 3 of that Resolution, this Conference:

> welcomes "Authority in the Church" (I & II), together with the Elucidation,[1] as a firm basis for the direction and agenda of the continuing dialogue on authority and wishes to encourage ARCIC II to continue to explore the basis in Scripture and tradition of the concept of a universal primacy, in conjunction with collegiality, as an instrument of unity, the character of such a primacy in practice, and to draw upon the experience of other Christian Churches in exercising primacy, collegiality and conciliarity.[2]

Rather more cautiously, two years earlier the General Synod of the Church of England had already agreed that the three texts on authority in the Final Report of ARCIC I:

> record sufficient convergence on the nature of authority in the Church for our communions together to explore further the structures of authority and the exercise of collegiality and primacy in the Church.[3]

Also during the 1980s, several Anglican Churches in different parts of the world noted, in their responses to the *Baptism, Eucharist, and Ministry* text, the omission of any reference to a universal ministry in the service of unity. They were not of course alone in noticing the implications of saying that "the ordained ministry should be exercised in personal, collegial and communal ways"[4] and suggesting that this principle applies at different levels of the Church's life.[5]

For example, the Episcopal Church in the U.S.A. noted "that there is no treatment of the Petrine ministry within the context of the ministry of bishops, and [felt] that this is a lack which ought to be remedied."[6]

---

[1] Anglican-Roman Catholic International Commission, *The Final Report, Windsor, September 1981* (London: SPCK/CTS, 1982).

[2] R. Coleman, ed., *Resolutions of the Twelve Lambeth Conferences 1867–1988* (Toronto: Anglican Book Centre, 1992) 203.

[3] General Synod of the Church of England, *Report of Proceedings* 17, 3 (1986) 944–76.

[4] World Council of Churches, Commission on Faith and Order, *Baptism, Eucharist, Ministry*, Faith and Order Paper 111 (Geneva: W.C.C., 1982) 25f, section on "Ministry," §26.

[5] *Ibid.*, 26 §27.

[6] M. Thurian, ed., *Churches respond to BEM: Official responses to the "Baptism, Eucharist, and Ministry" Text*, II, Faith and Order Paper 132 (Geneva: W.C.C., 1986) 61, §1.

The Scottish Episcopal Church went somewhat further, and, in assenting to the relevant paragraphs, recognized "that these principles point to the propriety of a personal embodiment of *episcopē* at world level."[7]

The subject of primacy was more widely referred to in the response of the Church of the Province of New Zealand. "We are conscious of the fact that, in the BEM document, there is no reference to a possible role of the Bishop of Rome as a central focus of unity. Nor is there any mention of the role of patriarchs, archbishops, and primates generally."[8]

The Church of England observed, rather coyly perhaps, that "the Church of England, together with the Anglican Communion as a whole, needs to consider the structures of oversight that properly belong to the Communion and the relation of personal oversight, primacy and collegiality appropriate at a level above the provincial."[9] Elsewhere in its response the Church of England welcomed the "project on common structures of decision-making."[10] This last point has been a consistent concern of the Church of England in ecumenical dialogues in recent years.

Alongside these official comments, it is noteworthy that an increasing number of books and articles deal with the question of authority within the Anglican Communion and within its member churches. This interest has been aroused by a number of factors. Some undoubtedly relate to internal issues within Anglicanism,[11] but similar debates are taking place throughout the Church, and all this takes place against the background of an emerging world culture in which the nature and exercise of authority are under increasing scrutiny. It would be incredible if questions of globalization and regionalization did not have their effect on the way Christians reflect on their own life and organization.

Thus the Inter-Anglican Theological and Doctrinal Commission, in its *Virginia Report*, one of the critical preparatory documents for the 1998 Lambeth Conference, has asked whether a universal primacy may not be necessary for the universal Church.[12]

---

[7] *Ibid.*, 50 §18.

[8] *Ibid.*, 68 §4.10.

[9] M. Thurian, ed., *Churches Respond to BEM*, III, Faith and Order Paper 135 (Geneva: W.C.C., 1987) 77, §158.

[10] *Ibid.*, 62 §116.

[11] See note 39 below.

[12] Inter-Anglican Theological and Doctrinal Commission, "The Virginia Report" in J.M. Rosenthal and N. Currie, eds., *Being Anglican in the Third Millennium—Panama 1996. The Official Report of the 10th Meeting of the Anglican Consultative Council* (Harrisburg: Morehouse Publishing, 1997) 223–88 see 3.54; 4.25; 5.20 and passim.

It is apparent therefore that "Anglicans are . . . by no means opposed to the principle and practice of a ministry at the world level in the service of unity."[13]

II. Anglican attitudes

This openness is the result of a process encouraged by the ecumenical movement over many years. It was not ever thus. Indeed as recently as 1938 the report of an Archbishops' Commission on Doctrine in the Church of England, which dealt extensively with questions of authority and episcopacy, appears not to mention primacy as such, even in its discussion of the episcopate, and the Petrine primacy only in a very thin note.

It must be stated frankly that the openness referred to still comes as a surprise even to some committed and practicing Anglicans. It comes as yet more of a surprise to non-churchgoing people in a country such as Great Britain where "no popery!" lies not far below the surface of much popular consciousness. Many English people still have their historical memories shaped by the juxtaposition of Bloody Mary and Good Queen Bess, by heroic if fanciful accounts of the defeat of the Spanish Armada, and by the story of Guy Fawkes and Gunpowder plot. On the other hand, many thus surprised would not be surprised if they were more familiar with the diversity of treatments of the papacy in the Church of England since the Reformation.

For the sake of proportion, then, I turn to some earlier Anglican attitudes to the Bishop of Rome and to the idea of a universal Petrine ministry. These may be divided for convenience's sake into two broad categories. On the one hand there are those for whom the papacy was a hopelessly flawed institution, some of them going so far as to describe the pope as antichrist. The second group saw the papacy as a corrupted but reformable institution.

James Ussher, the Calvinistically inclined archbishop of Armagh from 1625 to 1640, was credited with the authorship of "A Body of Divinity; or the Sum and Substance of Christian Religion"–although he himself denied it. Whatever the truth about its authorship, the extreme sentiments expressed were "unhappily all too common in some quarters in the Seventeenth century."[14]

---

[13] House of Bishops of the Church of England, *May They All Be One. A Response of the House of Bishops of the Church of England to* Ut unum sint, House of Bishops Occasional Paper (London: Church House Publishing, 1997) §44.

[14] See note to text number 32 in P. E. More and F. L. Cross, eds., *Anglicanism. The Thought and Practice of the Church of England, Illustrated from the Religious Literature of the Seventeenth Century* (London: SPCK, 1962) 69.

He asked,
"Who is that Antichrist?"
and answered,

> He is one who under the colour of being for Christ, and under title
> of His Viceregent, exalteth himself above and against Christ, op-
> posing himself unto Him in all his offices and ordinances, both in
> Church and Commonwealth; bearing authority in the Church of
> God; ruling over that City with seven Hills, which did bear rule
> over nations and put our Lord to death; a Man of Sin, a harlot, a
> mother of spiritual fornications to the kings and people of the na-
> tions, a child of perdition, and a destroyer, establishing himself by
> lying miracles and false wonders. All which marks together do
> agree with none but the Pope of Rome. . . .[15]

Even an archbishop of Canterbury, William Sancroft (archbishop
from 1678 until deprived for refusing to take the oath to William and
Mary in 1689), could write that:

> The bishops of this church are really and sincerely *irreconcilable* [ital-
> ics mine] enemies to the errors, superstitions, idolatries and tyran-
> nies of the church of Rome.[16]

Those who spoke and wrote so intemperately did so not because
they rejected the Catholic Church but because they believed that the
Roman Church had rejected the Catholic Church. At meetings of Convocation, the ancient assembly of the clergy in the Church of England,
the plea was made in the daily prayers:

> that we, who according to the rule of our holy reformation, justly
> and earnestly repudiated the errors, corruptions and superstitions
> at that time surrounding us and also the tyranny of the pope, may
> all hold firmly and constantly the apostolic and truly catholic faith,
> and may serve Thee duly and intrepidly with a pure worship.[17]

And lest the faithful forget, they too were urged to pray to be delivered from "the tyranny of the Bishop of Rome and all his detestable
enormities."[18]

---

[15] J. Ussher or Ps.-Ussher, *A Body of Divinity; or the Sum and Substance of Christian Religion*,
first published 1645. See P. E. More and F. L. Cross, eds., *Anglicanism . . .* , 69.

[16] E. Cardwell, *Documentary Annals of the Reformed Church of England* (Oxford: University
Press, 1844) II, 375–76 quoted in N. Sykes, *Old Priest and New Presbyter: Episcopacy and Pres-
byterianism since the Reformation with especial Relation to the Churches of England and Scotland*
(Cambridge: University Press, 1957) 177.

[17] Quoted in N. Sykes, *Old Priest . . .* , 177.

[18] First and Second Prayer Books of King Edward VI from the *Litany*.

Rightly or wrongly, the Anglican theologians rejected the papacy precisely because it had not proved a safeguard against doctrinal error. They may not always have been right in what they believed the common witness of the early Church to have been, but that at any rate was their intention.

As evidence of this, as far as it touches the papal primacy, we might take the testimony of Bishop Jewel:

> If any learned man of all our adversaries, or if all the learned men that be alive, be able to bring any one sufficient sentence out of any old catholic doctor or father, or out of any general council, or out of the holy scriptures of God, or any one example of the primitive church: whereby it may be clearly and plainly proved . . . that the Bishop of Rome was then called an universal bishop or the head of the universal church. . . . I promised then that I would give over and subscribe unto him.[19]

Among those taking this more moderate position there were some who believed quite simply that Rome had overreached itself. They did not want to separate from the Bishop of Rome, but could not accept that the Catholic Church could be in such thrall to one particular Church.

Archbishop Laud, for example, martyred in 1645 could write:

> The Roman Church and the Church of England are but two distinct members of that Catholic Church which is spread over the face of the earth. Therefore Rome is not the house where the Church dwells; but Rome itself, as well as other particular churches, dwells in the great universal house.[20]

It followed then, that

> the Roman patriarch, by ecclesiastical constitutions, might perhaps have a primacy of order; but for principality of power, the patriarchs were as even, as equal, as the Apostles were before them.[21]

Indeed, speaking of Peter and the other apostles, he wrote:

> A "primacy of order" was never denied [S. Peter] by the Protestants; and an "universal supremacy of power" was never granted him by the primitive Christians. . . . "Christ promised the keys to S. Peter" . . . but so did He to all the rest of the apostles; and to their successors as much as to his. So it is *tibi et illis*, not *tibi non illis*.[22]

---

[19] J. Jewel, *Works* I, 20–21 quoted in N. Sykes, *Old Priest . . .* , 179–80.
[20] W. Laud, *The Works*, II: *Conference with Fisher*, Library of Anglo-Catholic Theology (Oxford: John Henry Parker, 1849) 346.
[21] *Ibid.*, 186.
[22] *Ibid.*, 208.

John Bramhall (1594–1663) who ended a turbulent life as arch-bishop of Armagh, was one of many classical Anglican theologians who looked particularly to Cyprian of Carthage.

> . . . we dare not rob the rest of the Apostles to clothe St. Peter. We say clearly with St. Cyprian, . . . "The rest of the Apostles were even the same thing that Peter was, endowed with an equal fellow-ship both of honour and power; but the beginning cometh from unity, the primacy is given to Peter, to signify one Church and one Chair." It is well known that St. Cyprian made all the Bishoprics in the world to be but one mass, *"Episcopatus unus est Episcoporum multo-rum concordi numerositate diffusus"*; "whereof every Bishop had an en-tire part,"–*"cujus a singulis in solidum pars tenetur."* All that he attributeth to St. Peter is this "beginning of unity," this primacy of order, this pre-eminence to be the chief of Bishops, to be Bishop of "the principal Church from whence Sacerdotal unity did spring."
> . . . This primacy neither the ancients nor we do deny to St. Peter– of order, of place, of pre-eminence. If this "first movership" would serve his turn, this controversy were at an end for our parts. But this primacy is over lean; the Court of Rome have no gusto to it. They thirst after a visible monarchy upon earth, an absolute eccle-siastical sovereignty, a power to make canons, to abolish canons, to dispense with canons, to impose pensions, to dispose dignities, to decide controversies by a single authority. This was what made the breach, not the innocent primacy of St. Peter.[23]

One reason for quoting Bramhall at some length has been to show how central the appeal to the early Fathers was in the whole debate. This was no mere controversy between *sola Scriptura* on the one hand and Scripture and Tradition on the other, still less a simple dispute over the interpretation of scriptural texts.

With the benefit of hindsight, continued scholarship and a less polemical environment we may well question many of the assumptions made at a time of religious and political turmoil about the nature of "primitive" Christianity and the teaching of the Fathers. We ought how-ever at the very least to do our ancestors the courtesy of believing what they said about themselves and their motivations.

Simon Patrick, bishop of Chichester, then of Ely, wrote "The Reli-gion of the Church of England, by Law established, is the true Primitive Christianity; in nothing new, unless it be in rejecting all that novelty

---

[23] J. Bramhall, *Schism Guarded,* section I, chapter i quoted in P. E. More and F. L. Cross, eds., *Anglicanism . . . ,* 66, no. 28.

which hath been brought into the Church."[24] The so-called Vincentian canon provided something of a touchstone for many Anglican writers in the sixteenth century, *"Quod semper, quod ubique, quod ab omnibus . . . ."* "In the Catholic Church we take great care that we hold that which has been believed everywhere, always, by all. For that is truly and properly catholic . . . which comprehends everything almost universally. And we shall observe this rule if we follow universality, antiquity, consent . . . What if some novel contagion seek to infect the whole Church and not merely a small portion of it? Then the Catholic Christian will take care to cling to antiquity, which cannot now be led astray by any novel deceit."[25]

Anyway, let us return to our more immediate purpose with William Wake, archbishop of Canterbury from 1716 to 1737, who was in correspondence with certain Gallican theologians at the Sorbonne:

> As to the pope's authority, I take the difference to be only this; that we may all agree, without troubling ourselves with the reasons, to allow him a primacy of order in the episcopal college. They would have thought it necessary to hold communion with him, and to allow him a little canonical authority over them, as long as he will allow them to prescribe the bounds of it. We say fairly we know of no authority he has in our realm. But for actual submission to him, they as little mind it as we do.[26]

With such texts we are no longer in the realm of outright rejection, and indeed some place may be found for a papacy, even one conceived as inheriting some part of Peter's own ministry. Nevertheless, some basic questions of principle remained.

Isaac Barrow (1630–1677), in a posthumously published work on the papal supremacy, drew attention to one particular area of concern:

> The Scripture hath enjoined and empowered all Bishops to feed, guide, and rule their respective Churches, as the *ministers, stewards, ambassadors, angels of God; for the perfecting of the saints, for the work of the ministry, for the edification of the Body of Christ;* to whom God hath committed the care of their people, so that they are responsible for their souls.
>
> All which rights and privileges of the episcopal office the Pope hath invaded, doth obstruct, cramp, frustrate, destroy; pretending (with-

[24] S. Patrick, *The Second Note of the Church Examined, viz. Antiquity,* quoted in P. E. More and F. L. Cross, eds., *Anglicanism . . .* 141, no. 71.

[25] St. Vincent of Lerinum, *The Commonitorium,* R. S. Moxon, ed., Cambridge Patristic Texts (Cambridge: University Press, 1915) II.4, 7.

[26] W. Wake quoted in N. Sykes, *Old Priest . . .* , 199–200.

out any warrant) that their authority is derived from him; forcing them to exercise it no otherwise, than as his subjects, and according to his pleasure. . . .[27]

Even so, there were those who longed to see the Church of Rome and its bishopric reformed and serve again the unity of the Catholic Church. Bishop Jewel said that the Church of England "would be willing to yield to Rome all the honour Irenaeus gave her if she would return to the doctrine and traditions of the apostles."[28]

Or again, Richard Field (1561–1616) could declare:

> We deny not . . . to the Roman Bishop his due place among the prime bishops of the world, if therewith he will rest contented; but universal bishop . . . we dare by no means admit him to be, knowing right well that every bishop hath in his place, and keeping his own standing, power and authority immediately from Christ, which is not to be restrained or limited by any but the company of bishops.[29]

I conclude this highly selective survey with another quotation from Bishop Bramhall. This is included to indicate that even at a time of heightened polemic it was possible for certain universal functions still to be accorded to him:

> Let him [i.e. St. Peter] be "first, chief, or prince of the Apostles" in that sense wherein the ancient Fathers styled him so. Let him be the "first" ministerial "mover." And why should not the Church have recourse to a prime Apostle or Apostolical Church in doubtful cases?[30]

III. Anglican experience

By definition Anglicans have been separated from visible communion with the see of Rome since the Reformation. The Thirty-nine Articles of Religion stated baldly "The Bishop of Rome hath no jurisdiction in this realm of England."[31]

---

[27] I. Barrow, *A Treatise of the Pope's Supremacy,* first published posthumously in 1680. See P. E. More and F. L. Cross, eds., *Anglicanism . . .* , 63, no. 27.

[28] J. Jewel quoted in P. Avis, *Anglicanism and the Christian Church: Theological Resouces in Historical Perspective* (Edinburgh: T & T Clark, 1989) 25.

[29] R. Field, *On the Church* III, 264f quoted in P. Avis, *Anglicanism and . . .* , 72.

[30] J. Bramhall, *op. cit.* quoted in P. E. More and F. L. Cross, eds., *Anglicanism . . .* , 65, no. 28.

[31] *Article xxxvii.* It is however to be noted that this article is specifically about the civil magistracy.

This does not however mean that Anglicans have been strangers to either the principle or the experience of primacy. Indeed, a rather central principle of the English Reformation was precisely the location of primacy in a regional, that is to say a national, setting. Notwithstanding the important issue of the "royal supremacy," this was not a matter of replacing the pope by the sovereign. Indeed the Article already quoted declares "we give not to our Princes the ministering either of God's Word, or of the Sacraments,"[32] and referred to Queen Elizabeth's 1559 Injunctions which had denied that "the kings and queens of this realm may challenge authority and power of ministry of divine offices in the church."[33]

The ordinal attached to the Book of Common Prayer makes clear the intention of the reformed Church of England to continue the orders of bishops, priests, and deacons which have come from the time of the apostles.[34] The ordinal as such is concerned with these orders, all of which can only be conferred by a bishop.

In the case of episcopal ordination we note that a bishop is to be ordained or consecrated by the archbishop of the province (and other bishops present), and to be presented to him by two other bishops. Nevertheless another bishop may be appointed to act for the archbishop. An archbishop is thus a special kind of bishop, a bishop with special authority. He is not more than a bishop. The difference is one of jurisdiction not of order.[35]

Within the Church of England, the archbishops of Canterbury and York have extensive primatial jurisdiction in their respective provinces, and may hold visitations during which they have jurisdiction as ordinaries. They also have an appellate jurisdiction. They have the right of confirming the election of diocesan bishops in their provinces and of assenting to the ordination of bishops. Certain legal actions are only valid when the archbishops assent. In addition to being primate and metropolitan within his own province both archbishops have some jurisdiction, greater in the case of the archbishop of Canterbury, throughout England.[36]

The Anglican Communion consists of autonomous churches or "provinces" each of which has some form of primatial jurisdiction, al-

---

[32] *Article xxxvii.*

[33] P. Avis, *Anglicanism and . . .* , 38.

[34] *The Form and manner of Making, Ordaining and Consecrating of Bishops, Priests and Deacons according to the Order of the Church of England.* Preface.

[35] *The Form of Ordaining or Consecrating of an Archbishop or Bishop.*

[36] *Canon C17.* See Appendix.

though the character of this varies. For Anglican Communion purposes, the two provinces of Canterbury and York are deemed to form a single province, namely the Church of England, of which for most practical purposes the archbishop of Canterbury is reckoned to be the primate.

The *Virginia Report* is explicit in linking primacy and collegiality as "complementary elements within the exercise of *episcopē*."[37] Neither does the Report forget the "communal" element in BEM trinity of "personal, collegial and communal."

Specifically on primacy, the Report observes that:

> The role of primacy is to foster the communion by helping the bishops in their task of apostolic leadership both in their local church and in the Church universal. A Primate's particular role in *episcopē* is to help churches to listen to one another, to grow in love and unity, and to strive together towards the fullness of Christian life and witness. A Primate respects and promotes Christian freedom and spontaneity; does not seek uniformity where diversity is legitimate, or centralize administration to the detriment of local churches.[38]

and further that:

> A Primate exercises ministry not in isolation but in collegial association with other bishops. If there is a need to intervene in the affairs of a diocese within the Province, the Primate will consult with other bishops, and if possible act through the normal structures of consultation and decision-making. The Primate will strive never to bypass or usurp the proper responsibility of the local church.[39]

The growth of the Anglican Communion has raised questions about relationships between the member churches and the bonds of communion which hold them together. The Lambeth Conference (first meeting: 1867) is one of these; others are the Anglican Consultative Council (1971) and the Primates' Meeting (1979). Of a somewhat different character, but still relevant within the overall network of structures in support of communion, are the Inter-Anglican Theological and Doctrinal Commission (set up after a resolution at Lambeth 1978) and the Eames Commission (1988).[40]

---

[37] "Virginia Report" 5.13 in J.M. Rosenthal and N. Currie, eds., *Being Anglican . . .* , 267.

[38] *Ibid.*, 5.14, 268.

[39] *Ibid.*, 5.15, 268.

[40] See chapter on Women in the Episcopate in Church of England, Commission on Communion and Women in the Episcopate, *The Eames Commission. The Official Reports* (Toronto: Anglican Book Centre, 1994) 27–34.

None of these have binding or juridical force, but stand somewhere between a rather generalized "sense of family feeling," a common liturgical tradition and inheritance of theological method, on the one hand, and the clear confessional or juridical positions that characterize some other churches on the other.

Nevertheless, of the role of the primates' meeting the 1988 Lambeth Conference urged "that encouragement be given to a developing collegial role for the Primates' Meeting under the presidency of the Archbishop of Canterbury, so that the Primates' Meeting is able to exercise an enhanced responsibility in offering guidance on doctrinal, moral and pastoral matters."[41]

Another bond of communion is the personal ministry of the archbishop of Canterbury. The *Virginia Report* refers openly to the primacy of the archbishop of Canterbury within the Communion as a whole and sees this together with the Primates' Meeting as reflecting provincial primacy and collegiality at the world level of the Communion as a whole.[42] As I have already said he has no intrinsic or ordinary canonical rights outside England (apart from those few extra-provincial dioceses that depend directly upon Canterbury). On the other hand, the moral authority of his office is considerable and Anglican Churches around the world receive encouragement and a practical link with other Churches through their common communion with him. In some cases, most notably the recent civil war in Rwanda, the archbishop has been invited to and has uniquely been able to exercise a ministry of oversight which lay for a time beyond the capacity of the local church itself.

These developments have made it increasingly necessary to explain the role of the archbishop of Canterbury in relation to the Anglican Communion as a whole. That he has at present no juridical or canonical role is unambiguous, except to the extent this is accorded him by autonomous provinces. Typically, the Episcopal Church of the Sudan ". . . accepts the archbishop of Canterbury as holding the first place among the Metropolitans of the Anglican Communion," although it is not defined what this means.

On the other hand, communion with the see of Canterbury is part of the definition of what it means to be Anglican:

[41] Lambeth Conference 1988–Resolution 18 Section 2 (a) in *The Truth Shall Make You Free. The Lambeth Conference 1988. The Reports, Resolutions and Pastoral Letters from the Bishops* (London: Church House Publishers, 1988) 216.

[42] "Virginia Report" 5.16 in J. M. Rosenthal and N. Currie, eds., *Being Anglican . . .* , 269.

The Anglican Communion is a fellowship, within the One Holy Catholic and Apostolic Church, of those duly constituted Dioceses, Provinces or Regional Churches in communion with the See of Canterbury . . . bound together not by a central legislative and executive authority, but by mutual loyalty sustained through the common counsel of the Bishops in conference.[43]

The 1930 Lambeth Conference went even further and said that the Anglican Communion

is part of the Holy Catholic and Apostolic Church. Its centre of unity is the See of Canterbury. To be Anglican it is necessary to be in communion with that See.[44]

It is the archbishop of Canterbury who calls the Lambeth Conference together, although the Resolution of the 1978 Conference which affirmed this practice was careful in its expression:

In order that the guardianship of the faith may be exercised as a collegial responsibility of the whole episcopate, the Conference affirms the need for Anglican bishops from every diocese to meet together in the tradition of the Lambeth Conference and recommends that the calling of any future Conference should continue to be the responsibility of the Archbishop of Canterbury, and that he should be requested to make his decision in consultation with the other primates.[45]

The archbishop of Canterbury exercises his role by virtue of his ministry as "Primate of All England and Metropolitan"—in other words his worldwide ministry arises from his ministry of primacy in a particular church, in which he is both a diocesan bishop and an archbishop. For Anglicans, therefore, the question of universal primacy as actually experienced is inseparable from the question of provincial primacy and diocesan episcopacy.

None of this is, I hasten to add, an attempt to claim the archbishop of Canterbury as a rival or alternative pope. All Anglicans (and I hope Roman Catholics as well) will agree that one pope is enough and the questions are mainly (1) is such a ministry required, (2) if so, is it required *de*

[43] Lambeth Conference 1930–Resolution 49 in *The Lambeth Conference 1930. Encyclical Letter from the Bishops with Resolutions and Reports* (London/New York: SPCK/Macmillan, n.d.) 55.

[44] Quoted in the "Virginia Report" 3.32 in J. M. Rosenthal and N. Currie, eds., *Being Anglican . . .* , 249.

[45] Lambeth Conference 1978–Resolution 13 in *The Report of the Lambeth Conference 1978* (London: Church Information Office, 1978) 42.

iure divino or out of practical necessity and (3) how should it be exercised
(including how it relates to the organs through which it is exercised)?

Some of these concerns were well expressed by Michael Ramsey,
many years before he became archbishop of Canterbury:

> . . . a Papacy which acted as an organ of the Church's general con-
> sciousness and authority in doctrine, and which focused the unity
> of the one Episcopate might claim to fulfil the tests of true devel-
> opment. (. . .) at certain times in history the Papacy conspicuously
> failed to do this and has thereby been the means of perverting the
> real meaning of Catholicism. But this historical fact cannot justify a
> wholesale refusal to consider the Petrine claims. Other organs in
> the one Body have had their times of failure and of self-aggran-
> dizement, and we do not therefore conclude that they must be dis-
> carded. Hence it seems possible that in the reunited Church of the
> future there may be a special place for a *primus-inter-pares* as an
> organ of unity and authority. Peter will be needed as well as Paul
> and Apollos, and like them he will be chastened and repentant.[46]

At all events the current experience of Anglicans is pointing them
towards the need for a universal ministry of unity with greater canonical authority than at present possessed by the archbishop of Canterbury
and the other instruments at the world level. The question is directly put
by the *Virginia Report*:

> The world wide Anglican assemblies are consultative and not leg-
> islative in character. There is a question to be asked whether this is
> satisfactory if the Anglican Communion is to be held together in
> hard times as well as in good ones. Indeed there is a question as to
> whether effective communion, at all levels, does not require appro-
> priate instruments, with due safeguards, not only for legislation,
> but also for oversight. Is not universal authority a necessary corol-
> lary of universal communion? This is a matter currently under dis-
> cussion with our ecumenical partners. It relates not only to our
> understanding of the exercise of authority in the Anglican Com-
> munion, but also to the kind of unity and communion we look for
> in a visibly united Church.[47]

It follows that along with the need for a universal primacy Anglicans are also having to explore the relationship between such a ministry,
essentially personal, with the necessary bureaucracy such a worldwide

---

[46] A.M. Ramsey, *The Gospel and the Catholic Church*, 1st published in 1936 (London:
SPCK, 1990) Appendix I, 227f.

[47] "Virginia Report" 5,20 in J.M. Rosenthal and N. Currie, eds., *Being Anglican . . .* ,
269.

ministry needs. They are already of course familiar with a primatial bureaucracy at provincial level. The significance of such organization varies enormously of course if one moves from a primacy, whether regional or universal, seen primarily as a support and encouragement for the local churches and a servant of their unity and mission to a primacy envisaged as a source of authority in the Church. Here lies one of the real pressure points in Anglican–Roman Catholic dialogue about the universal Petrine ministry.

IV. Anglican Aspirations

From what has gone before it is clear that the Anglican Communion is conscious as never before of its character as a world-wide fellowship of Churches and is therefore becoming more aware of the instruments God provides or permits for ministry at the global level. It is also clear that while questions of unity are important here, so too are questions of mission. Indeed unity, holiness, apostolicity and catholicity are characteristic of the Church at every level. Anglicans look to the episcopate for collegial leadership of the church in each of these dimensions of its life. In the ordinal for bishops in the Alternative Service Book 1980, we read that:

> A bishop is called to lead in serving and caring for the people of God and to work with them in the oversight of the Church. As a chief pastor he shares with his fellow bishops a special responsibility to maintain and further the unity of the Church, to uphold its discipline, and to guard its faith. He is to promote its mission throughout the world.[48]

Primacy is a particular form of *episcopē* in support of local churches in a wider area. It is not an intrinsically superior form of *episcopē*, and, except in emergency situations, it lacks higher ordinary jurisdiction for its exercise. This principle is important for the integrity of the local church. Nevertheless at both regional and, many would now agree, the universal level, primacy is needed for the integrity of the Church at these levels too.

The questions this raises have been sharpened by other voices, especially from the two-thirds world, asking for a clearer centre and authority for Anglican doctrinal pronouncements.[49]

[48] Church of England, "Ordination of a Bishop" §13, *The Alternative Service Book 1980. Services Authorized for Use in the Church of England in Conjunction with the Book of Common Prayer* (London: SPCK, 1980) 388.

[49] E.g., the "Kuala Lumpur Statement" in *Second Anglican Encounter in the South, Kuala Lumpur, West Malaysia, 5–10 February 1997* (London: Anglican Consultative Council, 1997) 2–7.

This development needs to be seen in the light of two characteristic principles of Anglican ecclesiology over the past half century. The first is the tendency to speak of the dispersed nature of authority. This expression is frequently used and abused. Although it is, almost by definition, not easy to explain precisely, it is important as an analysis of Christian authority itself rather than as a particular theory of Anglicanism. The report *Towards a Church of England Response to BEM & ARCIC* puts it like this:

> Anglicans are accustomed to thinking of authority as diffused through many media by which God guides the Church and protects his people from error. A unique and supreme place is occupied by the Bible, accessible to every one of the faithful, together with the apostolic creed and the rule of faith for its interpretation, within the universal communion which Christ intended his Church to be. Of this communion a common baptism and shared eucharist are effectual signs; the episcopal ministry is the sign and instrument of unity and continuity in time and space.[50]

The principle of "dispersed authority" does not only mean such "faith and order" elements. Indeed the reference to all the faithful having access to Scripture is itself an indication of the role the informed conscience and reason of individuals have to contribute. Few Anglicans are satisfied with the present balance between the various elements in their churches' current understanding and practice of dispersed authority, but all consider the principle itself to be central to a truly catholic understanding of the Church.

Anglicans have also spoken much in recent years of the principle of provincial autonomy. This rests both on the historico-political foundation of ex-colonialism and on some theological convictions about the integrity of a local church and its responsibility for ministry and mission in its own area. It is of course precisely at the level of the province that the highest level of juridical canonical primacy in current Anglicanism is to be found.

As in the case of dispersed authority, here too we have a principle containing an important value, but one which needs clarification and the development of appropriate structures and safeguards. The past decades have seen a developing commitment on the part of member Churches to consult one another on matters which concern the common life of the Communion. Needless to say, consultation is not always enough, and

---

[50] General Synod of the Church of England, *Towards a Church of England Response to BEM & ARCIC*, GS 661 (London: CIO Publishing, 1985) §233, 90.

Anglicans still lack any wider primacy with sufficient canonical authority to maintain unity when fundamental issues of faith are at stake.

Thus, the twin principles of dispersed authority and provincial autonomy for so long perceived as a strength can also appear as a threat unless balanced by appropriate primacy to safeguard the identity of the one church at local, regional and universal levels.

At all events, there appears to be an increasing demand for a greater clarity about the central doctrinal or dogmatic teaching of the church, especially by bishops and theologians in Africa, Latin America and Asia resentful of what they see as the neo-colonialism of English and North American liberal power. What are the fundamentals of the Gospel, the heart of the message proclaimed by and embodied in the life of the Catholic Church?

The *Virginia Report* observes that

> At all times the theological reflection and *praxis* of the local church must be consistent with the truth of the gospel which belongs to the universal Church. The universal doctrine of the Church is important especially when particular practices or theories are locally developed which lead to disputes. In some cases it may be possible and necessary for the universal Church to say with firmness that a particular local practice or theory is incompatible with Christian faith.[51]

Wise and possibly brave words—but how is the universal Church to speak with or even without firmness. There must be organs and ministries for this if the universal Church is not to be a mere abstraction.

The question is urged both by the need for integrity in each of the separated denominations and by the need for the one Church to be effective in its witness to the saving message of the Gospel. In other words mission no less than faith and order is at stake—perhaps better, the reason why faith and order are concerned is for the sake of mission.

At the same time as the demand for greater cohesiveness and clarity is made, and indeed sometimes by the same people, an appeal is also made for a greater respect for the diversity of cultural expressions of the faith. The world missions of the various churches have all struggled with issues of imperialism and indigenization over the years.

None of this is of course a peculiarly Anglican problem. In recent years the question of authority has moved center stage for most world communions. Anglicans depressed about the difficulties they experience

---

[51] "Virginia Report" 4.25 in J. M. Rosenthal and N. Currie, eds., *Being Anglican . . .* , 263.

are mildly consoled but not reassured when they contemplate the contrast between the apparent clarity of Roman Catholic positions and the actuality of Roman Catholic life in many parts of the world.

Anglicans observe that a professedly infallible magisterium is scarcely more successful than their own principle and practice of dispersed authority in guaranteeing either an unambiguous proclamation of gospel truth or even compliance!

In this they are, however, only mildly consoled rather than reassured because they, like others, want to have confidence that the Lord of the Church has kept his promise not to abandon his Church, and further that the Holy Spirit, the Paraclete, still leads the Church into the whole truth. At the end of the day it is no encouragement to discover that other Churches have similar problems—or perhaps it would be more accurate to say that the one Church is almost bound to experience similar difficulties at all times and in all places during its earthly pilgrimage!

This seems to me to be the overall context in which primacy should be discussed. The function of *episcopē* personally and collegially is always to care for the life of the Church in its entirety. One of the specific functions of primacy at every level is to strengthen the brethren. All primacy is thus a Petrine ministry. This must include the safeguarding of both unity and diversity, a diverse unity and a united diversity. It is to be a focus (and locus) of unity for communities whose inner reality is the same but whose external forms of expression may vary significantly. The public recognition by popes at least from John XXIII onwards that there is a difference between the faith and the forms in which it is expressed increases the urgency of the ecumenical debate on this issue.

I have already indicated that the question of universal primacy is already an internal question for the Churches of the Anglican Communion as well as a matter for ecumenical discussion with Roman Catholics and others. The fact that the question is being asked is of course far from an indication of approval for any particular form of such primacy.

Indeed, there remain Anglicans who profess themselves implacably opposed to any consideration of universal primacy, whether or not linked to the see of Rome. Theirs is, however, a minority view and on 13 November 1986 the General Synod of the Church of England passed a resolution recognizing that the three texts on authority in the Final Report of ARCIC I "record sufficient convergence on the nature of authority in the Church for our Communions together to explore further the structures of authority and the exercise of collegiality and primacy in the Church."[52]

[52] General Synod of the Church of England, *Report of Proceedings* 17, 3 (1986) 991.

Later the same day the Synod passed another motion recording its conviction that "further attention to the case for a universal primacy necessarily based at Rome, including the official Roman Catholic claim that the Pope is the Vicar of Christ on earth" was a priority.

Nevertheless as one senior member of the General Synod of the Church of England put it during an earlier debate on the Final Report of ARCIC I: "We have only just begun tentatively, fearfully, to think out what kind of presidency over the world wide college of bishops is right, a position for which in practice the Bishop of Rome is the only candidate."[53] Immediately before this he had said, "We have only just begun to think out what kind of a patriarchate Canterbury is. We avoid the very word, yet it is a patriarchate in all but name."

It is no coincidence that the worldwide role of the archbishop of Canterbury and the universal primacy of the Bishop of Rome should be brought together in this way. Whatever may be said about the hand of providence in the development of papacy, it is evident that history and politics also played their part. So too in the case of Canterbury, the same factors in the twentieth century and in a divided church have forced the Communion of Anglican churches to develop worldwide instruments. Maybe providence should not be denied a hand here too.

If the vision of full visible unity to which Anglicans are committed is true, it seems unlikely that we are being led to establish a parallel papacy or a rival papacy. Even the suggestion sounds absurd. More probable is that Anglican churches are being given a foretaste of the experience of universal primacy which has been absent from the experience of their ancestors since the Reformation. My own conviction is that this is so, and further that the way in which under God *this* worldwide ministry is developing has something to offer to a future papacy which might become a more universal sign and service of unity than is possible in the present divided state of the Church.

Another factor which encourages me in this line of thinking is the way in which Roman Catholics and Anglicans, and indeed not only Roman Catholics and Anglicans but members of other confessional groups as well, are facing the same question in remarkably similar ways. Of course the precise form of the question varies according to different

[53] D. L. Edwards (Provost of Southwark) in the debate *Towards a Response to BEM and ARCIC* February 1985 in General Synod of the Church of England, *Report of Proceedings* 16, 1 (1985) 55. Cf. *Towards a Church of England Response* . . . (=GS 661) 93 §242: ". . . many agree on the value of a universal primate as a sign of the visible fellowship of the Church, and even upon the Roman primatial office as the obvious candidate for such a primatial see. . . ."

starting points, but everywhere the issues are: How can the Church be faithful to Jesus Christ in diversity as well as in unity? How does the local church (however defined) stand in relation to the world wide church? To what extent are the answers to these questions and the structural forms in which such answers are to be expressed already indicated by God, and to what extent are these pragmatic matters in which a number of different options might be available?

A closely related question is the relationship between historical development and theological principle. This is an area in which a number of Anglican critics challenged an apparent "sanctifying" of history in the ARCIC account of the emergence of the papacy. Certainly there is a need for further work on our common understanding of the sources and authorities for Christian truth. Nevertheless the divisions on this are within rather than simply between denominations, and theological investigation can and does take place within the ecumenical community. This enables members of separated churches both to be loyal to their own inheritance of faith and also to the possibility that some apparently divergent formulations may in fact be different forms of expression of the same truth.

Ecumenical method involves trying to go behind the differences to discern whether or not there is a common understanding at the level of faith. This does not mean trying to turn the clock back. Catholic Christians honored the ministry of Peter in their midst for many centuries before Boniface VIII and *Unam Sanctam* with the assertion that "for every human creature it is an indispensable condition of salvation that he should be subject to the Roman Pontiff."[54] Again, Byzantine Christians honored Peter as *coryphaeus* of the apostles and the Bishop of Rome as the one who presided over the revered Church of Peter and Paul even when Rome had begun to interpret some of the same biblical texts to support a universal Roman power which they utterly rejected.[55]

Such an approach should enable us to overcome the historic polarities in which the acceptance and rejection of the universal ministry of the Bishop of Rome have been expressed. An example may be seen in the way ARCIC *Authority II* treats the subject of *jus divinum* as applied to the primacy of the "successor in the chair of Peter" the Decree *Pastor Aeternus* having described this primacy *"ex ipsius Christi Domini institutione seu iure divino."* The Commission comments:

[54] Boniface VIII, *Unam Sanctam* (1302).

[55] J. Meyendorff *et al.*, *The Primacy of Peter in the Orthodox Church*, 1st ed. 1963, The Library of Orthodox Theology 1 (Bedfordshire: The Faith Press/American Orthodox Book Services, 1973).

While there is no universally accepted interpretation of this language, all affirm that it means at least that this primacy expresses God's purpose for his Church. *Jus divinum* in this context need not be taken to imply that the universal primacy as a permanent institution was directly founded by Jesus during his life on earth. Neither does the term mean that the universal primate is a "source of the Church" as if Christ's salvation had to be channelled through him. Rather, he is to be a sign of the visible *koinonia* God wills for the Church and an instrument through which unity in diversity is realized. It is to a universal primate thus envisaged within the collegiality of bishops and the *koinonia* of the whole Church that the qualification *jure divino* can be applied.[56]

One may suspect that this was not how the Fathers of the First Vatican Council saw the matter, and it was certainly not how other Churches interpreted it. But it may be an indication of a divine irony that God gives us tools which divide in one age and yet may become tools for unity in another. It is of course evidence that despite our sins and failures in understanding God does unerringly lead his Church.

One of the great ecumenical leaders of the Church of England of an earlier generation, Bishop Oliver Tomkins of Bristol, wrote in his journal, during a visit to Rome in the 1960s:

> How gladly I would accept him (the Pope) as supreme *Pastor pastorum* in the total episcopate. Please God, "collegiality" will lead on to possibilities of corporate reconciliation for *Ecclesia Anglicana* which need not imply total repudiation of our corporate past—and how important to remember how I feel vis-à-vis Rome when thinking of relations with Methodism and Presbyterianism.[57]

By writing thus, Bishop Tomkins was not, of course, suggesting that he wanted to turn his back on Methodists and Presbyterians as he looked towards Rome. Rather he wanted his vision of unity to be sensitive to the treasures every authentically Christian "tradition" brings with it, and always to be conscious of the ways in which churches can so easily "unchurch" each other. In this way, and typically, he testified to the Anglican policy of "all round and every level" ecumenism.

---

[56] "Authority II" in Anglican-Roman Catholic International Commission, *The Final Report . . .* 86, §11.

[57] A. Hastings, "Proclaiming the Gospel in the Twentieth Century: Michael Ramsey and Oliver Tomkins," *One in Christ* 32, 1 (1996) 19.

V. Conclusion

The Church of England bases its approach to ecumenism in general and to the question of primacy in particular on several interdependent principles:

- that the unity of the Church is a gift of God
- that visibility is inherent to this unity and is necessary if the Church is to be a credible sign of the unity God wills for the whole creation
- that the divisions between Christians are normally divisions *within* the Church
- that "the care of all the churches" is one of the central functions of the ministry of oversight
- that primacy has a role within the episcopate
- that the unity of the world church needs instruments of unity at the world level

On these bases the Anglican Communion rejoices at Pope John Paul II's invitation and looks forward to the development of the papacy as a ministry in the service of the unity of the whole Church—"a pope for all Christians."

APPENDIX

The Canons of the Church of England

Canon C17

1. By virtue of their respective offices, the archbishop of Canterbury is styled primate of All England and metropolitan, and the archbishop of York primate of England and metropolitan.

2. The archbishop has throughout his province at all times metropolitical jurisdiction, as superintendent of all ecclesiastical matters therein, to correct and supply the defects of other bishops, and, during the time of his metropolitical visitation, jurisdiction as ordinary, except in places and over persons exempt by law or custom.

3. Such jurisdiction is exercised by the archbishop himself, or by a vicar-general, official, or other commissary to whom authority in that behalf shall have been formally committed by the archbishop concerned.

4.   The archbishop is, within his province, the principal minis-
     ter, and to him belongs the right of confirming the election of
     every person to a bishopric, of being the chief consecrator at
     the consecration of every bishop, of receiving such appeals in
     his provincial court as may be provided by law, of holding
     metropolitical visitations at times or places limited by law or
     custom, and of presiding in the convocation of the province
     either in person or by such deputy as he may lawfully ap-
     point. (. . .) The two archbishops are joint presidents of the
     General Synod.

5.   By ancient custom, no act is held to be an act of the convo-
     cation of the province unless it shall have received the assent
     of the archbishop.

4

"The Gift Which He on One Bestows, We All Delight to Prove"

A Possible Methodist Approach to a Ministry of Primacy in the Circulation of Love and Truth

Geoffrey Wainwright

Anecdotal Impressions

To begin anecdotally, even journalistically: In September 1997 the executive committee of the World Methodist Council met in Rome at the invitation of the Methodist Church in Italy. At the request of the officers of the WMC, the Pontifical Council for Promoting Christian Unity kindly arranged for the members of the executive committee to be received in audience by His Holiness Pope John Paul II. Already before the meeting, the President of the Methodist Church in Italy, the Rev. Valdo Benecchi, wrote frankly and fraternally to the General Secretary of the WMC to explain why he could not participate in such an event as a papal audience, even though he was himself a member of the executive committee: "In the Italian context, whatever gesture by Protestants that, on account of the procedures adopted, could appear as a recognition of the role of the pope as defined by Roman Catholic doctrine, would not be accepted and would disturb the consciences of Italian Methodists and of Italian Protestants of all denominations."

In the same letter, Pastor Benecchi reported that "we rejoiced at the latest Synod of the Waldensian and Methodist Churches in Italy over the progress that has been made in relations between Protestants and

Catholics here. In particular, we appreciated the signing (last June) of a 'Common Text' concerning interconfessional marriages, and the gestures of reconciliation by Catholic authorities before and after the second European Ecumenical Assembly (in Graz)." The Italian Methodist President wrote also of a working document on ecumenism generated by the joint Waldensian-Methodist Synod and now being studied in the local congregations: it lays out a proposal that "sees the unity of the church in the direction of 'conciliar communion' and of 'reconciled diversity'": "The means of practicing this communion would be an universal council in which all the churches are present with equal standing." The document "reaffirms that the way in which the papacy is defined doctrinally and exercised practically remains an obstacle on the path to the unity of the church."

As matters turned out, the papal health did not permit a full schedule of audiences in September 1997, so the Methodists were included in the public occasion of a Wednesday in St. Peter's Square, where they were seated in front of the basilica in honorable proximity to the Pope; their chief officers were presented to His Holiness, who also spoke informally with several others at the conclusion of the event. In his allocution to the assembled pilgrims in the square, Pope John Paul continued his weekly series of addresses on the subject of the Blessed Virgin Mary according to the teaching of the Second Vatican Council. Afterwards, some members of the executive committee of the World Methodist Council expressed their concern, both in conversation and in council, at the Pope's development of a Marian theme. In particular, they had been made anxious by press reports of petitions among Roman Catholics to have the Mother of the Lord dogmatically defined as "Co-Redemptrix." Those with long enough memories recalled Pope Pius XII's definition of Mary's Assumption, which had in 1950 set the cat among the ecumenical pigeons. In 1997 some comfort was taken in the fact that a specially appointed commission of distinguished mariologists had recently discountenanced a new definition. Nevertheless, the Pope's address in St. Peter's Square had served to bring into sharp focus some issues of doctrinal substance and magisterial process that are inevitably involved in ecumenical consideration of a Petrine office such as it is defined and practiced in the Roman Catholic Church.

Pursuing Agreement

This anecdotal evidence suffices to show that a hard road still has to be travelled in any engagement between Methodists and the Roman see on the question of a universal ministry of pastoral oversight and dogmatic teaching. All the same, the World Methodist Council has been in official conversations with the Roman Catholic Church since 1967,[1] which is surely a sign of that "real but imperfect communion" within which John Paul II in his ecumenical encyclical of Pentecost 1995 invited "a patient and fraternal dialogue" on the subject of the ministry of the Bishop of Rome.[2] It should be possible to discuss that topic, which the Pope considers both delicate and indispensable, in a theological and ecclesiological framework such as has been constructed between Catholics and Methodists in their joint commission.

At the conclusion of its Singapore Report of 1991 on *The Apostolic Tradition*,[3] the Joint Commission noted in paragraph 100 that "Catholic and Methodist formularies differ over the concrete location of the Church which they both confess." Yet "while Wesley and the early Methodists could recognize the presence of Christ in the lives of individual Roman Catholics," "more recently Methodists have become more willing to recognize the Roman Catholic Church as an institution for the divine good of its members." On its side, "the Roman Catholic Church since Vatican II certainly includes Methodists among those who, by baptism and faith in Christ, enjoy 'a certain though imperfect communion with the Catholic Church'; and it envisages Methodism among those ecclesial communities which are 'not devoid of meaning and importance in the mystery of salvation'" (*Unitatis redintegratio*, 3). As a result of the dialogue up to that point, the report claimed that "a large measure of common faith has been brought to light, so that the increase in shared life that has begun may confidently be expected to continue. The need now is to consolidate the measure of agreement so far attained and to press forward with work on those areas in which agreement is still lacking. Continuing doctrinal progress should both encourage and reflect the growth in mutual recognition and in sharing in the life of the Triune God."[4]

In that spirit, the Joint Commission between the Roman Catholic Church and the World Methodist Council worked to produce its Rio de Janeiro Report of 1996 under the title *The Word of Life: A Statement on*

---

[1] For an overview see G. Wainwright, *Methodists in Dialogue* (Nashville: Abingdon/Kingswood, 1995) 37–56 ("Roman Catholic-Methodist Dialogue: A Silver Jubilee").

[2] John Paul II, *Ut unum sint. That They May Be One: On Commitment to Ecumenism* (Washington, D.C.: United States Catholic Conference, 1995) §96 (hereafter cited *Ut unum sint*).

[3] For the text, see Pontifical Council for Promoting Christian Unity, *Information Service,* no. 78 (1991–III/IV) 212–25 (hereafter cited "The Apostolic Tradition" followed by paragraph number).

[4] "The Apostolic Tradition," 101.

Revelation and Faith.[5] It concluded that, with the establishment of some "broad theological perspectives acceptable to both Roman Catholics and Methodists" and "a considerable commonality of outlook," the "time may have come for concentration, in the directions thus shown, on some of those more detailed questions that have recurrently caused difficulty among us. In particular, future study could address the related topics of pastoral and doctrinal authority, the offices of oversight in the Church and succession in them, and the offer made by Rome of a Petrine ministry in the service of unity and communion. We should thus be encouraged to pursue, more immediately and at a deeper level, the understanding that we both have of ourselves and of our partners in respect to the one Church of Jesus Christ and the communion which belongs to the body of Christ."[6] The renewed Commission has taken up that challenge as its work for the current *quinquennium* of 1997–2001. Thus the invitation of John Paul II was issued *au bon moment*.

Fundamental Categories

Methodist tongues and ears are not familiar with the language of a "universal power of jurisdiction" and of an "infallibility in defining doctrine" such as the First Vatican Council used in connection with the primacy of the Roman pontiffs as successors of the apostle Peter in a ministry of pastor and teacher instituted by Christ the Lord for the sake of the unity and faithfulness of the entire Church. They will resonate much more readily with the language of John Paul II when he speaks of "a ministry which presides in truth and love," so that the ship of the Church "will not be buffeted by the storms and will one day reach its haven."[7] Those are the terms—"truth and love"—under which the notion of a "presiding ministry" may begin to find understanding among Methodists; and perhaps also, in the long run, the idea that it is as a "function of Peter" that such a ministry "must continue in the Church, so that under her sole Head, who is Jesus Christ, she may be visibly present in the world as the communion of all his disciples";[8] and just possibly, in the even longer run, the thought that such a Petrine function belongs historically and theologically to the bishops of Rome.[9]

[5] For the text see *Information Service*, no. 92 (1996–III) 108–25 (hereafter cited "The Word of Life" followed by paragraph number).

[6] "The Word of Life," 131f.

[7] *Ut unum sint*, 97.

[8] *Ibid.*

[9] *Ut unum sint*, 88–95.

Let us start modestly, with the fundamental categories of "truth and love." That is a biblical binome. It governs the Second Epistle of John, which begins: "The elder to the elect lady and her children, whom I *love in the truth*, and not only I but also all who know the truth, because of the truth which abides in us and will be with us for ever: Grace, mercy, and peace will be with us, from God the Father and from Jesus Christ the Father's Son, in *truth and love*" (verses 1-3); and "following the *truth*" and "following *love*" are conjoined, if not equated (verses 4-11). Then there is the Apostle's exhortation in Eph 4:15f: "Speaking [*or* doing] *the truth in love*, we are to grow up in every way into him who is the head, into Christ, from whom the whole body, joined and knit together by every joint with which it is supplied, when each part is working properly, makes bodily growth and upbuilds itself in love." God is characterized by truth and love and has been revealed as such in Christ, in whom Christians participate and whom they are to imitate.

Methodists are familiar with the hymn of Charles Wesley (1707–1788): "Thou God of *truth and love*, We seek thy perfect way."[10] They know that life in the body of Christ entails *mutual love* as well as *consensus in the truth*; and so they sing in another Wesleyan hymn:

> All praise to our redeeming Lord,
> Who joins us by his grace,
> And bids us, each to each restored,
> Together seek his face.
>
> He bids us build each other up;
> And, gathered into one,
> To our high calling's glorious hope
> We hand in hand go on.
>
> Even now we think and speak the same,
> And cordially agree;
> Concentred all, through Jesus' name,
> In perfect harmony.[11]

A third hymn on ecclesial *koinōnia* (and there are many such hymns on "Christian fellowship" in the Wesleyan *oeuvre* and in traditional Methodist use) makes clear that mutual care and instruction is to serve the common growth, as the Letter to the Ephesians puts it, of the entire body "into Christ, the Head":

[10] In *A Collection of Hymns for the Use of the People called Methodists* (1780), no. 496; and many later hymnals.

[11] In *A Collection* (1831 edition), no. 500; and many later hymnals.

> Help us to build each other up,
> Our little stock improve;
> Increase our faith, confirm our hope,
> And pérfect us in love.
>
> Up into thee, our living Head,
> Let us in all things grow. . . .[12]

Clearly, then, Methodists have appropriated into their ecclesiology the scriptural categories of *unity* in *truth* and *love*. That provides at least a basis on which Methodists and Catholics can begin to discuss Pope John Paul's redescription of his own office as a ministry of truth and love in and for the sake of the whole Church. The question then becomes that of whether such a ministry may properly be seen as concentrated in some special way in one member of the body. Methodists have no problem with the diversity of gifts and tasks. In a Wesleyan hymn that has achieved ecumenical popularity in the English-speaking world ("Christ, From Whom All Blessings Flow"), those who make up Christ's "Mystic Body" pray thus to their Head:

> Move, and actuate, and guide:
> Divers gifts to each divide;
> Placed according to thy will,
> Let us all our work fulfil.[13]

The previously quoted hymn "All Praise to Our Redeeming Lord" recognizes the singularity of a particular gift that may bring delight to all, through whom grace flows from a single Source:

> The gift which He on one bestows,
> We all delight to prove;
> The grace through every vessel flows,
> In purest streams of love.

The question implied by the adoption of the first couplet of that stanza as the title of the present *ballon d'essai* is whether there is any way from what is there doubtless intended as a general experience of ecclesial life among the brothers and sisters (where all rejoice in the gifts of each) to what Pope John Paul writes about a very particular gift and responsibility that falls to one among the bishops of the Church: The "service of unity, rooted in the action of divine mercy, is entrusted within the Col-

---

[12] From an early hymn of 1742, entitled "A Prayer for Persons joined in Fellowship"; in the 1780 *Collection*, no. 489.

[13] *A Collection* (1780), no. 504, and many later hymnals.

lege of Bishops to *one* among those who have received from the Spirit the task, not of exercising power over the people—as the rulers of the Gentiles and their great men do (cf. Matt 20:25; Mark 10:42)—but of leading them towards peaceful pastures."[14] If such a road exists, it will be a long and difficult one, both theologically and, for Methodists (as was hinted in the opening anecdotes), experientially.

The next step may consist in showing that Methodist ecclesiology also in practice knows structures and organs in the Body that serve the maintenance of *truth* and the furtherance of *love*—and is even receptive to a ministry of *presidency*.

Methodist Functions

The most characteristic Methodist institutions intending to serve the maintenance of truth and the furtherance of love in the ecclesial body are the *Connexion* and the *Conference*. In Methodist practice, the Conference has the final oversight of "our doctrines" and "our discipline" within the fellowship of the Connexion.

"Connexion" is a notion dating from John Wesley (1703–1791) and the rise of Methodism. In a common eighteenth-century usage (and British Methodists retain the old-fashioned spelling), Methodists were those "in connexion with Mr. Wesley"—just as other evangelical leaders had those "connected" with them. People who responded to the itinerant preaching of the Anglican priest John Wesley and his associates ("Assistants" and "Helpers") were gathered into structured "Societies" for the mutual support and continued growth of the "Members" in faith and holiness (towards "perfect love"). In 1766 Mr. Wesley described the "connexion" of Methodists with him in terms of his "power of admitting into and excluding from the Societies under my care; of choosing and removing Stewards [i.e., officers of the Societies]; of receiving or not receiving Helpers [i.e. preachers]; of appointing them when, where and how to help me; and of desiring any of them to meet me, when I see good."[15] (That passage may evoke for Roman Catholics the notions of central appointment of bishops and of *ad limina* visits; and indeed many of Wesley's robustly Protestant English critics accused him of exercising a "papal" authority; but that is not the point just now.)

---

[14] *Ut unum sint,* 94; emphasis added.

[15] From the Conference of 1766, in *Minutes of Several Conversations between the Rev. John Wesley, A.M. and the Preachers in Connexion with Him, from the Year 1744* (Leeds: printed by Edward Baines, 1803) 23.

John Wesley spoke of all the Methodists in Britain as "one connected people" and indeed thought of them, as Methodism spread overseas, as "one people in all the world."[16] Methodists spoke of themselves, in an extended use, as "our connexion." The "bonds which gave substance to this connectedness" of eighteenth-century Methodism have recently been summarized by Brian Beck, current secretary of the British Methodist Conference, in his study of "connexionalism":

> All societies, their constituent bands and classes, their leaders and stewards, are furnished with the same rules. They are subject to the same discipline as to personal godliness and the quest for perfection. Members can be transferred from one society to another. The preachers similarly are held under obedience to Wesley and act in his name in the discipline of the societies. They are furnished with their own rules, and answerable to him for faith, personal behavior, doctrine, and the conduct of their ministry. By having their station changed each year, they travel widely among the societies and help to give them a sense of belonging to a single family. As time goes on, other factors enter into the picture, such as Wesley's publications and the hymns. Central funds are raised, for the general debt on the chapels, for Kingswood School, and to assist the preachers. All is under the supervision of the annual Conference of the preachers, which meets to consider points of doctrine and discipline, receive reports of the societies, and station the preachers. Wesley regarded the Conference as advisory (so that the connexion is with him, not, at this stage, with the Conference), although not all the preachers saw it in quite the same terms.[17]

(In reference to that last issue, one might perhaps speak, by analogy with the Roman Catholic view of the relation between the Pope and the College of Bishops, of "the Conference *una cum* Wesley"!)

Beck goes on to note concerning early Methodism that "the whole movement was motivated by three convictions about the Gospel: Christ died for all, all are called to a life of holy love, and there is no such thing as solitary religion": Methodism functioned to supply the failures of the established Church "to proclaim universal redemption, to nurture growth in holiness, and to provide for every seeker after salvation to be joined to others in fellowship." Correspondingly, John Wesley held that

---

[16] Respectively letter of March 3, 1790 to "Friends in Trowbridge" and letter of February 1, 1791 to "Ezekiel Cooper, of Philadelphia"; see *The Letters of the Rev. John Wesley*, ed. John Telford (London: Epworth Press, 1931) VIII, 205 and 260.

[17] See B. Beck, "Some Reflections on Connexionalism," *Epworth Review* 18, 2 (1991) 48–59, and 18, 3 (1991) 43–50; quotation from the first part, p. 50. This article provided initial references to some of the earlier texts cited on the theme.

"the end," or purpose, "of all ecclesiastical order" was to "bring souls from the power of Satan to God, and to bring them up in His fear and love. Order, then, is so far valuable as it answers these ends; and if it answers them not, it is nothing worth."[18]

As long as Wesley lived, he was at the very least a central point of reference for the entire Connexion. As he approached the age of seventy, he addressed the "travelling preachers in our connexion" thus:

> You are at present one body. You act in concert with each other, and by united counsels. And now is the time to consider what can be done in order to continue this union. Indeed, as long as I live, there will be no great difficulty: I am, under God, a centre of union to all our Travelling as well as Local Preachers. They all know me and my communication. They all love me for my work's sake: and, therefore, were it only out of regard to me, they will continue connected with each other. But by what means may this connexion be preserved when God removes me from you?[19]

The answer, in Britain, was to be "the Conference," legally established by the Deed of Declaration in 1784, with one hundred travelling preachers at its heart—"the Legal Hundred." In the first part of the nineteenth century, the Wesleyan Methodist Conference was familiarly called "the living Wesley." It met annually and exercised oversight of the whole Connexion, which more and more took on the character of a distinct "denominational church." The preachers—who from 1836 onwards were admitted into "full connexion with the Conference" by the laying on of hands—accepted and administered a common "doctrine" and a common "discipline" (to use the pair of terms that run the course of Methodist history).[20] Thus were truth and love served within what James Harrison Rigg (1821–1909) spoke of as an ecclesial "fellowship, which joins into one loving brotherhood the general society of believers, so that each

[18] Letter of June 25, 1746 "to 'John Smith'" in *Letters* . . . , II:77f. See further, G. Wainwright, *Methodists in Dialogue* . . . , 73–87 ("The End of All Ecclesiastical Order").

[19] From the Conference of 1769, in *Minutes of Several Conversations* (as in note 15) 56f.

[20] For example: Charles Wesley, *Journal* for June 25, 1744, at the first Conference ("our doctrines, practice, and discipline"); Joseph Benson (1748–1821), *An Apology for the People called Methodists* (London: printed by G. Story, 1801) 203, referring to the early Conferences ("The grand points in respect both to doctrine and discipline were then laid down, methodized and established, which have continued even to the present day"); Richard Watson (1781–1833), *An Affectionate Address* (1829), in *Works*, twelve volumes, (London: John Mason, 1834–1837) VII (1835) 90 ("a common bond of doctrine and discipline"); and so on, down to the questions still put synodically each year concerning every minister of the Methodist Church in Great Britain ("Does he believe and preach our doctrines? Does he faithfully observe and enforce our discipline?").

believer may have actual spiritual comradeship with some company of other believers, and be linked to the whole body in vital and organic connexion, and so that all may have an opportunity of using their spiritual faculties and gifts."[21] Benjamin Gregory (1820–1900) and Robert Newton Flew (1886–1962) developed similar notions under the heading of "the communion of the saints."[22]

A vital feature of the connexional system, ensuring the flow of truth and love throughout the Body, was what J. H. Rigg called a "circulating pastorate."[23] Again, Brian Beck notes that, for British Methodism in the nineteenth century, "itinerancy is important if the fidelity of preachers and congregations to the gospel is to be maintained. The argument is carried forward from Wesley's day that frequent changes of ministerial appointment guard both pastor and congregation against collusion in heresy or decline, and have the added advantage of providing varied ministry to meet different needs in each congregation, and a varied stimulus to the pastor to keep him at his best."[24]

From the beginnings of Methodism, the itinerancy of the preachers was seen not only as serving the doctrinal and pastoral needs of the gathered Societies but also, and perhaps in the first place, the opportunities for spreading the Gospel in new areas: souls needed to be brought "from the power of Satan to God" before they could be brought up in God's "fear and love"; evangelism precedes edification. This dual function of an itinerant ministry was expressed by Thomas Coke and Francis Asbury, the two men named by John Wesley as "Superintendents" of the Methodist work in North America, who from 1787 received the designation "Bishops" in the "Methodist Episcopal Church" that had been set up at the 1784 Christmas Conference in Baltimore. In their notes to the *Discipline* of 1798, Coke and Asbury wrote: "Our grand plan, in all its parts, leads to an itinerant ministry. Our bishops are travelling bishops. All the

---

[21] J. H. Rigg, *A Comparative View of Church Organizations, Primitive and Protestant* (1878), 3rd ed., revised and enlarged, (London: Charles H. Kelly, 1897) 11. Rigg is speaking normatively on the basis of the primitive Church in Jerusalem as described in the Acts of the Apostles; stereoscopically, he has Methodism in mind.

[22] B. Gregory, *The Holy Catholic Church, The Communion of Saints* (1873); R. N. Flew, "Methodism and the Catholic Tradition," in N. P. Williams and C. Harris, eds., *Northern Catholicism: Centenary Studies in the Oxford and Parallel Movements* (London: SPCK, 1933) 515–30. From its beginnings, Methodism has had a strong sense of the transhistorical character of the communion of saints; see G. Wainwright, *Methodists in Dialogue . . . ,* 237–49 ("Wesley and the Communion of Saints").

[23] J. H. Rigg, *The Principles of Wesleyan Methodism* (London: Partridge & Oakey, 2nd ed. 1850) 90.

[24] B. Beck, "Some Reflections . . . ," 53.

different orders which compose our conferences are employed in the travelling line; and our local preachers are, in some degree, travelling preachers. Everything is kept moving as far as possible. . . . Next to the grace of God, there is nothing like this for keeping the whole body alive from the centre to the circumference, and for the continual extension of that circumference on every hand."[25] To this day, the bishops of the United Methodist Church are "kept moving"–although scarcely at the rhythm of the old "circuit riders"–and collectively have the responsibility of a "general superintendency" over the whole Connection.[26]

The classical work of British Wesleyan Methodist ecclesiology in the nineteenth century, *Holy Catholic Church* by Benjamin Gregory, found an apostolic precedent for an "itinerant superintendency" that might even now stimulate in an interesting direction the incipient dialogue between Catholics and Methodists on a Petrine ministry. Tracing the stages of the initial spread of the Gospel according to the Acts of the Apostles, Gregory notes that

> the unity of the Palestinian churches with each other and with the Mother-Church at Jerusalem, and the Apostles at its centre, was realized and strengthened by the itinerant superintendency of Peter, who, we are told, "passed throughout all" (Acts ix.32). . . .
>
> Whilst Peter is on his tour of superintendency, he receives direct instructions from the Master to use his golden key, and open "the door of faith unto the Gentiles" (Acts xiv.27). . . . This work is assigned . . . to Peter, that it might be fulfilled which was spoken by Christ Himself, "I will give unto thee the keys of the kingdom of heaven" (Matt. xvi.19).
>
> . . . In [this] continuous evolution of the Church we cannot but recognize the essential oneness of the work, attesting the Oneness of the Worker, amidst the most beautiful and instructive diversities

[25] *The Doctrines and Discipline of the Methodist Episcopal Church in America, with Explanatory Notes by Thomas Coke and Francis Asbury,* facsimile ed. (Rutland, Vt.: Academy Books, 1979) 42.

[26] The word "Connection" was frowned on at times in nineteenth-century American Methodism (see the Journal of the General Conference of 1816, in *Journals of the General Conference of the Methodist Episcopal Church,* vol. 1: 1796–1836 (New York: Carlton & Phillips, 1855) 172–perhaps because it was (regrettably!) thought less appropriate to a "Church" than to a "Society." But the idea and practice were not lost; and the word itself, which had never in fact disappeared, has enjoyed a remarkable recovery in recent decades, not least as the United Methodist Church seeks to conceptualize its "global" character; see B. W. Robbins, "Connection and *Koinōnia*: Wesleyan and Ecumenical Perspectives on the Church" (paper presented at the Oxford Institute of Methodist Theological Studies, August 1997). On the episcopate in American Methodism, see G. F. Moede, *The Office of Bishop in Methodism: Its History and Development* (Nashville: Abingdon Press, 1964).

of adaptation to varying characters and circumstances. An unbroken uniformity of sequence, in the developmental processes by which the Church is extended, testifies to the ever-active superintendence of an intelligent Power, a Divine Personality, Whose energy is throughout the motive force. We see purpose, plan, prevision; but the purpose, plan, prevision is not man's, but God's.[27]

Noting how classic Wesleyan writers on early Methodism—and the same is true of John Wesley's own vision—saw it as "a revival of primitive Church life,"[28] David Carter comments thus in reference to the "itinerant superintendency" of Peter:

In the ecumenical era, we are engaged not merely in monitoring the faithfulness of our own communities to the fullness of apostolic life, but in endeavoring to discern that same life in other churches. Methodists should now re-examine both the historical achievement of the papacy and present papal practice in order to see how far they can discern in it a petrine tradition that is compatible with their reading of the New Testament and tradition in the light of their experience. They might particularly want to point to the "resumption" of a tradition of papal "itinerancy" in the practice of Paul VI and John Paul II with their frequent visits to Churches across the world. They should then be able to speak back to the Pope with their insights into his ministry as requested in *Ut unum sint.*[29]

That imaginative suggestion might gratifyingly allow a positive and particular contribution from the side of Methodism to the conversation which John Paul II has invited; but before that can become timely, the clarificatory dialogue between Methodists and Catholics requires further general work on the notion of a unitive "superintendency"—and eventually a universal "presidency"—in the service of love and truth.

Within the Methodist Connexion, the principal organ of oversight is the Conference.[30] Throughout Methodist history the Conference, in its evolving forms, may be regarded as having constantly exercised "a

---

[27] B. Gregory, *Holy Catholic Church* . . . , 43f.

[28] See T. A. Campbell, *John Wesley and Christian Antiquity* (Nashville: Abingdon/Kingswood, 1991).

[29] D. Carter, "A Methodist Reaction to *Ut unum sint,*" *One in Christ* 33, 2 (1997) 125–37, here 133f. Carter is a British layman, keenly interested in ecumenism.

[30] For early British Methodism, see W. L. Doughty, *John Wesley: His Conferences and His Preachers* (London: Epworth Press, 1944); for the nineteenth century, J. C. Bowmer, *Pastor and People: A Study of Church and Ministry in Wesleyan Methodism from the Death of John Wesley (1791) to the Death of Jabez Bunting (1858)* (London: Epworth Press, 1975); for America, R. E. Richey, *The Methodist Conference in America: A History* (Nashville: Abingdon/Kingswood, 1996).

corporate *episkopē*" in the internal matters of doctrine and discipline as well as in guiding the missionary outreach and evangelistic work of the Connexion. In British Methodism, the officers primarily responsible for local supervision have historically been the "Superintendent Ministers." Appointed by the Conference to geographical "Circuits," they are responsible for the doctrine preached in the Methodist chapels there, for the disciplined fellowship within and between the various local Societies, and for evangelistic extension in their area. A focal role is played by the President of the Conference, who is elected annually, who is regarded as occupying "Wesley's chair" (from the start, John Wesley assumed the part for himself), and who travels throughout the Connexion for a year (chief among the insignia of office being John Wesley's "field Bible").[31]

From 1878 onwards, the Conference of the Wesleyan Methodist Church in Britain included elected lay representatives; and since the union of the various branches of British Methodism in 1932 the number of matters reserved to the "ministerial session" has gradually declined.[32] Lay participation in the Conference may be viewed as building a communal dimension into the exercise of *episkopē* from the start, and the reception of the Conference's decisions by the Church at large is accordingly launched by active collaboration between ministers and lay people from the beginning of the process. In so far as Methodism may harbor any hints of "primatial" function (whether of Superintendent Ministers or of the President, who is always an ordained minister), their context must be that of the corporate *episkopē* of the Conference.

So far, the point has been, first, to show my fellow Methodists that, for Roman Catholics, the "petrine office" is fundamentally about the service of truth and love in the Church as a whole–a scriptural goal that Methodists share; and secondly, to introduce Catholics to the terminology and institutions by which Methodists characteristically express their concern for unity in doctrine and discipline–the connexion and the conference, superintendency and fellowship, and even the notion and

---

[31] In this description I have British Methodism principally in mind; things vary somewhat in American Methodism. The differences depend partly on the territorial range of the two countries and partly on the presence of bishops in American Methodism. American bishops are "consecrated" to the office but are not viewed as constituting an "order" distinct from the Elders/Presbyters; they remain subject to the General Conference; they exercise their "general superintendency" in part through regular meetings of a "council of bishops." The president pro tem of that council does not have the status or function of the President of the Conference within British Methodism.

[32] In the United States, the Methodist Episcopal Church, South "approved lay representation in 1866," while the Methodist Episcopal Church "conceded the issue in 1872"; see R. E. Richey, *The Methodist Conference . . . ,* 118f.

practice of an itinerating ministry. The last part of this essay will survey what has been said up to now in the official dialogue between the World Methodist Council and the Roman Catholic Church on the subject of a petrine ministry. Attention cannot be limited to direct and explicit references to the papacy, for several closely adjacent themes are needed as part of the context if the discussion is not to be determined sheerly from the Roman Catholic side.

Official Dialogue

There are six reports so far to examine; they are informally designated by the place and year in which, simultaneously with their presentation to the Vatican, they were presented to the meetings of the World Methodist Council: Denver 1971, Dublin 1976, Honolulu 1981, Nairobi 1986, Singapore 1991, and Rio de Janeiro 1996.

Denver 1971

Under the section heading of "authority," the meandering first report of the international commission made the following comments:

> 100. From the beginning of our discussions it was recognized that problems of authority were implicit in some of the deep "crevasses" between us, and notably the Mariological dogmas and the doctrines of the Infallibility or Indefectability of the Church on the one hand; while on the other hand the whole question of the origin and development of Methodism as a work of the Spirit, of an extraordinary and prophetic character, has at some point to be related to the Catholic view of church order and its understanding of the authority of Christ in his Church. We agreed to postpone these important questions because it seemed to us fundamentally important to begin, not with our differences and disagreements but with our agreements and with that fundamental unity without which all our conversations would cease to be conversations between Christians.

> 106. . . . Only an authority given in love and received in love expresses the deepest meaning of the word for Christians. . . .

> 108. . . . The various elements in the holy tradition, which we all accept and on which our continuing life as Churches also depends— theologies, liturgies, devotion, the sacraments, preaching of the Word and study of the Bible, the authority of the ministry and of Pope and bishops or of the Methodist Conferences and ministry—it is likely that the two lists of authorities might not turn out to be as dissimilar as we might expect. But almost certainly we should place

them in a differing order and lay more stress here on one element
and there on another.[33]

Dublin 1976

On the topic of "Ministry," the report of "Dublin 1976" was able to
affirm as "our common understanding" that "the fundamental ministry
is Christ's own ministry, whose goal is to reconcile all people to God and
to each other and to bring them into a new community in which they
can grow together to their full freedom as children of God. This ministry was focused in Christ's life and death and resurrection. It did not
end with his life on earth, but by the power of the Spirit continues now
in and through his church. Christ still chooses and equips people for his
ministry, just as he did in the beginning" (77). Further, "the apostles
were the first 'ministers of the gospel'" (82), and "we all agree that the
church's apostolicity involves continuous faithfulness in doctrine, ministry, sacrament and life to the teaching of the New Testament" (84).
Again, "Roman Catholics and Methodists agree that *episkopē* (pastoral
care and oversight) belongs essentially to the ordained ministry. Such
episkopē is exercised in different ways in their churches, but in each case
it is carefully ordered with the purpose of the building-up and discipline
of the faithful, the training of the young, the maintenance of the unity
and peace of the church, and in the planning and direction of mission
and evangelism" (88). The Roman Catholic bishop "exercises the fullness of the ordained ministry" and has "the overall responsibility of
teaching and governing, but he is related to the whole church as a member of the college of bishops, of which the Pope is head, and as pastor
of his own people shares the ministry with presbyters and deacons" (89).
In Methodism, "primacy" is recognized to the Conference (90–91).[34]

Honolulu 1981

More coherent and systematic reports start with "Honolulu 1981":
Towards an Agreed Statement on the Holy Spirit. In the section on "The Holy
Spirit and Authority in the Church," it is recognized that "there is no disagreement that the Church has authority to teach. In the Church, the
revelation of God in Christ comes to us through Scriptures, and to maintain God's people in the truth is the loving work of the Spirit in the

[33] Text in Secretariat for Promoting Christian Unity, *Information Service,* no. 21
(1973–III) 22–38.
[34] Text in *Information Service,* no. 34 (1977–II) 8–20.

Church" (34). Two paragraphs follow that deal directly with the authority and ministry of the papacy (emphases added):

> 35. Ours is not the only dialogue in which special difficulties have been voiced, and persist, in the matter of papal claims and the character of dogmatic definitions. . . . We believe that emotions surrounding such relatively modern terms as infallibility and irreformability can be diminished if they are looked at in the light of our shared doctrine concerning the Holy Spirit. *The papal authority, no less than any other within the Church, is a manifestation of the continuing presence of the Spirit of Love in the Church or it is nothing.* Indeed it should in its exercise be preeminently such a manifestation. It was declared at Vatican I to be "for the building up and not the casting down of the church"–whether of the local Church or the communion of local Churches.
>
> 36. This primary aspect has been obscured by the emotions and polemics surrounding such terms as infallibility and universal and immediate jurisdiction. As with other dogmas, the terms which express the dogma of 1870 belong to their time, and must be understood in the context of that time and of the debates of that era. The truth behind them is capable of fuller understanding in new settings by all concerned. Already Vatican II's Constitution on the Church, *Lumen gentium*, and other documents have done something to adjust an imbalance left by the unfinished business of Vatican I.
>
> The terms referred to are not to be explained away: from different standpoints we are agreed that this would be neither useful nor honest. Yet they are not claims about human qualities or glorifications of an office. They are to be understood in the light of *the total conception and the total responsibility of teaching and disciplinary office in the Church–a pastoral office mirroring the constant presence and solicitude of the Spirit within the Church, leading into truth and disciplining in love.* Thus, and thus only, whatever its forms and nomenclature, can any authority be understood and legitimized.
>
> However the claims implied in such terms are circumscribed and clarified, it is unlikely that Methodists in the foreseeable future will feel comfortable with them. But Methodist awareness of the papacy has enlarged and greatly altered in recent times, and *the general idea of a universal service of unity within the Church, a primacy of charity mirroring the presence and work in the Church of the Spirit who is love, may well be a basis for increased understanding and convergence.*[35]

---

[35] Text in *Information Service*, no. 46 (1981–II) 84–96.

Nairobi 1986

Under the general title *Towards a Statement on the Church*,[36] the next report, "Nairobi 1986," devoted thirty-seven paragraphs (39–75) to "The Petrine Office." The previous section, on "Structures of Ministry," ends with a reference to "Catholic belief in the primacy of the Bishop of Rome"; and, while recognizing that "for Methodists the concept of primacy is unfamiliar, even if historically John Wesley exercised a kind of primacy in the origins of the Methodist Church . . . and today's Conference continues to embody certain elements of this function," the joint commission saw that "questions of the Petrine office and the primacy of the Bishop of Rome" would have to be treated as part of the search for "full unity in faith, mission and sacramental life." Four sub-headings structure the section on "The Petrine Office": "Peter in the New Testament" (41–47), "Primacy and the Petrine Ministry" (48–60), "Jurisdiction" (61–62), and "Authoritative Teaching" (63–75).

Under the exegetical guidance of Raymond E. Brown, at that time a member of the joint commission and a previous participant in a Lutheran-Roman Catholic dialogue in the United States that had produced *Peter in the New Testament*,[37] the report surveys the scriptural testimony to Peter, who at Matthew 10:2 "is called 'first'" and who is depicted "in a plurality of images and roles: missionary fisherman (Luke 5, John 21); pastoral shepherd (John 21, Luke 22:32, 1 Pet 5); witness and martyr (1 Cor 15:5; cf. John 21:15-17, 1 Pet 5:1); recipient of special revelation (Matt 16:17, Acts 10:9-11, 2 Pet 1:16-17); the 'rock' named by Jesus (Matt 16:18, John 1:42, Mark 1:42); recipient of the keys of the kingdom of heaven (Matt 16:18); confessor and preacher of the true faith (Matt 16:16, Acts 2); guardian against false teaching (2 Pet 1:20-21, 3:15-16, Acts 8:20-23); and weak human being and repentant sinner, rebuked by Christ and withstood by Paul (Mark 8:33, Matt 16:23; Mark 14:31, 66-72, John 21:15-17, Gal 2:5)." It is noted that "most of these images persist through two or more strands of the New Testament tradition and several recur in subsequent Church history."

Moving to "Primacy and the Petrine Ministry," the report begins with an apparent acceptance, as a sociological principle, of "unity focused around leadership" and shifts quickly to the factual historical development of the local episcopate and then wider provincialates and

[36] Text in *Information Service,* no. 62 (1986–IV) 241–59.

[37] R. E. Brown, K. P. Donfried, and J. Reumann, eds., *Peter in the New Testament: A Collaborative Assessment by Protestant and Roman Catholic Scholars* (Minneapolis/New York: Augsburg/Paulist, 1973).

patriarchates; next it is asked, sociologically, "whether the whole Church needs a leader to exercise a similar unifying role in service to the worldwide *koinōnia*," and again history records the claim–"essentially complete by the fifth century"–that "the Roman see already exercises such a ministry of universal unity." The "special position and role of the Roman see in the early Church" is seen to have depended on the convergence of several factors: its strategic importance for the global mission of Christianity as the capital city of the Empire; its dual association with Peter and Paul and the place of their martyrdom; the listing of Peter as its first bishop; its role in the establishment of orthodoxy through the repudiation of Marcion and Valentinus. From the fourth and fifth centuries, when Christianity became the imperial religion, papal language took more of a juridical turn, which "sharpened the issue of authority" and, in calling forth resistance, "contributed to the origin and continuation of divisions in Christianity, first in the East and eventually in the West." While Roman Catholics consider that "being in communion with the see of Rome" has always served as "the touchstone of belonging to the Church in its fullest sense," it is noted that "Methodists give less doctrinal weight than Roman Catholics to long and widespread tradition." In view of the urgent need to recover Christian unity, however, it is hinted that Methodists might become receptive to a pragmatically formulated justification of the Roman claim in the present: "Methodists accept that whatever is properly required for the unity of the whole of Christ's Church must by that very fact be God's will for his Church. A universal primacy might well serve as focus of, and ministry for, the unity of the whole Church" (58).

The next section gives a brief indication that Roman Catholic theology may in fact be moving from a narrow view of the papal office in terms of "jurisdiction" towards a more varied view of the Pope's calling to be "an effective symbol of the unity of the Church in faith and life": "He is a reminder of the Apostles witnessing to the resurrection, of Paul preaching to the Gentiles, and of Peter professing faith in Christ and being sent to feed the sheep. In a particular way, the Pope is a sign of Peter. 'Vicar of Peter' is an ancient title that indicates that Peter, a saint in heaven, is present in the Church on earth and is as it were made visible in the Pope" (61). In the context of Catholic-Methodist dialogue, the thought is then prolonged from the previous section: "It would not be inconceivable that at some future date in a restored unity, Roman Catholic and Methodist bishops might be linked in one episcopal college, and that the whole body would recognize some kind of effective leadership and primacy in the bishop of Rome. In that case Methodists might justify such an acceptance on different grounds from those that now prevail in the Roman Catholic Church" (62).

The final section on "authoritative teaching" stands under a soteriological emphasis: "Because God wills the salvation of all men and women, he enables the Church, by the Holy Spirit, so to declare the truth of divine Revelation in Jesus Christ that his people may know the way of salvation. The Scriptures bear permanent witness to the divine Revelation in Christ and are normative for all subsequent tradition" (63–64). It is recognized on both sides that there is sometimes a particular need "to clarify the contents of the Christian Faith and even to define the limits of orthodoxy"; under "the supreme norm of the Scriptures," general councils have functioned in this way. Roman Catholics believe that "the bishops of the Church enjoy the special assistance of the Holy Spirit, when, by a collegial act with the Bishop of Rome in an ecumenical council, they define doctrine to be held irrevocably" (68); and that, exercised in carefully defined and limited circumstances "in and for the whole Church," "papal infallibility is another embodiment of the infallibility with which the Church has been endowed" (69). For their part, "Methodists have problems with this Roman Catholic understanding of infallibility, especially as it seems to imply a discernment of truth which exceeds the capacity of sinful human beings. Methodists are accustomed to see the guidance of the Holy Spirit in more general ways: through reformers, prophetic figures, Church leaders, and Methodist Conferences, for example, as well as through general Councils. Methodist Conferences, exercising their teaching office, formulate doctrinal statements as they are needed, but do not ascribe to them guaranteed freedom from error" (72). Methodists, it is claimed, set great store by the "assent of the whole People of God"—an assent really given, not merely assumed or expected—as "the final judge" of whether teaching is "in agreement with the Scriptures"; and they therefore (with special reference to the doctrines of Mary's immaculate conception and her assumption, which seem to Methodists to "lack assent and reception by all Christian people") welcome "the attention which Roman Catholic theologians are giving to the understanding of the reception of doctrine" and expect that "further study on the reception of doctrine will throw more light on the subject of infallibility" (72–73).

With hindsight, this treatment of Petrine office in terms of jurisdiction and infallibility may seem premature. Certainly the joint commission felt the need to investigate the broader and more fundamental theological perspectives characteristically adopted by Roman Catholics and Methodists *respectively*, and to engage in the attempt to discover or construct *common* such perspectives in which it might be possible eventually to face again the more obviously divisive questions.

Singapore 1991 and Rio de Janeiro 1996

In the two latest, and most systematic, reports, the Methodist-Roman Catholic international dialogue has treated the themes of "apostolic tradition" and "revelation and faith." "Singapore 1991" and "Rio de Janeiro 1996" move towards some common perspectives within which the question of a Petrine ministry can eventually be faced again.[38]

In *The Apostolic Tradition*, the attempt is made to reach a common reading of Christian history in which Catholics and Methodists discern together, with as much detailed agreement as possible, the constant "pattern" of "Christian faith," of "Christian life," and of "Christian community" that has been embodied down the centuries in fidelity to the apostolic witness as recorded in the Scriptures. "Ministry and ministries" are then located as "serving within the apostolic tradition." "Essentially pastoral in nature," and acting "in Christ's name and person" (71), the ordained ministry has "the special responsibility of exercising and holding together the functions of proclaiming the Gospel, calling people to faith, feeding the flock with word and sacrament, and making Christ known through the ministry of servanthood to the world" (81). Catholics and Methodists both "acknowledge the reality of *episkopē* (oversight) in the New Testament" and "agree that an ordained ministry which exercises *episkopē* is vital for the life of the Church": "Without the exercise of this gift of oversight, disorder and therefore disunity are inevitable. *Koinōnia* and *episkopē* imply one another" (92). Moreover, Catholics and Methodists agree that "central to the exercise of *episkopē* is the task of maintaining unity in the Truth." Thereafter, however, Catholics and Methodists can at this stage only state their continuing divergences in this area:

> In a Catholic understanding, the Church is united through its unity in faith and sacramental communion. The teaching of a common faith by the college of bishops in union with the successor of Peter ensures unity in the Truth. The succession of bishops through the generations serves the continued unity of the Church in the faith handed on from the apostles. In the Methodist tradition, Wesley accepted and believed in the reality of *episkopē* within the Church of England of which he was a minister. In relation to the Methodist societies he exercised *episkopē* over the whole; all his followers were

[38] Texts as above in notes 3 and 5.

bound to be in connexion with him. He expounded the main teachings of the Church by means of his Sermons, Notes on the New Testament, and Conference Minutes, and made available to his people authorized abridgements of doctrinal and spiritual work. His appointment of Francis Asbury and Thomas Coke to the superintendency in America was rooted in his belief that the Holy Spirit wished to bestow the gift of *episkopē* at that time and in that place for the sake of maintaining unity of faith with the Church of all ages. It was part of a fresh and extraordinary outpouring of the gift of the Spirit who never ceases to enliven and unify the Church (93).

While recognizing these remaining differences, the Joint Commission rejoiced in the progress made so far between Catholics and Methodists as part of the Spirit-led ecumenical movement for the unity of Christians and forecast that "when the time comes that Methodists and Catholics declare their readiness for that 'full communion in faith, mission and sacramental life' toward which they are working, the mutual recognition of ministry will be achieved not only by their having reached doctrinal consensus but it will also depend upon a fresh creative act of reconciliation which acknowledges the manifold yet unified activity of the Holy Spirit throughout the ages. It will involve a joint act of obedience to the sovereign Word of God" (94).

In *The Word of Life*, the "Rio de Janeiro 1996" statement on "revelation and faith," a strongly trinitarian narration is made of God's historical work of revelation and redemption through word and act; an agreed account is given of "the faith by which we believe," and "the faith which is believed" is set out in terms of the ancient creeds; moreover, there is agreement in principle that "the perception of the truth grows and is tested by the challenges of successive ages," and that "the fruitfulness of faith" shows itself in its periodically restated confession, in various forms of the spiritual life, in liturgical traditions as well as in spontaneous expressions of worship, and in service to individual and social needs. Tensions become apparent between Methodists and Catholics, however, when it comes to what is called "the discernment of faith." There is indeed agreement in principle that "the criteria for discernment" comprise "fidelity to Scripture," harmony with the mind and heart of the Church (*sentire cum ecclesia*), the "long-term reception" of "developments in Christian teaching or living" by "the wider Church," and the "spiritual holiness" which is produced by "conformity, in deep conviction, to Christian doctrinal and moral truth"; and it is even agreed that the "agents of discernment" are multiple (popular, prophetic, and pastoral), which ought to exist in "a growing interdependence and mutual recognition of those who exercise pastoral authority within the Church, those who offer prophetic vision, and all those who, by their response to revelation and their inspiration through the creative love of God, participate in active tradition of the Gospel and compassionate discernment of the will of God for his Church and the world" (72). Yet the nuances vary as they reflect the stubborn facts that in the Roman Catholic Church the teaching office is exercised by "the bishops in unity with the Bishop of Rome" (69), and that in Methodism "the teaching office is exercised by the Conference." In the current quinquennium (1997–2001) the renewed Commission is directed to "the differences between these approaches and their implications for the communion of faith" (71).

In addressing the theme of *koinōnia*-communion, *The Word of Life* achieved an agreement in principle on the basis of the apostolic witness deposited in 1 John 1:1-3, and the document recognized "some of the vital elements"—in the areas of faith, worship, and mission—"in the partial communion we already enjoy" with one another as Catholics and Methodists. Yet "the Roman Catholic Church . . . emphasizes that the whole teaching of the Church constitutes an organic unity" (116)—including its teaching concerning the teaching office (120). Thereby the discussion is brought once more to the theme of a Petrine ministry. The final paragraphs of the 1996 report may therefore now serve to sum up the *status quaestionis* between Methodists and Roman Catholics.

According to paragraph 126, both parties agree that "the Church of God has universal dimensions in regard to both time and space." Then paragraphs 127 and 128 respectively state the diachronic and synchronic issues:

> 127. Although we may differ in our evaluations about what have been signs of faithfulness and perseverance in the Church's history, we certainly agree that God's faithfulness has preserved his Church despite the faults, errors and shortcomings evident in its history.

> 128. In the same way, we acknowledge the importance of a structure which binds together local churches to testify to the global nature of the Gospel and of the Church universal. But we have different perceptions about the nature and the theological weight of those structures.[39]

[39] The ninety-four Methodist and related United Churches that hold membership in the World Methodist Council, representing a global community of some seventy million Christians, are mostly autonomous bodies. The World Methodist Council has no legislative authority; but it fosters collaboration through such instruments as its division for world evangelism, it is entrusted by the member churches with conducting the bilateral dialogues with other Christian world communions, and in 1996 the Council approved a statement of "Wesleyan Essentials of Christian Faith."

The two sides finally repeat once again the divergence of their respective perceptions and practices:

> 129. The Roman Catholic Church relies on the promise which it believes to have been given to St. Peter and the Apostles (see e.g., Matt 16:18) and to have been fulfilled throughout history in the apostolic succession and the episcopal college together with its head, the Bishop of Rome as the successor of St. Peter. The hierarchical structure of the Church is an important means and guarantee given by God's grace to preserve the continuity and the universality of the Catholic Church.

> 130. Methodist churches see the continuity of the apostolic tradition preserved by the faithfulness to the apostolic teaching. The teaching office which decides what is faithful and what is not lies in the hands of conciliar bodies, the Conferences. All Methodist churches recognize the necessity of a ministry of *episkopē*, "oversight," and in many Methodist churches this is expressed in the office of bishop. . . . Local churches are bound together by connexional structures which have to mediate the needs of local churches and of the Church as a whole. Methodists anticipate that more unity and a growing communion between churches of different traditions may be achieved by new conciliar structures.

The judgment made thus far by the Commission in 1996 was that "Roman Catholics and Methodists share a common concern regarding the Church universal as an expression of communion in Christ. But they differ widely in their beliefs about the means which God has given to attain or preserve this goal. These differences may be the greatest hindrances on the way to full communion."

Personal Suggestion

Rather than seek to nuance that summary perception of the Roman Catholic-Methodist Joint Commission by recapitulating the material of the present essay, I want my conclusion to take the form of a personal suggestion. My proposal may perhaps be dismissed as naive, but I hope that it will not be considered disingenuous. It is stimulated by the linkage made by the Holy Father—and in fact characteristic of the modern ecumenical movement from its nineteenth-century beginnings—between unity and evangelism. Negatively put, "it is obvious that the lack of unity among Christians contradicts the Truth which Christians have the mission to spread and, consequently, it gravely damages their witness."[40]

[40] *Ut unum sint,* 98.

Positively put, evangelization demands, for its fuller credibility, ecclesial unity in the substance and practice of the Gospel.

My respectful suggestion is that the pope should invite those Christian communities which he regards as being in real, if imperfect, communion with the Roman Catholic Church to appoint representatives to cooperate with him and his appointees in formulating a statement expressive of the Gospel to be preached to the world today. Thus the theme of the "fraternal dialogue" which John Paul II envisaged would shift from the *theory* of the pastoral and doctrinal office to the *substance* of what is believed and preached. And the very *exercise* of elaborating a statement of faith might—by the process of its launching, its execution, its resultant form, its publication, and its reception—illuminate the question of "a ministry that presides in truth and love." *Solvitur ambulando.*

5

The Primacy of the Successor of the Apostle St. Peter from the Point of View of the Oriental Orthodox Churches

Archbp. Hon. Prof. Dr. Mesrob K. Krikorian

Introduction

Before starting with a presentation and discussion of the Petrine office, it is suitable and useful to remember the words of our Lord Jesus Christ concerning preeminence and exaltation. In chapter 9 of the Gospel according to St. Luke, we learn that there arose a question among the disciples "which of them should be greatest."[1] Jesus said unto them: "He that is least among you all, the same shall be great."[2] In the same Gospel Jesus tells the parable of the wedding and suggests that the guests should not take the highest place at the dinner, unless they are asked by the host to do so.[3] At the end of the story Jesus says: "For whosoever exalteth himself shall be abased; and he that humbleth himself shall be exalted."[4] On the Holy Thursday Jesus washed the feet of his disciples and gave for all generations an example to be modest and honest and to serve the Christian fellowship for the prosperity of the mankind. After washing the feet, he said: "If I then, your Lord and Master, have washed your feet; ye also ought to wash one another's feet. For

---

[1] Luke 9:46 (all quotations are from the King James Version).
[2] Luke 9:48b.
[3] Luke 14:7-11.
[4] Luke 14:11.

I have given you an example, that you should do as I have done to you."[5]

Let us remember that the late Pope Paul VI kissed the foot of an orthodox bishop in Rome in order to show that he is not a master, but the first servant in the Christian Church. It is also noteworthy that His Holiness Pope John Paul II in his encyclical letter *Ut unum sint* states that the Bishop of Rome "is the first servant of unity"[6] and like his predecessors calls himself *"servus servorum Dei."*[7] Likewise the Armenian *catholicoi* in all their encyclicals use the expression "servant of Christ."

1. Sister Churches

Until the Second Vatican Council (1962–1965), the Roman Catholic Church used to identify herself with the one, Catholic, apostolic, holy Church and excluded all other Christians as schismatics and heretics from the body of the universal Church. A typical example is the encyclical letter *Mystici Corporis* of Pope Pius XII, issued in 1943, which clearly declares that in reality only Roman Catholics are to be accounted as members of the Church:

> Only those are to be accounted as members of the Church in reality who have been baptized and profess the true faith and who have not had the misfortune of withdrawing [separating themselves][8] from the Body or for grave faults been cut off by legitimate authority. . . . It follows that those who are divided in faith and government cannot be living in one Body such as this, and cannot be living the life of its one divine Spirit.[9]

With Vatican Council II came the great breakthrough: all the Christians baptized in their respective particular Churches were accepted as members of the one Catholic Church, though without fully participating in the unity of the Church. The Decree on Ecumenism (*Unitatis redintegratio*) states that the non-Roman Catholics "have a right

---

[5] John 13:14-15.

[6] John Paul II, *Ut unum sint. That They May Be One: On Commitment to Ecumenism* (Washington, D.C.: United States Catholic Conference, 1995) §94 (hereafter cited *Ut unum sint*).

[7] *Ibid.*, 103 ("Exhortation").

[8] *The Documents of Vatican II*, ed. W.M. Abbot and J. Gallagher (New York: Herder and Herder, 1966) 345 (=*Unitatis redintegratio* 3, hereafter cited *UR*) footnote 12. Unless otherwise noted all citations of Vatican II texts are from this edition.

[9] J. Neuner and J. Dupuis, eds., *The Christian Faith in the Doctrinal Documents of the Catholic Church*, 4th rev. ed. (Bangalore: Theological Publications in India, 1987) 238, no. 849/3802.

to be honored by the title of Christian, and are properly regarded as brothers in the Lord by the sons of the Catholic Church."[10] This document underlines and explains the special position of the Eastern Churches, praises the liturgical, spiritual, and canonical treasury of these Churches, Byzantine, Chalcedonian and Oriental non-Chalcedonian, and directly or indirectly calls them "Sister Churches." Here I quote the argument: "As a result, there prevailed and still prevails among Orientals an eager desire to perpetuate in a communion of faith and charity those *family ties which ought to thrive between local Churches, as between sisters.*"[11]

In the Dogmatic Constitution on the Church (*Lumen gentium*) Vatican II accepted as valid the baptism and other sacraments, as well as the episcopate, the Holy Eucharist and the Service of prayer of non-Roman Catholic Churches and ecclesial communities. In paragraph 15 we read: "that the Church recognizes that in many ways she is linked with those who, being baptized, are honored with the name of a *Christian*, though they do not profess the faith in its entirety or do not preserve unity of communion with the successor of Peter."[12]

Although under the designation "The Church" is meant the Roman Catholic Church, still it is pleasing and encouraging that the Church of Rome recognizes the validity of baptism of other Churches and regards herself "linked" in bonds with other Churches. Especially paragraph (or section) 8 of *Lumen gentium* is being appreciated and esteemed by many Roman Catholic theologians as an important milestone in the understanding and definition of the Church. The document says:

> This Church, constituted and organized in the world as a society, *subsists in the Catholic Church,* which is governed by the successor of Peter and by the bishops in union with that successor, although many elements of sanctification and of truth can be found outside of her visible structure. These elements however, as gifts properly belonging to the Church of Christ, possess an inner dynamism towards Catholic unity.[13]

If we have rightly understood the expression "the one, Catholic and Apostolic Holy Church *subsists* in the (Roman) Catholic Church," it means that the Roman Catholic Church has abandoned for ever her customary practice of identifying herself with the universal Church and accepts the other Churches as belonging to the same body of Jesus

---

[10] *UR* 3.

[11] *UR* 14.

[12] *Lumen gentium* 15 (hereafter cited *LG*); cf. *Ut unum sint,* 11 and 12.

[13] *LG* 8; cf. *Ut unum sint,* 10.

Christ. Especially the Eastern and Oriental Orthodox Churches after Vatican II are regarded as "Sister Churches." In this respect *Ut unum sint* quotes the apostolic brief *Anno ineunte* (25 July 1967) and *Tomos agapis* in which the Eastern Orthodox Churches are repeatedly called "Sister Churches."[14]

2. Ancient Churches of the East

Ut unum sint has dedicated two special paragraphs to the "Relations with the Ancient Churches of the East."[15] In this section are considered the Ancient Oriental Orthodox Churches and the Assyrian Church of the East; for a long time the latter, which rejects the dogmatic formulations of the Council of Ephesus (431), was named the "Nestorian Church." During the past thirty years all patriarchs of the Oriental Orthodox Churches have paid visits to the Roman pontiffs and signed common declarations stating their mutual agreement in many questions of faith, sacraments, rites, spiritual life and of canon law. The encyclical appreciates and praises not only these visits and the declarations, but also the ecumenical dialogue which clarified and solved the christological dispute in connection with the Council of Chalcedon (451). The letter says:

> Ecumenical contacts have thus made possible essential clarifications with regard to the traditional controversies concerning Christology, so much so that we have been able to profess together the faith which we have in common. Once again it must be said that this important achievement is truly a fruit of theological investigation and fraternal dialogue.[16]

This "fraternal dialogue" in fact was conducted in Vienna by the ecumenical Foundation *Pro Oriente* from 1971 to 1988 in five international theological consultations (1971, 1973, 1976, 1978 and 1988). As a participant and co-chairman of these consultations, I would like to present shortly the main results or the christological agreement which is now widely known as "The Vienna Formula."

In reality the Vienna dialogue followed the example of the dialogue of the Eastern and Oriental Orthodox Churches who had began their consultations in 1964 at Aarhus, Denmark, and continued them until 1971. In 1985 the dialogue was carried on officially, until November 1993, when both sides signed a historical document of union which

---

[14] *Ut unum sint*, 55–58.
[15] *Ibid.*, 62–63.
[16] *Ibid.*, 63.

ended the christological disputations. In 1971 when the unofficial dialogue of the Eastern and Oriental Orthodox Churches came to an end, a similar ecumenical conversation started in Vienna between theologians of the Roman Catholic Church and the Oriental Orthodox Churches. Already in the first meeting (Vienna-Lainz, September 1971) the participants succeeded to achieve a christological agreed formula which reads as follows:

> We believe that our Lord and Saviour, Jesus Christ, is God the Son Incarnate; perfect in his divinity and perfect in his humanity. His divinity was not separated from his humanity for a single moment, not for the twinkling of an eye. His humanity is one with his divinity without commixtion, without confusion, without division, without separation. We in our common faith in the one Lord Jesus Christ, regard his mystery inexhaustible and ineffable and for the human mind never fully comprehensible or expressible.[17]

This christological agreed formula was blessed and sealed by the heads of both families. I wish to present here only the common declarations of the Coptic Orthodox and Armenian Apostolic Churches. On May 10, 1973, Pope Paul VI and His Holiness Pope Patriarch Shenouda III in their common declaration included a christological definition which almost word for word was taken from the Vienna formula as follows:

> We confess that our Lord and God and Saviour and King of us all, Jesus Christ, is perfect God with respect to His Divinity, perfect man with respect to His humanity. In Him His divinity is united with His humanity in a real, perfect union without mingling, without confusion, without alteration, without division, without separation. His divinity did not separate from His humanity for an instant, not for the twinkling of an eye.[18]

Due to political reasons and to the ecclesiastical policy of the Soviet Union, Catholicos Vasken I could not endorse such a christological for-

[17] "Non-official Ecumenical Consultation between Theologians of the Oriental Orthodox Churches and the Roman Catholic Church, Vienna-Lainz, September 7–12, 1971. Papers and Minutes," in O. Mauer, ed., *Wort und Wahrheit*, Revue for Religion and Culture, Supplementary Issue 1 (Vienna: Herder, 1972) 182. For a detailed analysis of this christological formula, see M.K. Krikorian, "The Christological Consensus," in *The Vienna Dialogue. Five PRO ORIENTE Consultations with Oriental Orthodoxy. Middle East Regional Symposium Deir Amba Bishoy*, The Vienna Dialogue Booklets 3 (Vienna: Pro Oriente, 1993) 85–98; cf. D.W. Winkler, *Koptische Kirche und Reichskirche* (Innsbruck/Vienna: Tyrolia) 263–71.

[18] *The Vienna Dialogue. Five PRO ORIENTE Consultations with Oriental Orthodoxy. Communiqués and Common Declarations*, The Vienna Dialogue Booklets 1 (Vienna: Pro Oriente, 1991) 109.

mula with Rome, but his successor His Holiness Karekin I in December 1996 signed a common declaration with His Holiness Pope John Paul II where we read the following christological agreement:

> They particularly welcome the great advance that their Churches have registered in their common search for unity in Christ, the Word of God made flesh. Perfect God as to his divinity, perfect man as to his humanity; his divinity is united to his humanity in the Person of the Only-begotten Son of God, in a union which is real, perfect, without confusion, without any form of separation.[19]

Ut unum sint mentions the return of fraternal relations between Rome and the Oriental Orthodox Churches and immediately points out: "This is a concrete sign of how we are united in Christ in spite of historical, political, social, and cultural barriers."[20]

To these obstacles one could add also the problem of primacy which is the main stumbling block on the way of unity of the Churches. Almost in all five ecumenical Consultations (1971–1988) and in the subsequent study seminars the question of primacy in general, the petrine office especially were discussed. The Roman Catholic theologians claimed that the Bishop of Rome, as successor of the Apostle Peter, has or should have authority and jurisdiction over the universal Church, whereas the Oriental Orthodox insisted that all Apostles were given the same authority by Jesus Christ to continue his mission, to evangelize all peoples and nations, to minister and administer and to lead them in the path of Salvation. According to Oriental Orthodox theologians, all Apostles are equal in honor and rank and their successors, patriarchs and *catholicoi*, equally possess authority within the jurisdiction of their respective Churches. For instance, canon 6 of the Council of Nicaea (325) confirms the ancient custom according to which the bishop of Alexandria holds jurisdiction on all the provinces of Egypt, Lybia, Pentapolis etc., as does the Bishop of Rome over his province. Likewise the see of Antioch also enjoys jurisdiction over all its dioceses.

The same canon 6 also states that if someone has been ordained bishop without the approval of the metropolitan, the majority of the general/provincial synod must take the final decision. The Second Ecumenical Council, the Council of Constantinople (381), in canon 2 reaffirms the jurisdiction or the primacy of Egypt, as well as the jurisdiction of Antioch over its dioceses. Furthermore, the council emphasizes—repeating the reg-

---

[19] *L'Osservatore Romano*, English edition no. 51/52 (18/25 December, 1996) 2; *Information Service* no. 94 (1997–I) 30.

[20] *Ut unum sint*, 62.

ulations of Nicaea—that bishops should not interfere in the ecclesiastical affairs of another diocese, and that the provincial synod is responsible for the affairs of the whole province. Since about this time, under the reign of the emperor Theodosius I (379–395), Christianity became the official religion of the Eastern Roman Empire, the council recognized the preeminence of honor of the bishop of Constantinople following the Bishop of Rome, "because this city is the new Rome" (canon 3). The most important canon of the Council of Chalcedon is number 28, which is concerned with the primacy of the see of Constantinople. The council recognizes the "preeminence" of the see of Constantinople, just after that of the see of Rome, because "the Imperial Capital is honored by the presence of the Emperor and the Senate" and enjoys the same civil privileges as Rome. In fact this canon, which has caused so much trouble and aroused controversy over the centuries, means nothing more than a "primacy of honor." It also grants to Constantinople the right to consecrate metropolitans for the dioceses of Pontus, Asia and Thrace, as well as for the dioceses of the regions occupied by the barbarians.[21] In all these canons there is no mention at all about the jurisdictional primacy of the bishop of Rome over the universal Church.

In June-July 1991 Roman Catholic and Oriental Orthodox theologians held in Vienna a study seminar on primacy. Of course, the results were interesting, but not sensational! Some of the observations of the Common Statement were:

a) All present structures are the result of a historical process of development. They express the Churches' ongoing theological reflection on what Christ wills for his Church, on how the Holy Spirit has been working in the Churches and on the Apostolic tradition which they inherited. . . .

b) In all Churches we observed some tensions, and sometimes even discrepancy, between ecclesiological perception and actual practice. Every Church recognizes the need to improve present practice in the light of the acknowledged ecclesiological norm.

c) It was also noted that all our Churches at various periods spread geographically and have become in one way or another world-wide. Their present structures reflect this process.[22]

---

[21] P.-P. Joannou, *Codificazione Canonica Orientale. Fonti. Discipline générale antique*, tome I, part 1: *Les Canons des Conciles Œcuméniques (IIᵉ-IXᵉ s.)* (Grottaferrata: Tipografia Italo-Orientale S. Nilo, 1962); see also M.K. Krikorian, "Authority and Jurisdiction in the Tradition of the Armenian Church," *Journal of the Society for Armenian Studies* 7 (1994) 16–19.

[22] *The Vienna Dialogue. Five PRO ORIENTE Consultations with Oriental Orthodoxy. On Primacy First Study Seminar June 1991*, The Vienna Dialogue Booklets 4 (Vienna: Pro Oriente, 1993) 77 (observations nos. 1, 3, and 4).

3. Unity of the Church in the First Millennium

In the sections on "Sister Churches" and "The ministry of unity of the Bishop of Rome," *Ut unum sint* examines and explains the ecclesiastical structures of the first millennium and suggests a return to the period of unity. The letter openly proposes the first millennium as "a kind of model": "In its historical survey the Council Decree *Unitatis redintegratio* has in mind the unity which, in spite of everything, was experienced in the First Millennium and in a certain sense now serves as *a kind of model*."[23]

The model of the first millennium is a subject which has attracted the attention of many theologians and hierarchs. Cardinal Joseph Ratzinger is one of the first who in 1976 in a lecture at Graz, Austria, spoke of unity of the Church in the first millennium and suggested to take it as example and objective. In this respect all Churches or their representatives are enthusiastic and in agreement, but apparently each side understands and means something different in connection with the situation in the first millennium; otherwise the restoration of unity of the Church should have been realized long ago. *Unitatis redintegratio,* in paragraph 14 mentions the "brotherly communion of faith and sacramental life" between the Churches of the East and West in earlier centuries. Literally it says: "*For many centuries,* the Churches of the East and West went their own ways, though a brotherly communion of faith and sacramental life bound them together. If disagreements in belief and discipline arose among them, the Roman See acted by common consent as moderator."[24]

This statement has been quoted in the encyclical, only instead of "for many centuries," it is said "for a whole millennium."[25] I am sure many Churches would accept the Petrine office as service of a "moderator" who to my understanding is a "mediator," presiding officer, without any jurisdictional authority. His moral authority would be to play the role of mediating, admonishing and reconciling, but apparently Rome under "moderator" understands more than the office of mediator. In the section "Sister Churches" we read that:

> the structures of the Church in the East and in the West evolved in reference to that Apostolic heritage. Her unity during the First Millennium was maintained within those same structures through the Bishops, Successors of the Apostles, *in communion with the Bishop of Rome.* If today at the end of the second millennium we are seeking

[23] *Ut unum sint,* 55.
[24] *UR* 14.
[25] *Ut unum sint,* 95.

to restore full communion, it is to that unity, thus structured, which we must look.[26]

"In communion with the Bishop of Rome" is an expression which needs some elucidation. Armenia as the first country was officially christianized in 301/314; from this time until the twelfth century the Armenian Church did not have any direct relation or communion with Rome. The Armenians participated only in the First Ecumenical Council of Nicaea (325), through Bishop Aristakes, the younger son of Gregory Illuminator. The decisions of Constantinople (381) and Ephesus (431) were accepted later, after the convocation of these councils. The first three or seven councils in the first millennium were in fact convoked and conducted by the Byzantine emperors and their commissioners. It is true that the Bishop of Rome through his legates conveyed his opinion or position, but his primacy was rather a moral authority and not an absolute power. The best proof in this respect is the case of canon no. 28 of the Council of Chalcedon (451), which, in spite of protests of the Roman legates, confirmed the preeminence of Constantinople as "new Rome." The deplorable and regrettable story of the "eighth Ecumenical Council" in 869–870, is another evidence which shows that the primacy of the Pope in the first millennium was not decisive. In 879–880 Patriarch Photius organized a new synod ("The Eighth Ecumenical Council of the Eastern Church") which rejected the decisions of the council of 869–870. The tragic schism between East and West had already started; its completion took place in 1054. Consequently we could conclude that the first millennium (325–870) is not such an excellent period in order to consider it as a pattern for the restoration of unity of the Church. Harmony among Churches prevailed only up to 451 when the Council of Chalcedon effected the first division; the Churches of Egypt, Syria, Armenia, and Ethiopia refused to co-operate further with the Church and State of Byzantium. The structural unity of the Church was already damaged. Therefore it won't be very helpful to return to the "structures of unity which existed before the separation (1054)."[27] To my modest opinion, it is rather necessary to continue the fraternal dialogue and try to formulate anew the Petrine office in such a form which would be acceptable to all sides.

---

[26] *Ibid.*, 55.
[27] *Ibid.*, 56.

4. Ministry of Unity of the Bishop of Rome

In *Ut unum sint* we find a new language and a new reconciling spirit. Instead of the terminus "primacy," very often is used the expression "ministry of unity,"[28] "ministry of mercy,"[29] "service of unity."[30] Pope John Paul II has joined his predecessor Paul VI in asking forgiveness for "certain painful recollections" or events for which the Roman Catholic Church feels herself responsible. Here are the words of regret of the Holy Father:

> On the other hand, as I acknowledged on the important occasion of a visit to the World Council of Churches in Geneva on 12 June 1984, the Catholic Church's conviction that in the ministry of the Bishop of Rome she has preserved, in fidelity to the Apostolic Tradition and the faith of the Fathers, the visible sign and guarantor of unity, constitutes a difficulty for most other Christians, whose memory is marked by *certain painful recollections*. To the extent that we are responsible for these, I join my Predecessor Paul VI in asking forgiveness.[31]

I would like to examine now some convictions and expectations of the Roman Catholic Church in connection with the position and mission of the Apostle Peter and his successors. The encyclical Letter quotes the well-known passage of St. Matthew 16:17-19, where our Lord Jesus Christ declares: "And I tell you, you are Peter, and on this rock I will build my Church and the powers of death shall not prevail against it."[32] Also the witness of St. John concerning the role of Peter, has been cited: "Simon, son of John, do you love me more than these? . . . Feed my sheep."[33] Furthermore, the letter explains that "the Bishop of Rome exercises a ministry originating in the manifold mercy of God" and then adds: "The authority proper to this ministry is completely at the service of God's merciful plan and it must always be seen in this perspective. Its power is explained from this perspective."[34] The nature of the power or authority of this ministry is not sufficiently expounded. In paragraph 94 the ministry of unity of the Bishop of Rome is described as a service of leading the people "towards peaceful pasture" and "not of exercising

[28] *Ibid.*, 88–96.
[29] *Ibid.*, 93.
[30] *Ibid.*, 94.
[31] *Ibid.*, 88; emphasis added.
[32] *Ibid.*, 91.
[33] *Ibid.*, 91; John 21:15-19.
[34] *Ibid.*, 92.

power over the people."[35] Of course this is an attitude which could be accepted by all partners with gratitude, but in practice how would the power be exercised, is not very clear. At the end of the same paragraph (section), we find some guidelines concerning the spheres and forms of a primacy exercised on various levels:

> First: This primacy is exercised on various levels, including vigilance over the handing down of the Word, the celebration of the Liturgy and the Sacraments, the Church's mission, discipline and the Christian life.
> Secondly: He [the Bishop of Rome] has the duty to admonish, to caution and to declare at times that this or that opinion being circulated is irreconcilable with the unity of the faith.[36]

In the first part of this statement are counted the areas where primacy should be exercised, and in the second part the role of admonishing of the primate has been underlined. It is quite evident that in the tradition of the Oriental Orthodox Churches there is no formal censorship; everybody is free to express his views, but if these views are wrong and tend to be dangerous, other theologians may refute them, and if necessary, the Church can suspend the adversary from his teaching post, without much whirlwind and formalities. However primacy as *a service of unity* whose aim and duty is *to admonish and caution*, hardly can be rejected by anybody, if it is practiced in conciliarity and collegiality together with bishops or patriarchs of other Churches. Here I would like to present two responses from the Oriental Orthodox Churches which were given at the Fourth Ecumenical Consultation between theologians of the Oriental Orthodox Churches and the Roman Catholic Church in September 1978 in Vienna-Lainz. Amba Gregorius from the Coptic Orthodox Church stated in a lecture:

> In conclusion, we may say that all bishops are of equal dignity. The Primate among his bishops enjoys a primacy of honor according to the grandeur of his city and its historical importance. The primate, whether called bishop, archbishop, pope, patriarch or catholicos, is also on the same footing of honor among all primates in the whole Christendom.
> The unity of the Church Universal is manifested in the one faith, confessed and professed by all Churches throughout the whole Christendom. The unity of the Church Universal is embodied in an inseparable unity of all bishops. In St. Cyprian's words,

---

[35] *Ibid.*, 94.
[36] *Ibid.*

"The episcopate is one, so that each shares the whole, and the whole is in each part *(episcopus unus est, cuius a singulis in solidum pars tenetur)*."

Whenever a need for one voice in a matter that challenges the whole Christian world, an ecumenical council has to be convened. The Ecumenical council is to be chaired by the Bishop or the Primate of the place or the Chairman has to be elected from among the primates of equal honor as brothers in Christ.[37]

The late Metropolitan Paulos Mar Gregorios in his paper on the International Anglican-Roman Catholic Commission's document concerning authority in Church, said the following:

This conceding of the primacy of honor . . . is conditional upon questions of faith in dispute (filioque, infallibility, etc.) being amicably settled and communion being restored. Such a primacy of honor will have whatever content the Churches in concord agree upon. It will certainly exclude certain elements like immediate jurisdiction outside the Western Church. Whether the right of spokesmanship on behalf of the Churches everywhere and the right of convoking ecumenical synods with the agreement of all the Churches and other similar privileges should be granted to the Bishop of Rome after communion is restored is a matter for the Churches to decide in mutual agreement.[38]

5. Conciliarity and Collegiality

In all the Eastern Churches, Chalcedonian and non-Chalcedonian, conciliarity and collegiality are two important principles and forms of administration which belong to the traditional structures of their organization. The patriarchs and *catholicoi* as heads of the Churches decide and act within the framework of their respective synods and ecclesiastical councils; they are not entitled to take any decision on important matters of faith and discipline as well as in election of bishops. Infallibility is foreign to their tradition, and only the Tradition enjoys the highest authority in all Eastern/Oriental Churches. In many administrative synods or organs of these Churches the laity plays an important role, and especially in the Armenian Church the laymen participate even in discussions and decisions concerning questions of faith and reforms. Almost

---

[37] "Fourth Ecumenical Consultation between Theologians of the Oriental Orthodox Churches and the Roman Catholic Church, Vienna-Lainz, September 11–17, 1978. Papers and Minutes," in O Mauer, ed., *Wort und Wahrheit*, Revue for Religion and Culture. Supplementary Issue 4 (Vienna: Herder, 1978) 164.

[38] *Ibid.*, 224–25.

in all councils on various levels, they form two-third of the members, and the *catholicos* as well as diocesan bishops are elected by delegates who to larger extent are lay people. Each parish or diocese possesses a council which together with the priest or bishop governs the life and organization of the community.

In administration and governing boards of the Roman Catholic Church, after the Council of Vatican II, the situation has changed remarkably, but still in general the decision-makers are the bishops in dioceses, and the pope represents the absolute authority in all matters of administration, faith, morals and discipline. Obviously the administrative structures of the Eastern Churches and of the Roman Catholic Church are entirely different, not to say, contrary to each other. How could the ecumenical dialogue reconcile these two systems, is a question which I hope through discussions and negotiations can be solved. In the encyclical letter under discussion, several times the communion which relates and unites the Bishop of Rome with other pastors or bishops has been mentioned and it is stated that they all are "vicars and ambassadors of Christ."[39] In fact this approach is based on the Dogmatic Constitution on the Church *(LG)* of Vatican II, where we find a detailed presentation concerning the bishops as "vicars and ambassadors of Christ" and their sacred power and authority. According to this conception, "the supreme authority of the Church" belongs to the Roman Pontiff, whereas all other bishops have authority only in the framework of their respective particular Churches and the exercise of that sacred power "is ultimately regulated by the supreme authority of the Church, and can be circumscribed by certain limits, for the advantage of the Church or of the faithful."[40] In any case it is appeasing and pleasing to know that the non-Roman Catholic bishops and patriarchs have full and complete freedom in the ordering of worship and liturgy, in pastoral office, apostolate, and discipline. Here is what we understand and learn from *Lumen gentium*:

> In virtue of this power, bishops have the sacred right and the duty before the Lord to make laws for their subjects, to pass judgment on them, and to moderate everything pertaining to the ordering of worship and the apostolate.
>
> The pastoral office or the habitual and daily care of their sheep is entrusted to them completely. Nor are they to be regarded as vicars of the Roman Pontiff, for they exercise an authority which is proper to them, and are quite correctly called "prelates," heads of the people whom they govern. Their power therefore, is not

[39] See *Ut unum sint,* 94f.
[40] *LG,* 27.

destroyed by the supreme and universal power. On the contrary it is affirmed, strengthened, and vindicated thereby, since the Holy Spirit unfailingly preserves the form of government established by Christ the Lord in His Church.[41]

In the documents of Vatican II, the Bishop of Rome as successor of the apostle Peter is vested with all powers and rights and consequently he possesses the highest authority and enjoys the greatest honor in the Church. Even in case of the ecumenical councils their confirmation or acceptance by the pope is regarded as a prerequisite, whereas for the Eastern and Oriental Churches the universal reception of a council by the Churches is the most important condition for its ecumenical character. In *Lumen gentium* we read that:

> the supreme authority with which this college is empowered over the whole Church is exercised in a solemn way through an ecumenical council. A council is never ecumenical unless it is confirmed or at least accepted as such by the successor of Peter. It is the prerogative of the Roman Pontiff to convoke these councils, to preside over them, and to confirm them.[42]

It is quite clear that I am not delegated to speak in the name of other Churches, but I think at least the Oriental Orthodox will not be able to accept the sole and highest authority of the Roman pontiff in respect to ecumenical councils. I can imagine that most of these Churches will accept the *primacy of honor* of the Bishop of Rome and probably they also will agree that in consulting the heads of other Churches, he could convoke an ecumenical council and preside over it. Here I wish to quote a response by the Coptic Orthodox metropolitan Amba Bishoy who in 1991 in Vienna, at a study seminar on primacy said: "Primacy of honor, following the historical events, we can accept. But this would not mean that the Pope of Rome could periodically convoke the councils unless the other Patriarchs so ask him. He could have the primacy of honor in the council and in the Eucharist. I cannot give a final reply."[43]

I would like to remind also the positive opinion of Paulos Mar Gregorios who in 1972 at the fourth International Consultation of *Pro Oriente* optimistically expressed the possibility of such procedure after a mutual agreement.

---

[41] *Ibid.*, 27.

[42] *Ibid.*, 22.

[43] *The Vienna Dialogue—On Primacy First Study Seminar* . . . , 71.

6. The Necessity of a Fraternal Dialogue

The proposal of John Paul II in *Ut unum sint*[44] to Church leaders and their theologians to enter in "a patient and fraternal dialogue" on the Petrine office, was sensational, but unfortunately it was not seriously and sufficiently taken into consideration. I think such a dialogue is an important ecumenical task for all Christian Churches. In my opinion especially the Eastern/Oriental Orthodox Churches are already in communion with the Roman Catholic Church in respect to the apostolic faith, mission, and sacraments. Therefore "a patient and fraternal dialogue" on the problem of primacy, can lead to a full visible unity among these Churches. In consideration of such a new chance which inspires hope and promises a solution acceptable to all sides, I would like to present here my modest reflections:

> 1. The primacy or the preeminent position of the Bishop of Rome as successor of Peter, is a fact, which nobody can ignore or neglect.
>
> 2. What kind of preeminence should be the primacy of the Pope? On the basis of biblical, theological, and canonical evidence, one can state, that in the First Millennium the primacy of the Bishop of Rome had neither administrative nor authoritarian character.
>
> 3. In case of reunion of Churches, it should be the privilege of the Pope, as the first among the equals (*Primus inter pares*), to convoque ecumenical council(s), and to preside over the assembly, alone or together with other patriarchs. However the decisions are valid only when the majority of bishops express their agreement and endorse them, i.e. the Pope possesses no right of veto.
>
> 4. In the light of these considerations, the primacy of the Bishop of Rome is an office of admonishing in service of unity of the apostolic Faith of the Church(es), to be exercised in charity and love, without jurisdictional power and authority. Such pretentions and claims in the past have led to schism and divisions; they may in the future again effect separations. The admonition is a privilege of the successor of Peter and a visible sign of primacy of the Pope, but there cannot be any reason to hinder or prevent the heads of other sister Churches to write and send recommendations and suggestions to Rome or directly to the patriarch of a particular Church.[45]

It is unfortunate that the fall of the Soviet Empire in 1990–1991 created new conflicts between Rome and the Eastern Orthodox Churches,

---

[44] *Ut unum sint,* 96.

[45] See my study on "Affiliation to the One Church" read on September 30, 1997 in Würzburg, at the Congress of Society on the Canon Law of Eastern Churches.

especially in West-Ukraine, and the ecumenical official dialogue, which was being carried on very smoothly, suddenly was interrupted. Apparently for the Orthodox the problem of proselytism has a priority on the agenda; in any case we hope and wish that the dialogue can be continued very soon. I am sure a positive solution to this question can be found; perhaps afterwards an international commission can start with the dialogue on primacy.

Concluding Words

Thirty years ago when I for the first time participated in the christological dialogue with theologians of the Eastern Orthodox Church, I thought it would be impossible to settle the controversy concerning Chalcedon. In spite of all difficulties, a miracle happened and already in 1971 an agreed christological formula, acceptable to all sides, was achieved. The same might happen with the problem of Petrine office: it is well possible that if the theologians of various traditions sincerely and seriously initiate an official dialogue, they might find a positive solution which would accelerate the desired unity of the Churches for the benefit of mankind and for the glory of God.

6

Papal Primacy in Eastern and Western Patristic Theology: Its Interpretation in the Light of Contemporary Culture

Dumitru Popescu

Introduction

There are few New Testament texts that have been analyzed more thoroughly and more comprehensively than the text of the Gospel according to St. Matthew 16:18, which is invoked in favor of papal primacy. In this text the Lord praises Peter for having shown himself worthy to receive a heavenly revelation which made him confess his faith in the messianic character and the divinity of the Son of God. And he said to him: "And I tell you, you are Peter, and on this rock I will build my church, and the powers of death shall not prevail against it." The question this text raised for Eastern and Western theologians was whether this "rock" refers to Peter or to Christ Himself; that is, whether the Church is built on Peter or on Christ. To find an adequate answer to this theological dilemma, whose consequences for an understanding of the Church are immense, we have turned to Eastern and Western patristic theology. And the result has been surprising.

Early Sources

In the first three Christian centuries the text "You are Peter" is used by the Fathers or by the ecclesiastical writers to affirm, against the heretics,

the messianic character and divinity of Christ. For them and in the consciousness of the Church, this text had a Christological meaning. That
is how it is understood in the writings of St. Hippolytus and St. Irenaeus.
That is still its meaning for Calixtus or Tertullian in the controversy over
the remission of sins, without reference to the question of interest here.
In Origen, as in St. Cyprian, we find the interpretation given by the
Apostle Paul: the cornerstone is Jesus Christ (Eph 2:20). The same line
is taken by Eusebius of Caesarea, Epiphanius, Ephrem the Syrian, the
Cappadocian Fathers (Basil of Caesarea and Gregory of Nazianzus)
John Chrysostom, Athanasius of Alexandria, Theodoret of Cyr, Cyril of
Alexandria, John Damascene and many others.

Also in Western exegesis we find the same interpretation until the
late Middle Ages, when the text is applied instead to the Pope. In Africa,
for instance, we find St. Cyprian's exegesis maintained by Optat of
Milevi, by St. Augustine and his disciples. In Italy we find it in Ambrose,
Rufinus and Jerome; in Gallia, in the writings of Hilary of Poitiers. In
Rome we find it at the time of Pope Siricius (384–399). This shows that
the exegesis is no different from that used in Alexandria, in Antioch, in
Caesarea of Cappadocia, in Carthage or Milan, and finally in Gallia.
The Pauline interpretation will be the starting-point and guide for all the
patristic exegesis both in the East and in the West, and so the Holy Fathers, and through them the ecumenical Church, will make it their own:
the Person of the Savior is the heart and foundation of the Church.

We have to stress, however, that for the Fathers the notion of
"pietra" in the biblical text with which we are dealing has also connotations other than that referring directly to Christ, without in any way di-
minishing the central role of the Lord. In the second century, St. Justin,
martyr and philosopher, and also St. Irenaeus use the Gospel text, "You
are Peter," on the one hand to affirm the messianic character and divinity of Christ against the Jews, whose imaginary spokesman was
Tryphon, and on the other hand, to affirm the divinity and divine Son-
ship of Christ against the Gnostics. St. Irenaeus opposes the term
"pietra"—the rock on which are built the disciples who will slake their
thirst from the spiritual rock that is to come—to the term "arena," the
"sand" that is the foundation for the heretics. This *pietra,* which bears
within it the principle of unity, signifies the teaching of Christ, while
"arena" is the doctrine of the heretics. Central to the thinking of the two
Fathers is the Person and the teaching of Christ, for they never thought
the teaching of Christ could be separated from his Person—as happens
today, making of it the object of theological speculations.

Eastern Fathers

Origen's exegesis of the text in question seems different, since, according to him, *pietra* refers not only to Christ, but to all Christians. "If, like Peter, we say, You are the Christ, the Son of the living God," Origen says, "we, too, become Peter, and it is also to us that the Son of God will say, 'You are Peter,' and what follows. For everyone who imitates Christ is *pietra,* from whom those will drink who come to slake their thirst at the spiritual 'rock.' And it is upon this rock that is built the teaching of the Church, and upon this teaching the life of the community. For the Church is built by God in each one of those who, being perfect, possess the fullness of knowledge and of life that leads to happiness."[1] In stressing Peter's confession, Origen makes no difference between Peter and the apostles or between the apostles and the Christians. Peter is spokesman of the apostles, but whoever confesses the faith of Peter becomes a rock for the building up of the Church. "All those who obey Christ can therefore rightly claim to be called '*pietra.*'"[2]

For St. Athanasius of Alexandria, as for Eusebius of Caesaria, the *pietra* is Christ. For both Christ is the rock upon which the Church is built. St. Athanasius declares that the Savior is the rock "upon which his Church is built for eternity," that is, as he calls it, the "city of the Lord."[3] St. Epiphanius, on the contrary, knows two interpretations of the text: according to the first, *pietra* is Peter, head of the apostles;[4] according to the second, it is the faith confessed by Peter.[5] This text has a special importance, because of the close link between the person of Peter and his profession of faith: Peter confesses his faith in Christ in the name of the apostles, and is therefore considered the head of the apostles, and his confession of faith becomes the norm which allows Peter, but also the other apostles, to become "solid rocks" in the foundation of the Church, which however is always Christ. That is why St. Ephrem the Syrian speaks of Peter as the rock upon which the Church is built, but at the same time sees Christ as the *pietra* in the foundation of the Church.

This is also the view of the Cappadocian Fathers. St. Basil affirms that "the soul of Blessed Peter was called the chosen stone because his roots were planted solidly in the faith and because he faced the blows of

---

[1] Origen, *Commentarii in Matthaeum,* ed. E. Klostermann (*Die griechischen christliche Schriftsteller der ersten drei Jahrhunderte* 12, 85–86 (hereafter cited *GCS* followed by volume number and pages).

[2] *Ibid.,* 12, 88.

[3] Athanasius, *Expositiones in Psalmos* (*PG* 27, 220).

[4] Epiphanius of Constantia (Salamis), *Panarion* 59, 7, ed. K. Holl (*GCS* 31, 372–73).

[5] Epiphanius, *Panarion* 80, 5–6 (*GCS* 63, 490–92).

temptation with unshakable courage."[6] St. Gregory of Nazianzus exclaims: "See how, among the disciples of Christ, who are all very great and worthy to be chosen, it is he (Peter) who is called *pietra,* becoming by his faith the foundation of the Church."[7] St. Gregory of Nyssa says the same thing: "Peter, the head of the apostles, is glorified, and with him are glorified all the other members of the Church, and the Church of God is sustained by him. For he, Peter, according to the gift given him by the Lord, is the firm, unshakable rock upon which God has built his Church."[8] By stressing the *pietra* of the confession of faith the Cappadocian Fathers are able to bring into relief the special role of Peter as the unshakable rock upon which God has built the Church, while at the same time seeing the other apostles also as stones in the foundation of the Church.

For Dydimus the Blind, the *pietra* is the confession of faith in the divinity of Christ by virtue of which all the apostles received the power to remit and retain the sins of humankind.[9] Asterius of Amasea also says that "Christ is the 'cornerstone' that guarantees the eternity and indestructibility of the Church";[10] that the Lord gave Peter the name *pietra* he had given to his faith, and that the Church, like the Christians, has been made solid and saved in this faith, firm as a rock, upon which we have all been built.[11] In St. John Chrysostom we find two approaches to the question which concerns us: On the one hand, "You are Peter" refers to Peter's confession of faith in the divinity of Jesus Christ, and Peter is the head of the apostles into whose hands the Church of the whole world has been given, for him to be its unshakable foundation";[12] on the other hand, "Peter is called the unshakable foundation, head of the brethren, because he has received the Church to transmit it to the whole world."[13] Although Chrysostom never puts Peter on a higher level than that of the other Apostles, we have to admit that, since he considers him head of the brethren, he attributes to him a primacy that we have not found in the Fathers already quoted. But it is a primacy of honor, for the Holy Doctor is careful to add elsewhere: "We, too, possess Peter, if we observe

[6] Basil, *Commentarius in Isaiam* 66 (*PG* 30, 233 B).

[7] Gregory of Nazianzus, *Sermo* 32 (*PG* 36, 193).

[8] Gregory of Nyssa, *In sanctum Stephanum* (*PG* 46, 735).

[9] Didymus the Blind, *De Trinitate,* 30 (*PG* 39, 416–17).

[10] Asterius of Amasea, *In sanctos Petrum et Paulum* (*PG* 40, 268).

[11] *Ibid.*

[12] John Chrysostom, *In Acta Apostolorum* (*PG* 60, 86).

[13] *Id., De Poenitentia, Homilia V* (*PG* 49, 308).

the faith of the apostles confessed by Peter."[14] The faith of Peter remains the foundation on which the Church is built.

Continuing our investigations, we find in Theodoret of Cyr two interpretations of the text in question. One that the *pietra* refers to all the apostles since they constitute the foundation of the Church. The other, that the *pietra* on which the Church is built is Christ himself.[15] Theodoret excludes from the outset any attempt to build the Church on a foundation that is human, subject even to corruption. St. Cyril of Alexandria gives priority to Peter's confession of faith, for "Christ said to the divine Peter: 'You are Peter, and on this rock I will build my Church', calling *pietra,* in my opinion, the unshakable faith of the Apostle."[16] Elsewhere, St. Cyril says also: "The *pietra* was nothing other than the unshakable and solid faith of the Apostles, a rock upon which the Church of Christ was built and consolidated against all danger."[17] As we can see, the exegesis of St. Cyril remains faithful to the Alexandrine school. We should also add that Anastasius of Sinai says that Christ built the Church on the faith confessed in his divinity,[18] and St. Sophronius of Jerusalem declares that the Church was built by Peter,[19] in the sense that Oriental theology gives to such a statement without implying a monarchical authority to govern the Church.

We conclude our investigations with St. John Damascene. On the one hand, he says that God chose Peter to be the primate of the Church, granting him the power to remit and to retain sins;[20] and on the other hand, that the Church is built on Peter's firm and unshakable faith in the divinity of Jesus, against which the power of death can never prevail.[21] "The rock is faith in Christ."[22] If the Church is built on the faith of Peter, this means that the honor given to Peter cannot go beyond a primacy of honor at the service of Christian unity. It is a well known fact that some of the Church Fathers already mentioned, among them Athanasius of Alexandria and John Chrysostom, appealed to Rome for support in

---

[14] *Id., In librum quod Christus sit Deus, contra Judaeos atque Gentiles (PG* 48, 829, 835, 885, 886); *In epistolam ad Galatas (PG* 61, 613).

[15] Theodoret of Cyr, *Homiliae in Ezechielem* 43, 16 *(PG* 81, 1232) and *id., Epistola* 146 *(PG* 83, 1396).

[16] Cyril of Alexandria, *Commentarium in Isaiam (PG* 70, 940).

[17] Cyril of Alexandria, *De sancta Trinitate (PG* 75, 865).

[18] Anastasius Sinaita, *Anagogicarum contemplationum in Hexaemeron* II, 2 *(PG* 40, 871ff).

[19] Sophronius of Jerusalem, *Vita Acephala sactorum martyrum Cyri et Joannis (PG* 87/III, 3692).

[20] John Damascene, *In transfigurationem Domini (PG* 96, 536 B).

[21] *Ibid.*

[22] *Ibid.*

solving certain questions concerning the unity of the Churches of which they were pastors. But that is precisely what shows that the bishops of Rome enjoyed a primacy of honor and not a juridical primacy. For all the Fathers of the Oriental Church, the *pietra* par excellence of the Church remains Christ. Nicephorus, patriarch of Constantinople, states that "the Church is founded on the unshakable rock that is Christ."[23]

The Western Fathers

The Western Fathers and writers give a similar interpretation of the text with which we are dealing. Although they have been in direct contact with Rome and given Rome their support, they do not speak of a monarchical government for the Church. Tertullian, going in the direction which will be that of St. Cyprian, Optat of Milevi or St. Augustine, says that Jesus Christ gave the keys of heaven to Peter and through Peter to the Church.[24] The power of binding and unbinding sins was given to Peter and the other apostles, because the true recipient of the power of the keys remains the Church. It is true that Peter has a certain priority, but since the power of the keys was given to all the apostles, this means that his primacy is symbolic in character. Tertullian agrees with Pope Calixtus, who admits that all bishops have the power to bind and to loose, since this is a power that Christ gave to Peter and to the apostles.

In the second half of the third century, we find St. Cyprian using the text, "You are Peter," with two meanings. On the one hand, he affirms that "in every Christian community there can and should exist only one Church, one *cathedra,* founded on Peter through the Savior's words."[25] On the other hand, he declares that "the episcopate is one, each member having his share in solidarity with the others."[26] According to the former text, Christ built his Church on Peter; but, according to the latter, the Church is led not in a monarchical manner, but in solidarity. The bishop of Carthage professes an ecclesiology of communion, since he declares: *"Hoc erant utique et ceteri apostoli quod fuit Petrus, pari consortio praediti et honoris et potestatis."*[27] From the affirmation that what Peter was, every other apostle also was, it follows that "You are Peter" becomes a real charter for the episcopate. We cannot, however, overlook the fact that, in this ecclesiology of communion, St. Cyprian confers

---

[23] Nicephorus of Constantinople, *Apologeticus minor pro sacris imaginibus* (*PG* 100, 621 C).

[24] Tertullian, *Scorpiace X,* ed. W. Hartel (*CSEL* 21, 167).

[25] Cyprian, *Epistula* 43, 5, ed. W. Hartel (*CSEL* 3, 594).

[26] Cyprian, *De ecclesiae unitate,* ed. W. Hartel (*CSEL* 3, 214–15).

[27] *Ibid.*

upon Peter a place that we do not find given to him by any other Father of the Church. We shall return to this point later.

St. Hilary of Poitiers (Pictavium) makes two statements that seem contradictory. On the one hand, he says that "Peter is the rock upon which Jesus Christ built the Church, as reward for the confession of his faith in the divinity of the Savior";[28] on the other hand, that the Church is built on the objective truth of faith of Peter's confession,[29] which, ultimately, is Christ himself.[30] The coexistence of these two statements shows that St. Hilary favored an ecclesiology of communion which makes Peter and all who believe in the Savior's divinity into foundations and building-stones of the Church, coming from the one rock which is Christ. In the same way St. Ambrose of Milan speaks both of Christ as *pietra* of the Church[31] and of Peter as the foundation on which the Church is built.[32] The apparent contradiction between these two statements is overcome by St. Ambrose through the faith which he places at the foundation of the Church and which, in his work, is of primary importance: "for it is of faith that has been said the power of death will not prevail against it, and the confession will have the victory over hell."[33] Peter has a primacy, but it is the primacy of faith, which enables the apostles and the faithful to be stones for the building of the Church. In this context we have to understand the famous saying of St. Ambrose: *"Ubi Petrus, ibi Ecclesia"*–"Where Peter is, there is the Church."[34]

We find similar expressions in St. Jerome. On the one hand he speaks of the rock upon which Christ has build his Church;[35] but, on the other hand he shows that the rock is Christ. Like St. Ambrose, he reconciles these two statements by putting the emphasis on faith as foundation of the Church, since the rock is metaphorical, symbolizing the confession of faith which enables Peter and all who believe in Christ to be "rocks" on which the Church is built. Nevertheless, Jerome honors in a special way the successors of Peter: "I who do not want to follow anyone but Christ, I am united to your beatitude, that is, to the see of Peter. I know that the Church has been built on this rock."[36] Continuing

[28] Hilary of Poitiers, *Commentaria in Matthaeum XVI, 18* (*PL* 9, 109).

[29] Hilary, *De Trinitate* VI, 36–37 (PL 10, 186–87).

[30] *Ibid.*

[31] Ambrose, *Expositio Evangelii secundum Lucam,* 97–98 (*PL* 15, 1781).

[32] *Ibid.*

[33] *Ibid.*

[34] Cf. Haralambie Cojocaru, *Primatul lui Petru dupa Noul Testament* (=The primacy of Peter according to the New Testament) (Sibiu: Tipografia Arhidiecezana, 1940) 274.

[35] Jerome, *Commentarii in Matthaeum III* (*PL* 26, 121–22).

[36] Jerome, *Epistula 15 ad Damasum* (*CSEL* 54, 63).

our investigation with Rufinus of Aquileia and Paulinus of Nola, we find that for them also the *pietra* par excellence of the Church is Christ. The former justifies this opinion by the fact that Christ as God and Man is the rock by which we are raised from earth to heaven, from the devil to God;[37] and from which will drink those who are to come. "And he has not refused to give his disciple the grace of this name, saying that on this rock I will build my Church and the power of death will not prevail against it."[38] The Church in its totality could not have been built only upon one, or by one alone, but has been built on Christ.[39] The same theological approach is found in the Popes Siricius, Zosimus and Boniface, while Pope Leo I says clearly that "Peter is the type of all the Apostles, of all the leaders of churches, of the Bishops, of all to whom has been given the power to remit and to retain sins."[40]

St. Augustine synthesizes for the first four centuries the patristic exegesis of the text invoked in favor of papal primacy. Under his inspired pen, "You are Peter" is given three different connotations. Following his predecessors, Augustine sees the biblical text as referring to faith in Christ's divinity, the faith St. Peter had confessed in the name of the apostles and for all of them together, deducing from this a power not granted personally to Peter but to all the apostles and, through them, to the Church.[41] Augustine also maintains that the Church will never perish, for she is built on the cornerstone that is Christ.[42] In this regard, he remains attached to the Pauline teaching about the "rock." Finally, Augustine, in his vast theological work, only once points to Peter as foundation of the Church.[43] If we look together at the three meanings of Matthew's text, we come to the conclusion that they depend mutually on one another, and all on Christ, only to the extent that Peter can be said to be the representative and prototype of the totality and the unity of the Church.[44] The patristic exegesis of the text was continued by the disciples of St. Augustine, Fulgentius of Ruspe, and Vincent of Lérins. We will be returning to the latter. For the moment we have to stress that for John Cassian, contemporary of Augustine, "You are Peter" refers to faith in Christ's divinity;[45] and that Popes Gregory the Great and

---

[37] Rufinus of Aquileia, *In Psalmos* (*PL* 21, 739–40).

[38] Paulinus of Nola, *Epistula* XXIII, 43 (*CSEL* 79, 198).

[39] Siricius, *Epistula I ad Himerium* (*PL* 13, 1135–36).

[40] Leo the Great, *Sermo* 4 (*PL* 54, 151 A).

[41] Augustine, *Sermo* 61 (*PL* 38, 479).

[42] *Ibid.*

[43] Augustine, *Retractationes* 21 (*PL* 32, 618).

[44] Augustine, *Sermo* 245, 2 (*PL* 38, 1354).

[45] John Cassian, *De incarnatione Domini,* III, 14 (*CSEL* 17, 279).

Nicholas I also adopt this point of view. This is, in fact, the same Pauline interpretation of the *pietra* that is the foundation for a whole ecclesiology of communion and that was maintained for a long time throughout the Christian Church.

If we attempt to recapitulate the different meanings that the notion of *pietra* takes on in Eastern and Western patristic thought, we can say that we are in presence of three or four explanations. According to the first interpretation, the *pietra* upon which the Church is built is Peter. This affirmation, which occurs only once in St. Cyril of Jerusalem, is found, alongside other meanings of the notion of *pietra* in various Fathers of the patristic period. As our exposition shows, it is mentioned seventeen times in the work of various authors. The second explanation makes the term *pietra* refer equally to all the apostles; we meet it eight times in patristic writings. It intends to show that the faith affirmed by Peter in presence of the Lord was the faith of all the apostles, who together hold the power of the keys. The third explanation is the most frequent; it maintains that the rock upon which the Church is built is the faith in Christ's divinity confessed by Peter. We find it forty-four times in patristic works, and this frequency is of capital importance for the question with which we are dealing. It shows that the Fathers recognize a primacy of Peter, but it is the primacy of faith, since, in their overwhelming majority, they see the Church as being built on the faith of Peter, a faith against which—as St. Ambrose of Milan affirms—the power of death will not prevail. Finally, a significant number of Fathers identify the *pietra* with Christ himself; this interpretation appears sixteen times.[46]

This incursion into the patristic exegesis of the text, "You are Peter" has shown that the three meanings of the notion of *pietra* in patristic thought are organically linked, and that they are all dependent on the rock that is Christ, whom all the apostles have considered and confessed to be the Son of the Living God. In this way the Fathers remain in the line of St. Paul who shows, in masterly fashion, that the *pietra* par excellence of the Church, the cornerstone, remains Christ; but, at the same time, they are in line with an ecclesiology of communion, which gives to Peter and his successors a primacy of faith. If the Church of Christ remained united during the first millennium of Christian history, this was due to the fact that both Eastern and Western patristic theology gave proof of a remarkable unity of thought, remaining faithful to the principle stated by Vincent de Lérins in the following terms:

[46] H. Cojocaru, *Primatul* . . . , 297.

> In the Catholic Church itself, every care should be taken to hold fast to what has been believed everywhere, always, and by all *("quod ubique, quod semper, quod ad omnibus traditum est")*. This is truly and properly 'catholic,' as indicated by the force and etymology of the name itself, which comprises everything truly universal. This general rule will be truly applied if we follow the principles of universality, antiquity, and consent. We do in regard to universality if we confess that faith alone to be true which the entire Church confesses all over the world. [We do so] in regard to antiquity if we in no way deviate from those interpretations which our ancestors and fathers have manifestly proclaimed as inviolable. [We do so] in regard to consent if, in this very antiquity, we adopt the definitions and propositions of all, or almost all, the bishops and doctors."[47]

And yet, in spite of all that, another tradition developed in the Western Church, a tradition that would lead to an interpretation of the "rock" in the Gospel text that was different from the traditional patristic interpretation. This development was initiated by Pope Zosimus (417–418) and brought to completion by Pope Boniface I (418–422). In parallel with the patristic interpretation of the text "You are Peter," Zosimus maintains that Jesus gave Peter the power to remit and to retain sins, while adding the words: "Those who, with his permission, inherit the episcopal power, have the same power as he."[48] Peter, therefore, had received from Christ the power to remit and to retain sins, and those who inherit Peter's episcopate, inherit also his power. Peter's successors receive their power directly from Christ. Boniface goes even further in biblical justification of the primacy; he declares that the rights of the see of Rome derive from the prophesy made by the Lord *("Domini sermone concessa")*.[49] The Church of Rome is the head of all the Churches. Whoever separates himself from it, separates from religion. Peter has been placed by Jesus as foundation of the Church.[50] In asserting this, Boniface considered himself sovereign also over Illyricum; and he afterwards affirms that no one can enter the kingdom of heaven without the intervention of Peter, who is the gate-Keeper.[51] The Roman Church is heir to Peter, and supremacy in the Church has nothing in common with the

---

[47] Vincent of Lérins, *Commonitorium* (*PL* 50, 610). English trans. by R. E. Morris, "The Commonitories," in *The Fathers of the Church. A New Translation* (New York: The Fathers of the Church, 1966) 7, 271f.

[48] Zosimus, *Epistula* 11 (*PL* 20, 649).

[49] Boniface, *Epistula* 14 (*PL* 20, 777).

[50] Boniface, *Epistula* 15 (*PL* 20, 779).

[51] *Ibid.*, col. 781.

Council of Nicaea, which did no more than take note of this primacy enjoyed by the Bishop of Rome.[52]

Boniface's exegesis, which goes beyond the synodal theory of the primacy, is repeated by Celestine I. In his letter to the bishops of Illyricum, he says that the words addressed to Peter oblige him to concern himself with all the affairs of the Church (*"quibus necessitatem de omnibus tractandi Christus in Sancto Petro . . . indulsit"*).[53] We find this exegesis also in St. Leo the Great. In his third Discourse he says: "The authentic institution remains Blessed Peter, who keeps the capital role of foundation which he had received. He has not given up the role of governing the Church that was entrusted to him. The good that we do, and that we teach, the gifts that our prayers obtain from the mercy of God, come by his actions and from his merits, for his power and his authority remain in his see."[54] And, to crown this trend, there is the declaration contained in a document often attributed to Damasus and included in the *Decretum Gelasianum:* "It was not the decisions of the Councils that instituted the pre-eminence of the Roman Church over the other Churches, but the words of our Lord and Savior: 'You are Peter' that are inscribed in the Gospel."[55]

Although this new trend came in conflict with the conception of St. Cyprian, according to which the Church is guided in solidarity by the bishops, that is, in a synodal manner, it is none the less true that Cyprian's ecclesiology contains an aspect that came to the aid of the Roman exegesis. Metropolitan John of Pergamon speaks of this when he says:

> the first theologian . . . who altered decisively the Ignatian scheme as well as the Hippolytan synthesis so as to respond to this problem seems to have been St. Cyprian. With Cyprian the eschatological image of the apostolic college surrounding Christ—an image which was applied to the structure of the local Church by Ignatius and Hippolytus (the bishop surrounded by the presbyterium)—is changed to become an image of the apostolic college surrounding its head, *St. Peter.* Thus for him each episcopal throne is not, as it is for Ignatius, the "place of God" or Christ, but the *cathedra Petri.* The significance of this alteration is that we can now talk of *unus episcopatus* dispersed over the earth with Peter as its head. This leads to

---

[52] Boniface, *Epistula* 14 (*PL* 20, 777).

[53] Celestine I, *Epistola* 3, 3 (*PL* 54, 428).

[54] Leo the Great, *Sermo* 3 (*PL* 54, 146).

[55] Damasus, in *Decretum Gelasianum* (*PL* 20, 374; *PL* 59, 13); see also T. Andreas, *De Decretali Gelasii Papae de recipiendis et non recipiendis libris et Damasi Concilio Romano* (Brunsberg: Peter, 1866) 913.

the concept of episcopal collegiality, as it has been expounded today in Roman Catholic theology.[56]

An Ecclesiology of Communion

Beyond this Roman trend, the ecclesiology of the first millennium of Christian history was a theology of communion which remained faithful both to Eastern and Western patristics. Extremely enlightening from this point of view is a comment from the eminent Catholic theologian, Fr. Yves Congar. He clearly asserted that

> in the East, the authority of the see of Rome was never that of a monarchical prince. The history of the VI Ecumenical Council (680–681) is eloquent on this point. Pope Agaton was acclaimed, not because his authority would be obeyed but because the expression of the authentic faith was recognized in his words. The theory of the Pentarchy, mentioned in the *Novelle* 123 and 131 of the Emperor Justinian, was in no way anti-Roman; it was a way of structuring communication between the Churches and ensuring unity. Agreement between the five Patriarchs expressed the unanimity of the Churches, which was a criterion of conciliar ecumenicity, and remained as such, also at times in the West, until about the Sixteenth century. The Pentarchy was, in its way, an expression of the collegial sense of the synodal East insofar as it was a form of the communion of the Churches in homophony.[57]

Father Congar continues:

> The Body of Christ has no Head other than Christ Himself. Roman ecclesiology, the Greeks say, attributes to the Pope an unconditional discretionary power, although, like everyone else, he is obliged to observe the limits laid down by the Fathers and by the canons of the Ecumenical Councils. He is bound by the faith of the Church. His voice is recognized as the voice of Peter if he confesses the faith of Peter. It is only by virtue of their confession of faith that the Patriarchs accept one another into their communion. There is no autonomous authority with respect to the objective Tradition expressed in the writings of the Fathers and the Councils that are, equally, divinely inspired (*theopneustoi*). The Byzantine theologians very rarely relate the primacy of the see of Rome to the Apostle Peter, although

---

[56] J. D. Zizioulas, *Being as Communion. Studies in Personhood and the Church,* Contemporary Greek Theologians 4 (Crestwood, N.Y.: St. Vladimir's Seminary Press, 1985) 200.

[57] Y.-M. Congar, *L'Église de saint Augustin à l'époque moderne,* Histoire des dogmes III, christologie-sotériologie-mariologie 3 (Paris: Cerf, 1970) 78–79.

authors of prestige like Maximus the Confessor or Theodore the Studite do, at times, say something to this effect. The primacy of Rome is that of the first see *inter pares*; it is attributed to the capital of ancient Rome. The principle involved is that of adaptation of the Metropolitan sees to the political importance of the city, and not an apostolic principle. Through the priesthood and the celebration of the Sacrament each Church has the sacramental fullness of the divinizing life. Their communion is exercised in cases where a vital element is called in question or when a new decision is to be taken, in the Councils. It is structured in the system of five Patriarchs, or Pentarchy. A decision is only binding if it has been agreed upon by the five Patriarchs and, first of all, by the Bishop of ancient Rome.[58]

As for the West, "everyone recognized the Roman primacy, but not everyone gave it the same significance that it was given in Rome after St. Leo. Cyprian's interpretation of Matt 16:18 dominated among the authors of the century.[59] The Roman Church must judge according to the Holy Scriptures and the decrees of the holy canons."[60] Gerbert, who became pope with the name of Silvester II, wrote towards the end of the tenth century that "the Church is a communion of local churches and of bishops, presided over and governed by a *prima sedes*." The mandate to feed the flock that was entrusted to Peter, is shared by all the bishops. The Church is not a monarchy; she is a communion whose life is guided, not by the judgement of a single person, *unius arbitrium,* but by the common law of the Catholic Church. In the writings of Silvester II we find many statements indicating his awareness of the exercise of Peter's mandate, but not the monarchical declarations familiar to Nicholas I and to John VIII.[61] We have proof in this way that, during the first Christian millennium, the papal primacy was exercised within an ecclesiology of communion, in spite of all the monarchical tendencies prevailing at the time. And this way of exercising the primacy continued in the West, according to Father Congar, until the sixteenth century, until the papacy succeeded in imposing the Roman monarchical tradition on the whole of the Western world.

Conclusion

Today, over the entire face of the earth, the Church of Christ is more than ever in need of unity. Individualism, as a product of secularized

---

[58] *Ibid.*, 79.
[59] *Ibid.*, 65.
[60] *Ibid.*, 64.
[61] *Ibid.*, 66.

culture, is constantly fragmenting Christian unity. A Catholic, specialist in this field, writes that

> everything is happening as if Christianity had ceased to be an overall and unifying system that has to be seen as a whole becoming a collection of loose pieces, offered for free personal compositions, for selective adherence to a certain number of beliefs, practices and prescriptions. This system of *à la carte* religion means rejection of an institution that regularizes practices and beliefs–rejection of orthodoxy–in favor of the principle of individual sovereignty. The imaginary world of those who declare themselves Christians is often dismembered. Raymond Lemiex notes that it is made up mainly of four types of elements: Christian elements, cosmic elements (references to universal energy), the element of a sublimated Ego ("the essential Being," "the inner divine," "the force of psychic being"), reified values such as love, freedom, peace. Each one organizes his own universe of Christian and cosmic beliefs, psychospiritual and moral (gathered synchretistically from various religions). So, in a totally imaginary production, we find both Providence and the universal cosmic force, resurrection and incarnation, unlimited personal development, love and non violence, as stages in an individual quest for salvation.[62]

It is said that religion has been changed into a supermarket where each one chooses individually the religious product that suits him. Individualism leads to the dissolution of Christianity, understood as expression of the human person's communion with others and with nature. This fact is not without a direct link with the elimination of the Holy Spirit from the visible Church, to be relegated to the invisible, nor with the elimination of the Spirit from visible creation to be isolated, individualistically, in human subjectivity.

. We need unity, but for this unity to be accepted by all, it must be founded on Peter's confession of faith in presence of Christ. As long as the Church remained faithful to this principle, she kept her unity; as soon as she abstracted from it, her unity was broken. The importance of the confession of faith consists–as results from all we have said–in the fact that it generates communion and has at its center Christ, God and Man, One of the Holy Trinity, Creator and Redeemer of the visible and the invisible universe, Head of the Church and the living Stone from which have come all the other stones that make up the Church; it stresses the Apostles and their successors as fundamental stones of the Church built

---

[62] J. Delumeau, *Religiile lumii* (=The religions of the world), ed. Humanitas, (Bucarest, 1993) 707.

on the Cornerstone that is Christ, and gives to the first of the bishops an important role in safeguarding Christian unity; it sees in all the faithful stones with which the Church of Christ is built; that is, it considers the laity to be an integral part of the Church. Seen in this way, the papal primacy, understood as a primacy of service, can only be exercised in the context of an ecclesiology of communion, and not above it.

That is why His Holiness Bartholomew, ecumenical patriarch of Constantinople, declared: "God appointed apostles (Luke 6:13) all his disciples, equally and without distinction. He has given them authority over the unclean spirits (Matt 10:1) and has said to them all: 'Go and make disciples of all nations' (Matt 28:19; Mark 16:15). Consequently, each one of us bishops is responsible for the way in which the boat of the Church advances; we can either contribute to its progress or prevent it."[63] Orthodoxy accepts a primacy of the Bishop of Rome, but a primacy of service. As St. John Chrysostom said, each bishop has both a universal and a local function, since he has to watch over both the universal Church and his own local Church. The government of the Church is synodal or collegial. The experience of the papacy can be of great importance for Christian unity, but in order to be accepted by everyone, it has to be exercised in the context of an ecclesiology which situates communion both at the visible level and at the invisible level of the Church, that is, which relates communion to the institutional aspect of the Church, as Father Congar says.[64]

The unity of the Church is not only a Christological, monarchical unity, but also a pneumatological unity of communion. Patristic theology understood that individualism can only be overcome by an ecclesiology of communion, founded on the faith of Peter, which brings clearly to light the divinity and the Messiahship of Christ the Savior; only in this way can the Church be victorious over the powers of hell, transfiguring humanity and the whole of creation in Christ and in the Church, by the power of life, love and light of the Holy Spirit, according to the will of the Heavenly Father. We need unity more than ever, in order to face together the grave problems confronting the Church today. We have been one Church, and we will be one again, for that is the will of Christ our Lord.

---

[63] Bartolomée Ier, "Une déclaration sur les différences entre la conception catholique et la conception orthodoxe de la primauté dans l'Église," *Istina* 41, 2 (1996) 184–89, here 186.

[64] J. Fameré, "L'ecclesiologie du Père Yves Congar. Essai de synthèse critique," *Revue des sciences philosophiques et théologiques* 76, 3 (1992) 414.

7

Primacy in the Church:
An Orthodox Approach

Metropolitan John (Zizioulas) of Pergamon

I should like to begin by expressing my deep appreciation of the initiative to convoke this meeting in order to reflect on the thorny issue of primacy, particularly that of the Roman See. The fact that this meeting marks the 100th Anniversary of the Foundation of the Society of the Atonement indicates the ecumenical significance of this Society and of its *Centro Pro Unione,* which has become by now one of the most renowned centers of ecumenical studies in the whole world. The center, with its rich library and it various activities, including a great number of symposia and conferences which have made history in the Ecumenical Movement of our time, constitutes an example of how ecumenical work should be performed, if it is to bear fruit for the unity of the Church. Openness of mind, respect for every point of view and the encouragement of frankness for all those involved in ecumenical discussion have been characteristics of the work of this ecumenical center, and it is this kind of mentality and approach that is particularly needed at this critical moment in the history of the Ecumenical Movement. We are all, therefore, indebted to the work and inspiration provided by the *Centro Pro Unione,* and we wholeheartedly congratulate the Society of the Atonement both for its one-hundredth anniversary and for its remarkable achievements and contribution in the field of ecumenism. Our special thanks are due to the present director of the *Centro,* Fr. Jim Puglisi, who has been the leading force behind this and many similar meetings. May the Lord bless abundantly the efforts of all those who are eager to see the divisions of his Church healed and full unity and communion of all Christians restored as soon as possible.

We are approaching the third millennium since the coming of our Lord, and our generation seems to be loaded with the formidable task to accelerate the process towards the re-unification of Christendom, for which previous generations worked hard and laid the foundation. In this task we are assisted by work done so far in all areas of theology, particularly in ecclesiology, and we are now called to draw practical conclusions from the remarkable consensus that has arisen from this work. This is especially true with regard to the *rapprochement* that has taken place over these years between Western and Orthodox theology concerning the fundamental presuppositions of ecclesiology, as it is witnessed in the documents of the official theological dialogue between the Roman Catholic and the Orthodox Churches, as well as in the texts of Faith and Order and other ecumenical documents. It is the *rapprochement* that should be our starting point and basis as we attempt to tackle the thorny issue of the primacy of the Church.

The issue of primacy is perhaps the most important ecumenical problem. Its importance is underlined by the words of the pope himself who has called his Petrine ministry an obstacle to the restoration of the Church's unity. The recent papal document *Ut unum sint* also makes mention of the seriousness of the problem and invites us to study it and propose ways of resolving it. Needless to say that the issue is of decisive importance for the Roman Catholic-Orthodox relations. Historically the question of the papal authority and primacy has been the main cause for the gradual estrangement between the West and the East, leading finally to the Grand Schism of 1054 and the grave consequences that followed it. The same question lies also at the root of the division between Rome and the Churches of the Reformation, although the theological disagreements that led to the appearance of Protestantism were of a much broader nature. In the Roman Catholic-Orthodox relations, too, other theological issues became prominent, such as the *Filioque,* but I regard these issues as less difficult to solve, as it is evident from a recent document of the Vatican concerning the *Filioque.*[1] The most important and at the same time the most difficult problem in the Roman Catholic-Orthodox relations is the undoubtedly that of papal primacy.

Historical method and theological approach

There are basically two ways to approach this problem. One is the *historical* method which has been used in the past extensively and which

---

[1] See the Pontifical Council for the Promotion of Christian Unity, *The Greek and the Latin Traditions Regarding the Procession of the Holy Spirit*, edition published in French, Greek, English, and Russian (Vatican City: Tipografia Vaticana, 1996).

has led to no fruitful result. The question whether the primacy of the Bishop of Rome in the Church can be justified on the ground of biblical and Patristic evidence cannot decide the issue. There is undoubtedly a Petrine "primacy" in the college of the Twelve, as it is admitted even by Protestant biblical scholars of the authority of an Oscar Culmann. But it is difficult to establish on biblical grounds the link between the ministry of St. Peter and that of the Bishop of Rome. Oscar Culmann's point that in fact the ministry of the Twelve is unique and unrepeatable continues to be valid as long as continuity is understood strictly in historical terms, i.e. as a matter of linear historical succession.

An attempt to establish the link between the Petrine and the papal primacy through the fact that Peter died and was buried in Rome can hardly convince the historian that such a link can follow by logical necessity. Paul also died in Rome and so did many other martyrs of the Church, but there has been no claim of their succession by the Bishop of Rome. As it is indicated by the controversy concerning the celebration of Easter in the second century, other Churches in Asia Minor boasted for having hosted the tombs and relics of apostles in their territory, but none of them thought of using this as a justification for a claim of apostolic succession. As the late Francis Dvorník demonstrated in his work *The Idea of Apostolicity in Byzantium and the Legend of the Apostle Andrew*,[2] it was only much later that the argument of apostolicity on the basis of a Church's foundation by an apostle began to be used widely. The historical argument became popular in the Middle Ages, but it had for the most part to rely on historically spurious evidence, as it was shown later by historical research. The historical approach to the question of papal primacy has proved to be almost pointless in the debate and can be of very little use in the ecumenical discussion of the issue.

The other way to approach the problem is the *theological* one. This method seems to have been followed in the official theological dialogue between the Roman Catholic and the Orthodox Churches, and I personally believe that it can bear fruit, if it is followed with consistency by both sides. This method begins by raising the fundamental questions concerning the nature of the Church not in a scholastic way of compartmentalizing ecclesiology as a subject in itself, but by placing it in the broader context of Christian doctrine, including our faith in the trinitarian God, in Christ and in the Holy Spirit. If the Church is "the Church of God," it must be asked of *what kind of God* she is the Church.

---

[2] F. Dvorník, *The Idea of Apostolicity in Byzantium and the Legend of the Apostle Andrew*, Dumbarton Oaks Studies 4 (Cambridge: Harvard University Press, 1958).

If she is the "body of Christ" and the "Temple of the Spirit," her nature cannot but depend on a Christology conditioned fundamentally by Pneumatology. If, finally, the Church is revealed in its fullness in the sacrament of the Holy Eucharist, we cannot form our view of her structure and ministries without taking into consideration the structure of the Eucharist itself. All these considerations are fundamental presuppositions in a theological approach to the question of primacy.

Towards a theology of primacy

If we approach the problem with such a theological method, the fundamental theological principles for a theology of the primacy in the Church can be summed up in the following observations.

1. *The Church cannot but be a unity of the One and the Many at the same time.* This principle stems from trinitarian theology as well as from christology in its relation to pneumatology. It is also supported by the eucharistic nature of ecclesiology. In the triune God there is unity, but this unity does not precede multiplicity (the three Persons). The priority of the "One God" over against the "triune God," which we encounter in traditional dogmatic manuals in the West—and, also, in the academic dogmatic theology of the East—was rightly shown by theologians such as Karl Rahner to be wrong. We do not first speak of the One God (= divine substance) and *then* of the three persons as relations *within* the one substance—a favorite approach of medieval theology. The Trinity is just as primary as the one substance in the doctrine of God: the "many" are constitutive of the One, just as the One is constitutive of the "many."

The same principle applies also to christology. The fact that Christ is inconceivable without the Spirit makes pneumatology *constitutive* of christology. Given that the Spirit operates as a force of *communion* (2 Cor 13:13) and as the one who *distributes* the charismata and personalizes the Christ-event, Christ as the "anointed one" by the Spirit (Χριστὸς) is at the same time "one" and "many"—not "one" who *becomes* "many," but as "one" who is inconceivable without the "many," his "body." There can be no "head" without a "body," there is no "one" without the "many," no Christ without the Spirit.

The "one" and "many" principle is also fundamental in the case of the Holy Eucharist. St. Paul makes this clear in the interpretation he gives the Sacrament in Corinthians 11. The entire Christian tradition in both the East and the West repeats and supports this view. Every Eucharist is offered in the name and on behalf of the entire world. There is one Eucharist in the whole universal Church and yet this one Eucharist is at the same time many Eucharists. Which comes first, the one or the many? It is absurd even to pose the question. There is *simultaneity* between the one and the many, similar to that found in the very being of God as Trinity and in the Person of Christ as a pneumatic being. This mysterious simultaneity is of crucial importance in our Christian faith. Ecclesiology cannot depart from this, if it is not to become heretical throughout.

2. *The Church is local and universal at the same time.* There have been theological voices in my own Church which tried to reverse the priority traditionally preferred by Roman Catholic ecclesiology (see e.g., Rahner and Ratzinger) according to which the Church is *first* universal and only secondarily local. In reversing the position Orthodox theologians such as the late Afanassief and Meyendorff put forth the view that the local church comes first, both historically and theologically, and it is only in a secondary way, if at all (Afanassief would not allow even for that, at least until the time of St. Cyprian), that we can speak of the Church universal. My own personal view has always been different, and it was so because I have always believed that the nature of the Eucharist points to the simultaneity of locality and universality in ecclesiology, as I have tried to explain a moment ago. This is precisely the reason that the term καθολικὴ ἐκκλησία (Catholic Church) is marked in the early patristic sources with the ambiguity of indicating both the local and the universal Church. It was only St. Augustine that identified for the first time "catholic" exclusively with "universal" in order to react to the provincialism of the Donatists. St. Cyril of Jerusalem in the East offers a synthetic definition of the term and in Ignatius, the *Martyrium Polycarpi*, Tertullian and even Cyprian this term clearly indicated the *local* Church. All this is quite instructive as it shows that locality and universality are interdependent in ecclesiology, just as the "one" and the "many" are interdependent in trinitarian theology and in christology.

3. *The bishop is both a local and a universal ministry.* The bishop is ordained for a particular church in order to be its head and center of unity. In the exercise of his ministry he is the "one" who, however, cannot be conceived without the "many," his community. The bishop is the head, but as such he is conditioned by the "body," he cannot exercise authority without communion with his faithful. Just as he cannot perform the Eucharist without the *synaxis* of the people, his entire ministry requires the *consensus fidelium,* the "Amen" of the community. The reverse is equally true: there is no community without a head, the bishop; nothing can be done without him.

Now, the bishop may be ordained primarily for a specific local church, and yet he is at the same time a bishop of the Church universal. This is indicated by two canonical provisions: (a) ordination to episcopacy requires the participation of more than one bishop (whereas that of the presbyter and the deacon is a strictly local affair). And (b) once a bishop is ordained he is entitled or even obliged to exercise his *synodical* ministry. None, except secular force (cf. the case of certain bishops of the ecumenical patriarchate today) can deprive a bishop of his right and duty to be a member of the regional or the universal synod. In the person of the bishop locality and universality meet and form two aspects of one and the same ministry.

4. *The synodal system is a "sine qua non conditio" for the catholicity of the Church.* There can be no Church without a synod—this is a principle followed carefully by the Orthodox Church, albeit not always in a satisfactory way. Why is this principle so important? Some tend to see in the synodal system an expression of "democratic" spirit and a reaction against monarchical tendencies in ecclesiology. The movement of *konziliarismus* was historically such a reaction against the papacy, and there are still many Orthodox who think that synodality is an alternative to the papal primacy. Such views would imply that there is an incompatibility between primacy and conciliarity, which, as we shall see, is by no means true.

The reason why synodality is fundamental in ecclesiology is that through this institution the catholicity of the local church is guaranteed and protected. This is achieved through a double canonical provision. On the one hand *every* bishop has the right and duty to participate *on equal terms* with all the other bishops in a council, and on the other hand no council has the authority to interfere with the internal affairs of each bishop's diocese. The authority of a council or synod is limited to the affairs pertaining to the communion of local churches with one another. Such was, for example, the case in the early Church when canon 5 of I Nicaea instituted the convocation of synods in every region twice a year in order to examine cases of eucharistic excommunication: if a certain bishop excommunicated one of his faithful, the excommunicated person could not go to another local church to take communion. This could only be decided by a synod of which the bishop concerned would be also a member. The synod could not in this way become an institution *above* the local church. It would exercise authority only *via* the local church. Equally, the local church could not ignore the consequences of its decisions and actions for the other churches, as if it were a "catholic" church independently of its relations and communion with the rest of the churches. The catholicity of the local church cannot be turned into self-sufficiency, while the condition of communion with the rest of the churches should not lead to a loss of its catholicity through subjection to an institution existing and acting above the local church. This means that through the synodical system we do not arrive at a universal church; we rather arrive at a *communion of churches. Universality becomes in this way identical with communion.*

5. *Primacy is also a "sine qua non conditio" for the catholicity of the Church.* If the fundamental principles mentioned above are to be followed faithfully, the "one-and-the-many" idea which runs through the entire doctrine of the Church leads directly to the ministry of primacy. It also indicates the conditions which are necessary for primacy to be ecclesiologically justifiable and sound. Let us consider this in some detail.

(a) There is a primacy *within* each local church. The bishop is the *primus* at the local level. He is the head of the collegium of the presbyters, but at the same time he is the head of the eucharistic synaxis, which means that he is conditioned in his ministry by the entire community of which he is the head. The fact that there can be no eucharistic synaxis without his presidency (directly or indirectly through the authorized priest) shows that the *primus* is a *constitutive* element in the local church. Equally, however, the fact that the synaxis of the people is a condition for the bishop to function as the head of the community shows that his primacy requires the consent and participation of the community. In a similar manner, the bishop is the only one that can distribute the gifts of the Spirit as the sole ordainer in the Church (this includes also baptism and confirmation taken together as an unbreakable unity according to the ancient tradition and that of the Orthodox Church). Yet, the fact that the bishop cannot ordain in his study or in his home but only within a eucharistic synaxis indicates that he distributes the gifts only on condition that the community is involved in the ordination. The "many" cannot be a church without the "one," but equally the "one" cannot be the *primus* without the "many."

(b) Similar observations apply also to the *regional* level. The *metropolitan* system in the Church developed in close connection with the synodical institution. The bishop of the "metropolis," i.e., the capital city of the region, was automatically the *primus* of the synod and of the region. He was very early recognized as the πρῶτος (the first one) and as the "head" (κεφαλή) of all the bishops of the area, but his primacy was strictly conditioned by the involvement in all his decisions and actions of the rest of the bishops of whom he was *primus*. This is clearly laid down by canon 34 of the corpus known as "Apostolic Canons" which belong in all probability to the fourth century A.D., i.e., to the time when the metropolitan system was taking shape. This canon provides that all the bishops of a region (ἔθνος) must recognize their "first one" (πρῶτος) as their "head" (κεφαλή) and do nothing without him, while he should equally do nothing without them. The canon, significantly enough, ends with reference to the Holy Trinity, thereby indicating indirectly that canonical provisions of this kind are not a matter of mere organization but have a theological, indeed a triadological, basis.

(c) Mention should be made of a special kind of primacy which although regional in character rose above the metropolitan system to comprise all the metropolitan units of a certain broader area. This is what came to be known as *Patriarchates*. The basis of this institution was political as well as historical and ecclesiastical—never theological in the strict sense. Certain local churches acquired pre-eminence, either because they were important in the political structure of the empire or because they had an historic significance in the establishment of the Christian faith and the emergence of new churches (as mother churches). At the time of Byzantium these centers formed the well-known *pentarchy* which comprised the Churches of Rome, Constantinople, Alexandria, Antioch, and Jerusalem. The bishops of these Churches rose above the rest of the bishops and became each of them *primus* in his own area.

The Great Schism between Rome and Constantinople in the eleventh century opened the way to further developments in this matter. In the first place Rome, following and developing a tradition which started before the schism, claimed universal jurisdiction and was not satisfied with the primacy of the patriarchate of the West. This was not recognized by the Churches of the East (the other four patriarchates of the pentarchy) who formed their own structure and recognized the bishop of Constantinople as the first one among them—keeping for the rest of them the order of the pentarchy. In so doing the Churches of the East never recognized in their *primus* (i.e., Constantinople) a ministry of universal jurisdiction, but only one in the sense of canon 34 of the Apostolic Canons mentioned above. The patriarch of Constantinople could not interfere in the affairs of the other patriarchates, but would be responsible for the canonical order within them and intervene only when asked to do so in cases of emergency or disturbance and anomaly of some kind. He would also be responsible for the convocation of councils dealing with matters pertaining to the entire Orthodox Churches, always with the consent of the other patriarchs. The same principles continue to apply after the creation of the other patriarchates and autocephalous Churches that make up the present structure of the Orthodox Church. With the exception of occasional difficulties in their mutual relations, due mainly to nationalistic tendencies, the Orthodox Churches have accepted the idea of primacy as exercised within the Orthodox

Church by the patriarch of Constantinople in the spirit of canon 34 by the Apostles, as analyzed above. This primacy is sometimes called "primacy of honor," a misleading term since, as we have noted, it is not an "honorific" primacy but one that involves actual duties and responsibilities, albeit under the conditions just mentioned.

6. *The Primacy of Rome.* We can now address the specific question of the primacy of the Bishop of Rome. Is such a primacy necessary ecclesiologically, and if it is in what sense should it be understood and applied?

Let me begin by repeating what I said at the beginning of his paper. The question for me is not an historical but a theological one. If there is a necessity for the primacy of the Bishop of Rome this could not be because history demands it, for even if history demanded it (which is in my view doubtful, to say the least) it would not make it a necessary thing for the Church's *esse.* The same thing would have to be said if the reasons offered for such a primacy were to be practical and utilitarian. For if this were the case the primacy we are considering would not be a matter of the Church's *esse* but of her *bene esse,* and this would be less than satisfactory to a theologian. The primacy of the Bishop of Rome has to be theologically justified or else be ignored altogether. Speaking as an Orthodox theologian, I can see two possibilities for a positive appreciation of the papal primacy.

(a) The understanding of the primacy of the Roman bishop *in the traditional sense of the Byzantine pentarchy.* This would mean that the Bishop of Rome is *primus* only for the West; he is the patriarch of the West and should have no primacy whatsoever over the rest of the world. This would seem to satisfy fully the Orthodox, for it would appear to be a return to the Byzantine pentarchy from which Rome has departed by claiming universal jurisdiction.

Such an understanding of the Roman primacy could lead to a scheme of division of the world into two parts: the West and the East which would mean that Old Rome would have the primacy over the West (whatever that may involve: certainly the Protestant and Anglican world), whereas the New Rome will have the primacy it now has over the East (i.e. the Orthodox world, including the Oriental and non-Chalcedonians?). The problem that such an "arrangement" presents is that there are now parts of the world which are Christian and which were not known at the time of the Byzantine pentarchy. To whom will these belong in terms of primacy?

But there is also another difficulty. What would be the theological justification of such a division of primacies or of any such primacy at all? The pentarchy can hardly claim a theological *raison d'être,* and for this reason it was eventually amended and modified and can always be amended and modified in terms of number. There is nothing permanent about the number of the *primi;* the only permanent thing is that of the *sees* which hold the primacy, because these were chosen on the basis or irrevocable historical facts relating to the establishing of churches and their faith. Thus, although the limitation of the Roman primacy to the West would be a solution easily acceptable to the Orthodox, this solution would have its weaknesses.

(b) The understanding of the Roman primacy as a universal primacy. This would appear to be totally unacceptable to the Orthodox at first sight. And it *should* be unacceptable *unless it is fundamentally qualified.* These are qualifications that I think should be applied according to the theological principles presented above.

(i) The primacy should not be *primacy* of jurisdiction. The reason for this is that the exercise of jurisdiction means interference with the affairs of a local church and this means the destruction or negation of its catholicity and ecclesial integrity. This, as we noted, has not been allowed to any institution, be it the council or the patriarchate or the metropolitan. The local church headed by its bishop must be always allowed to feel like a "catholic church," totally free to run its affairs as long as this does not interfere with the life of the other local churches. This is part of what it means to call, together with Vatican II, each particular church a full church.

(ii) The primacy should not be the prerogative of an individual but of a *local church.* This means that in speaking of the primacy of the pope we mean the primacy of a see, i.e., the *Church of Rome.* There is a big difference between these two ways of understanding primacy. In an ecclesiology of communion we have not a communion of individuals but of *churches.* Even when councils or synods are composed only of bishops, these bishops are not there as individuals but as heads of churches, and it is this that makes the *reception* of conciliar decisions by the faithful a necessary condition for the final authority of these decisions. The bishops, at least according to Orthodox ecclesiology are not members of an "apostolic college" standing on its own feet and above the local churches. They are an integral part of each of its own local church. So must be also the bishop of Rome, if he is to exercise a primacy.

(iii) The primacy should be exercised *in a synodical context* both locally and regionally as well as universally. This means that the spirit and the provisions of the 34th canon "of the Apostles," as explained earlier on here, would have to be respected: the *primus* must always act together with the rest of the bishops on matters pertaining to or common with the other churches outside his own local church, while the bishops in similar cases should always act together with their *primus*.

(iv) Given the established structure of the Church the universal primacy of the Church of Rome would mean in the first instance that the Bishop of Rome will be in cooperation on all matters pertaining to the Church as a whole with the existing patriarchs and other heads of autocephalous churches. His primacy would be exercised *in communion*, not in isolation or directly over the entire Church. He would be the President of all heads of churches and the spokesman of the entire Church once the decisions announced are the result of consensus. But communion should not be exhausted at the level of heads of Churches; it should penetrate deeply into all levels of church life, reaching all bishops and all the clergy and all the people.

A universal *primus*

These are some conditions that would make a Petrine ministry of primacy acceptable to me as an Orthodox theologian. Under such conditions the catholicity of the local church is respected and at the same time the unity and oneness of the Church in the world is served and manifested. A universal *primus* exercising his primacy in such a way is not only "useful" to the Church but an ecclesiological necessity in a unified Church.

For such a primacy to be accepted and applied an ecclesiology of communion rooted deeply in a theology, and even an ontology of communion, would be necessary. I believe that the second Vatican Council has made an historic advance in this direction, and we can proceed in the deepening of such a theology of communion and apply it to all matters still dividing us, including that of the Roman primacy. The final outcome of our efforts can only be the gift of God. We trust in him and pray with him to the Father in the Holy Spirit that we all may be one, as God the Holy Trinity is One.

8

Conciliarity-Primacy in a Russian Orthodox Perspective

Nicolas Lossky

It is not possible to speak of one, common attitude towards the conceptions of conciliarity, of primacy, or of the relation between the two among Russian theologians and Church people. Especially of late, there have been many different, often contradictory conceptions and opinions on these notions.

Some hold a very simple view according to which the Catholics have the pope while the Orthodox have the council. Others will simply affirm that in Orthodoxy there has never been a primacy at the world level except perhaps a "primacy of honor," meaning practically nothing. In any case, many will tend to overemphasize the notion of conciliarity (or synodality) as a characteristic of Orthodoxy to the detriment of any other approach to authority in the Church. To them, since Orthodoxy is the Church of the Seven Ecumenical Councils, Orthodoxy is conciliar and the supreme authority in matters of doctrine and discipline is the Council. A few years ago, such an opinion was publicly voiced in the following terms: "If tomorrow a Pan-Orthodox Council tells me that it is lawful to ordain women to the priesthood, I shall accept," meaning that a Council is *necessarily* right, and its decisions are therefore binding for all Orthodox, just as a papal decision is binding for all Catholics.

Such oversimplifications are perhaps due to a certain distortion, a certain misunderstanding of Alexis Khomiakov's neologism *Sobornost,* derived from the slavonic adjective *sobornaia* which translates the Greek *Katholikē* in the Creed, adding an extra dimension to the notion of catholicity through the relation with the root *Sobor* which also means "council" or "synod." They may also be due to insufficient knowledge of church history and insufficient contact with the world of scholars abroad. This is understandable after seventy-five years of rather limited theological research and teaching, at least for the vast majority.

For the attitude of suspicion with regard to the notion of primacy, things are perhaps a little more complicated. Indeed, such an attitude may find its theoretical roots in certain opinions, certainly known to all, of an outstanding theologian who did not live in Russia but in Paris where he taught at Saint Sergius' Orthodox Theological Institute. Fr. Nicolas Afanassieff is known as one of the first to have developed the notion of a eucharistic ecclesiology for the Orthodox world. We must all be grateful to him for his rediscovery of the fullness of ecclesiality of the local church expressed in the celebration of the sacrament of the Eucharist.[1]

However, in his essay "The Church which Presides in Love,"[2] he distinguishes between a eucharistic and a universal ecclesiology basing the latter on St. Cyprian's conception of the unity of the episcopate which he tends to interpret in juridical terms. In his view, St. Cyprian's conception of the universal Church necessarily implies primacy. And primacy necessarily means power in a juridical sense. He then distinguishes between "primacy" understood as power and "priority" which, according to him, in an Orthodox perspective, implies not power but "grace" and "love." Although each local Church is "autonomous and independent" (the phrase is used several times) because it is the Church of God in all its fullness, one of them has "priority" among them and since priority does not mean power, a legalistic concept which belongs to primacy, it "presides in love" (St. Ignatius "To the Romans," salutation).

Now, this "presidency" in fact seems to imply a certain conception of universality which in a sense contradicts the insistence on the "independence" of local churches. Besides, the strong opposition between "primacy" and "priority" is not totally convincing. Why should "priority" have a monopoly of "grace" and "love" and why should "primacy" be necessarily understood as legalistic power? Is it not possible to envisage primacy as an exercise of presidency in love and over love, as a

[1] See *The Church of the Holy Spirit*, published posthumously in Russian and the French translation, *L'Église du Saint Esprit*, Cogitatio Fidei 83 (Paris: Cerf, 1975). That eucharistic ecclesiology among Western Catholic theologians was not derived from N. Afanassieff is shown by J.M.R. Tillard in *Chair de l'Église, chair du Christ*, Cogitatio Fidei 168 (Paris: Cerf, 1992) and in *L'Église locale: ecclésiologie de communion et catholicité*, Cogitatio Fidei 191 (Paris: Cerf, 1995).

[2] In J. Meyendorff, A. Schmemann, N. Afanassieff, N. Koulomzine, *The Primacy of Peter in the Orthodox Church*, The Library of Orthodox Theology 1 (Bedfordshire: The Faith Press, 1973) 91–143.

service, a ministry?[3] It might be suggested that the total rejection of the notion of primacy by some Orthodox proceeds from an excessive anti-romanism, based on a certain distortion of the office in the historical development of the Church of Rome.[4]

In a more positive perspective, in the same essay, Fr. Nicolas Afanassieff strongly emphasizes the fact that conciliarity and what he calls "priority" (which in fact could be understood as a form of "primacy") not only do not represent a polarization between two ecclesiologies but are absolutely linked together, the one necessarily implying the other. This is unfortunately not always clearly understood by many Russians who retain from Fr. Nicolas Afanassieff's teaching only his insistence on the "independent" character of the local church. The positive basis for this rather unfortunate notion tends to be left on one side (the fullness of ecclesiality in the celebration of the Eucharist) and only the idea of "independence" or self-sufficiency is emphasized. The result is the development of an ecclesiology based on the idea that each autocephalous church is by definition the "local church" and being fully self-governing does not really need the others and leads an "individual" life. This is of course a caricature. But the tendency exists and some of us call this an "autocephalist" ecclesiology. It entails not so much a spirit of communion as the tendency to speak mainly in terms of the "rights" of the local church defended in the name of what some call "historical justice." As a result, relations among the "sister churches" tend to resemble more and more the relations between sovereign states, all the more so as a strong dose of nationalism (condemned in 1872 as "phyletism," which paradoxically all unanimously denounce as a heresy and many, at the same time, profess it in practice) is mixed with this notion of "independence."

It is interesting to note that together with the development of "autocephalist" ecclesiology which is often linked with a simplistic anti-romanism and therefore anti-papism, the notion of primacy, rejected in connection with the Roman Church, tends to reappear in the context of the local autocephalous church. Many are the members of the people of God (not excluding some church leaders at various levels) who in fact consider the patriarch to be something of a "super-bishop" who has

---

[3] Cf. John Paul II, *Ut unum sint. That They May Be One: On Commitment to Ecumenism* (Washington, D.C.: United States Catholic Conference, 1995) §§88, 94 where "power" is explicitly refused; (hereafter cited *Ut unum sint*).

[4] See chapter 8 of O. Clément, *Rome autrement. Une réflexion orthodoxe sur la papauté* (Paris: Desclée de Brouwer, 1997) 65–73 where these distortions are briefly described. See also N° 88 of *Ut unum sint* which ends with a reference to "certain painful recollections" and the concluding sentence: "To the extent that we are responsible for these, I join my predecessor Paul VI in asking forgiveness."

more power than any of his brothers in the episcopate, practically a power over the other bishops of the territory of the autocephalous church. Needless to say that such a "multiplied papism" is largely due to mere ignorance of church history and canon law.

If the somewhat simplified views of conciliarity, eucharistic ecclesiology and primacy described so far may be said to represent a certain majority among Russian Orthodox Christians (in Russia there is the excuse of the long period of the Dark Ages), is it lawful and scientifically correct to judge of ecclesiological opinions in terms of what a majority thinks and expresses? This would amount to a purely phenomenological approach to Church History. Such an approach is perhaps sometimes necessary in order to discover the state of mind of people but we all know that we cannot draw from the discovery conclusions as to what the real theological opinions of a Church consist in. The minority, most of the time, is much more important in this respect than the majority. Thus, the present patriarch of Moscow, a few bishops and a few theologians hold views in the area of ecclesiology very different from what has been described so far.

Such views, in terms of primacy, conciliarity and ecclesiology more generally, are best expressed by Russian theologians of the emigration such as Fr. Georges Florovsky, Fr. John Meyendorff, and particularly Fr. Alexander Schmemann. The latter's essay, "The Idea of Primacy in Orthodox Ecclesiology" in the volume already referred to (*The Primacy of Peter in the Orthodox Church*), is remarkably clear. First of all, he does not hesitate to use and clarify the notion of "primacy" (not "priority") which he examines at different levels, culminating with "the highest and ultimate form of primacy: *the universal primacy.*"[5] He also refers to "an age long anti-Roman prejudice [which] has led some Orthodox canonists simply to deny the existence of such primacy in the past or the need for it in the present."[6] And he adds something which, it seems, all Russian Orthodox should read and meditate in the present atmosphere of disagreement: "But an objective study of the canonical tradition cannot fail to establish beyond any doubt that, along with local 'centers of agreement' or primacies, the Church had also known a universal primacy."[7]

As for the nature of this primacy, it is defined as a "center of communion" and in no way as a notion to be identified with a form of "supreme power," a notion "incompatible with the nature of the Church

---

[5] A. Schmemann, "The Idea of Primacy in Orthodox Ecclesiology," in J. Meyendorff *et al.*, *The Primacy . . .* , 163, the author's italics.

[6] *Ibid.*

[7] *Ibid.*

as Body of Christ." It is interesting to note, again in the present atmosphere of doubt, that Fr. Alexander Schmemann adds that primacy is not to be understood as "a mere 'chairmanship' if one understands this term in its modern, parliamentary and democratic connotations."[8] Implicitly complementing Fr. Nicolas Afanassieff's eucharistic ecclesiology, Fr. Alexander Schmemann goes to the heart of the nature of primacy by stating that no local Church can live in isolation: "A local Church cut from this universal *koinonia* is indeed a *contradictio in adjecto*, for this *koinonia* is the very essence of the Church. And it has, therefore, its *form* and *expression:* primacy. Primacy is the necessary expression of the unity in faith and life of all local Churches, of their living and efficient *koinonia*."[9]

For the manner of understanding the exercise of primacy at all the different levels, including the universal one, like so many of us after him, Fr. Alexander Schmemann refers to the famous thirty-fourth so-called apostolic canon which everyone probably knows by heart nowadays: "The bishops of each nation must know who is first among them and acknowledge him as their head; they are to do nothing of weight without his opinion and let everyone of them look after the affairs of his diocese and the regions depending thereon. But neither let him do anything without the advice of all and thus, concord will prevail to the glory of the Father, the Son and the Holy Spirit." The final doxology clearly is not perfunctory politeness but points to the fact that the model, both for the exercise of primacy and of conciliarity is nothing less than the Holy Trinity.

Some might say that canon 34 speaks of bishops and therefore concerns primacy and conciliarity among bishops only. Certainly, in a literal sense this is true. However, as many of us say with insistence today, a bishop (theoretically at least) does not exist outside or above his Church.[10] The bishop is within the community of the people of God, being himself a member of the *laos*.[11] Certainly, he receives a special gift

---

[8] *Ibid.*, 164.

[9] *Ibid.*, 165.

[10] See in particular, Metropolitan John Zizioulas's remarkable contribution to the World Conference on Faith and Order at Santiago de Compostela in 1993: Metropolitan John (Zizioulas) of Pergamon, "The Church as Communion: A Presentation on the World Conference Theme," in T. F. Best and G. Gaßmann, eds., *On the Way to Fuller Koinonia. Official Report of the Fifth World Conference on Faith and Order*, Faith and Order Paper 166 (Geneva: W.C.C. Publications, 1990) 103–11. Though he is not a Russian theologian, it is difficult to resist from referring to him in this context for he expresses this ecclesiology of communion so well for all of us.

[11] On the unity of the community of the baptized, who are all of them *"Christifideles,"* it seems impossible not to refer once again to a theologian who is not a Russian nor even

of the Holy Spirit for exercising his pastoral duties as teacher, preacher, president of the eucharistic community, and as such, it is his charism to express the truth of the Church. But if it is a gift, it must be received and the reception consists in doing his best to correspond to his function. There is nothing automatic about this. If the eucharistic prayer is heard by God, whatever the indignity of the minister, it is because of the promise of Christ and his own prayer to the Father. But the truth of the Church is voiced by the bishop only provided that it is the truth of the Church, however unhelpful and simplistic this may sound. The only criterion is the Holy Spirit himself. It is therefore in communion, in the unity of the one Spirit, that the magisterium is to be exercised. As a pastor, the bishop must strive to be *servus servorum Dei*.[12]

This brings us back to the notion of conciliarity. When bishops meet, never severed from their communities, it is a council or a synod (there is no difference in spite of the fact that some Churches use the Latin form "council" and others, particularly in the Reformation world, will tend to use the Greek form "synod"). It is one level of conciliarity in which notions such as democracy or monarchy in the worldly, political sense of these words, have no place; a Council works by consensus, and it is the primate's particular duty to serve the search for this consensus or unity in Spirit. But when a bishop presides, especially the eucharistic Synaxis of his Church, it is another level of the same conciliarity. One might say that whenever the Eucharist is celebrated, the Church is in council because there is an affirmation of communion in the fullness of the Apostolic faith with all the local churches throughout the world and throughout time in the mention of the primate, of the bishops of the province, and of course in the offering "for" (St. John Chrysostom) or "with" (St. Basil) the Communion of Saints, all the living, all the dead.[13]

However communion should not be understood as a fusion in which all are merged in an indistinguishable whole. It is a communion

---

an Orthodox: J.M.R. Tillard whose *Église locale* . . . contains excellent pages on the subject. See chapter III, "L'Église locale, Église des baptisés."

[12] St. Gregory the Great, readopted by Pope John Paul II in *Ut unum sint,* 88.

[13] Metropolitan John of Pergamon (Zizioulas) writes: "Just as a eucharist which is not a transcendance of divisions within a certain locality is a false eucharist, equally a eucharist which takes place in conscious and intentional isolation and separation from other local communities in the world is not a true eucharist. From that it follows inevitably that a local Church, in order to be not just local but also Church, must be in full communion with the rest of the local Churches in the world," J. D. Zizioulas, *Being as Communion. Studies in Personhood and the Church,* Contemporary Greek Theologians 4 (Crestwood, N.Y.: St. Vladimir's Seminary Press, 1985) 257.

of *persons,* of "living stones" (1 Pet 2:5). The community of the people of God is composed of persons who do not, as it were, "disappear" in the Body of Christ. Diversity is as absolute as unity. Each one, in baptism–chrismation/confirmation, receives the Holy Spirit who incorporates us in the Body of Christ and "guides us into all the truth" (John 16:13), and the whole Truth is Christ. With the help of the Holy Spirit who dwells in our hearts, everyone is called to become a *co-responsible* member of the body, an active member, active in his or her function. There are no passive members of the Church. But the activity is in communion, both with the other members, our contemporaries, and with the witnesses of all times, the communion of saints. There must be unity because the Spirit is one: "the same Spirit" (1 Cor 12:4).

And yet, as a "living stone" building up the edifice (1 Pet 2:5), everyone is fully responsible for the whole body, for the whole Church. When I act, I am never severed from the Church; the Church acts through me if I am a conscious member of the Church. This at least is our calling. This is what another Russian theologian who lived in Paris, Vladimir Lossky expressed in speaking of everyone's vocation to become a "catholic consciousness of the Church." This, according to him, can only be achieved through a renunciation of seeking my own consciousness, through a constant replacement of my self-consciousness by an *ecclesial* consciousness, hence a *catholic* consciousness.[14] If this point is taken seriously, it will clearly have important consequences in the realm of ethics and will throw light on the painful problem of eucharistic hospitality in an Orthodox perspective.

All the Russian Orthodox theologians of the so-called diaspora who have written about ecclesiology will agree in saying that the petrine office, the succession of St. Peter is inherited by every bishop because Peter is the "rock" on account of his confession of Jesus-Christ as "the Son of the living God" (Matt 16:16). This means that any bishop is a successor to Peter only in so far as he confesses the fullness of the apostolic faith in Christ. And one may add, in the light of what has been said about the tight communion that should exist between the bishop and his flock, and about the necessary growth in catholicity (catholic consciousness) of every baptized member of this flock, that every true Christian, moved by the Holy Spirit, who confesses the fullness of divine revelation and the divinity of Christ is in a certain sense a successor to Peter. But this, of course, can only be conceived in the full communion of the

---

[14] V. Lossky, "Catholic Consciousness: Anthropological Implications of the Dogma of the Church," in id., *In the Image and Likeness of God* (New York: St. Vladimir's Seminary Press, 1974) 183–94.

Church where there can be no place whatever for any form of individualism (to quote once more the Greek theologian, Metropolitan John of Pergamon whose admirable contribution to Orthodox theology clearly leads us to abandon any references to nationality and to seek together what is universal Orthodox theology).

It should clearly appear from all that has been said that conciliarity should be understood in terms of communion at all levels: among the members of the body of Christ, among the local Churches in the person of their bishops who voice the faith of the Church; in other words, it is profoundly eucharistic. It is not to be understood in terms of the "conciliarism" of the Great Schism of the West which raised a question that has no place in true conciliarity: "Is the pope above the council or is the council above the pope?" "Conciliarism" also tended to introduce a certain form of "democracy" in conciliar decisions.

In a conciliarity of communion, the primate and conciliarity necessarily imply one another. The primate's duty, or special charism, is to serve the search for consensus, for unanimity that is unity in the Spirit, and thereby a constant reconstruction of true conciliarity, true communion. Conciliarity without primacy tends towards either a form of fusion or a form of democracy which amounts to individualism, not personhood. Primacy without conciliarity tends towards a kind of concentration of episcopacy in one super-bishop above the community, a form of domination tantamount to dictatorship which is a negation of communion.

As a conclusion, I would like to draw attention to two points. One is the recognition by many Orthodox theologians of Rome (on condition of course that full communion is restored) as the court of appeal (excluding intervention before an appeal) in disputes among bishops, such as this is defined by the Council of Sardica (ca. 343, canons 3, 4, 5).[15] The other is that most of these Orthodox theologians would accept the restoration of the primacy of Rome such as it was understood, with ups and downs, it is true, and not always in the same spirit in the East and in the West, during the first millennium of the existence of the Christian Church. The best expression of a common understanding of this place of Rome and of Church relations more generally is probably to be found in the Council of Constantinople of 879–880 which reha-

[15] See e.g., Comité mixte catholique-orthodoxe en France, *La primauté romaine dans la communion des Églises*, Documents des Églises (Paris: Cerf, 1991) 123 (=common conclusion of the Commission); for an English translation, see "'The Roman Primacy within the Communion of Churches': French Joint RC-Orthodox Committee," *One in Christ* 29, 2 (1993) 162f.

bilitated St. Photius as patriarch of Constantinople and marked a full reconciliation between Rome and Constantinople, and through them, the reconciliation of the whole Chalcedonian Church in the East and in the West. May I be permitted to reiterate at this stage the strong plea made by Fr. John Meyendorff for a common reception as the Eighth Ecumenical Council of the Council of Constantinople of 879–880?[16]

[16] J. Meyendorff, "Églises-sœurs. Implications ecclésiologiques du Tomos Agapis," *Istina* 20, 1 (1975) 35–46.

9

The Ministry of Unity and the Common Witness of the Churches Today

Lukas Vischer

A Reformed View

What can be said from a Reformed perspective about the significance of papacy for the common witness of the churches? Is there room in the Reformed understanding of the Church for a ministry serving the unity of the Church world-wide?

I. Papacy in Calvin's writings and in subsequent Reformed tradition

To understand the Reformed attitude towards papacy, two aspects need to be underlined.

1. From its early beginnings the Reformed tradition has always been characterized by a particularly radical rejection of papacy. Calvin did not confine his critique to denounce the corruption of papal Rome but called into question the institution of papacy as such. True, his opposition to papacy had its primary reason in the fact that Rome was not only not prepared to undertake the reforms which in his eyes were long overdue but sought actively to suppress the proclamation of the Reformers. This experience inevitably raised for Calvin the question of the legitimacy of papacy as such. The conclusion could be but negative. The claims of the Bishop of Rome went well beyond the evidence found both in the Bible and in the writings the Fathers of the early centuries. Papacy in the form it acquired in the course of the centuries up to the Reformation has to be considered the result of an erroneous development.

Calvin develops this thesis with great care in the fourth book of his *Institutes*.[1] Having briefly described the nature and order of the Church of Jesus Christ as he understands them, he begins to deal with the subject of papacy. His first concern is the biblical passages usually used to legitimize the papal ministry. He refutes one by one the interpretations which were generally accepted at his time.[2] Special attention is devoted to the words of promise Jesus addresses to Peter in the Gospel according to Matthew (16:18). Calvin offers an interpretation which had been taught by many Fathers and theologians before him. The rock, on which Christ builds his church, is the confession of faith uttered by Peter–Jesus Christ himself, the one foundation (1 Cor 3:11). The words of promise seek to emphasize the significance of the proclamation of the apostles. Calvin also underlines that there is no passage in the Bible which would allow the promise addressed to Peter to be applied to the bishop of Rome. Peter was never a bishop but regarded himself, according to the First Epistle of Peter, as "co-elder among elders" (5:1).

For Calvin the papal ministry is therefore no divinely instituted structure. It is the result of a complex historical development. The biblical legitimation was added *a posteriori*. In a remarkable historical study which extends over several chapters (7-11) Calvin shows how in the course of the centuries the claims of the Roman see were expanded step by step, eventually resulting in the universal jurisdiction of the Roman see over all other sees. In Calvin's view the original structure of communion characteristic for the early centuries was destroyed in the course of this process. A pyramidal structure took its place. The concentration of power in one person had devastating effects. It prevented the action of the Holy Spirit in the Church. In Calvin's view, Jesus had never named one person over all others as his "lieutenant."[3]

The pope is therefore Antichrist. Like other Reformers, Calvin also felt inevitably driven towards this conclusion.[4] Because, what else can an institution be which prevents Christ from being present in the church? "Encore que j'accorde que Rome ait été jadis la mère de toutes les Églises, depuis qu'elle a commencé d'être le siège de l'Antichrist, elle a

---

[1] English edition: *Calvin: Institutes of the Christian Religion*, ed. J. T. McNeill, The Library of Christian Classics 20, 21 (Philadelphia: Westminster Press, 1967). Hereafter Calvin's *Institutes* will be cited *ICR* followed by Roman numeral for the Book, then the chapter number, and finally the section number. Reference to the English edition will be cited between parentheses as McNeill followed by volume number and then page number.

[2] *ICR* IV, 6 (McNeil 2, 1102–18).

[3] *ICR* IV, 6, 10 (McNeill 2, 1110f).

[4] *ICR* IV, 7, 24ff (McNeill 2, 1143–49).

laissé d'être ce qu'elle était."[5] This view was generally accepted by the Reformed churches and has also found its place in Reformed confessional statements, especially in the Westminster Confession.[6] Today it is held only by a few, and some Presbyterian churches, e.g., the Church of Scotland, have even explicitly amended the text of the Westminster Confession. But there should be no illusions. This does not mean that the Reformed Churches are on the way to recognizing papacy. In Reformed eyes papacy continues to be incompatible with the spirit of the New Testament.

2. This leads to a second observation. The radical rejection of papacy by the Reformed Churches has its real reason in their understanding of the church. It excludes such a ministry. Calvin understands the Church as a communion called into existence by the preaching of the Gospel and the administration of the sacraments according to Jesus' instruction. For the stream of the Spirit to flow abundantly, the fountain providing the living waters must be freed from all obstacles. The proclamation of the word leads to a communion accepting Christ's discipline. Various ministries—in Reformed ecclesiology the term normally appears in the plural—are instituted to make sure that the fundamental tasks of the Church are fulfilled. Pastors (or bishops) have the obligation to preach, deacons recall through word and deed the duty of solidarity of the whole community, the elders (or presbyters) see to it that the "fruits of preaching can be harvested";[7] their tasks are pastoral care and the exercise of discipline. All these ministries loose their raison-d'être as soon as their purpose is not fulfilled.

What about governance in the Church? There is a striking emphasis in Reformed ecclesiology on decision making through representative bodies. This applies to all levels of church life—the local community, the region, and the nation. In the local community authority lies with the council of pastors and elders. At the level of the region and nation, representative synods have the task to preserve truth and to ensure common witness. Reformed churches have generally a deep,

---

[5] *ICR* IV, 7, 24 (McNeill 2, 1145): "Of old, Rome was indeed the mother of all churches; but after it began to become the see of Antichrist, it ceased to be what once it was."

[6] 25, 6 see P. Schaff, *The Creeds of Christendom. With a History and Critical Notes,* vol. III: *The Evangelical Protestant Creeds,* 4th revised and enlarged ed., Bibliotheca Symbolica Ecclesiae Universalis (Grand Rapids: Baker Book House, 1977) 658f (hereafter cited Schaff followed by page).

[7] *The First Book of Discipline in Scotland (1561),* ed. J. K. Cameron (Edinburgh: St: Andrew Press, 1972).

sometimes even an excessive, mistrust of all forms of personal authority. Again and again Reformed statements of faith emphasize that there is no hierarchical order in the Church but that all ministries are of equal importance. Again and again they maintain that no congregation has more rights than any other. "We believe that all true pastors, wherever they may be, have the same authority and equal power under one head, one only sovereign and universal bishop, Jesus Christ; and that consequently no church shall claim any authority or dominion over any other."[8] According to Calvin, the historical development of papacy was devastating because it gradually led to the reduction and even suppression of the freedom of the people of God. Direct access to the Bible was prohibited. People's consciences were bound by unbiblical prescriptions and rules. The community lost its dignity because it had no longer the right to elect its own bishop.

Reformed theologians and even some statements of faith place strong emphasis on the need for synods and councils.[9] It is the task of synods and councils, "to determine controversies of faith, and cases on conscience; to set down rules and directions for the better ordering of the public worship of God, and government of the Church; to receive complaints in cases of mal-administration, and authoritatively to determine the same."[10] Evidently, councils can err and their decisions may be, or may even have to be, corrected in the light of new insights gained from God's Word in the Bible. But they are to be accepted with "reverence and submission, not only for their agreement with the Word of God but also for the power whereby they are made, as being an ordinance of God, appointed thereunto in his Word."[11] Reformed theologians normally see the value and the purpose of synods in the "common and mutual edification." They emphasize that councils have to discuss and determine issues which cannot be solved at the next lower level, especially in situations when "the truth and purity of the faith needs to be defended against heretics and appropriate moral behavior and order against the schismatics." They have to serve "the edification, integrity and peace of the church."[12] Synods have become an integral and indis-

---

[8] *Confessio Gallicana* 1559, 30 (Schaff 377).

[9] Scottish Confession 1560, 20 (Schaff 465f.); Second Helvetic Confession 1561, 2 (Schaff 239f.); Irish Articles 1615, 75–80 (Schaff 539f): and especially the Westminster Confession 1647, 31 (Schaff 668–70).

[10] Westminster Confession 31 (Schaff 669).

[11] Westminster Confession 31 (Schaff 669ff.)

[12] Synopsis purioris theologiae disputationibus quinquaginta duabus comprehensa ac conscripta per Johannem Polyandrum, Andream Rivetum, Antonium Walaeum, Antonium Thysium, Lugduni Batavorum 1881, disp. 49, Thesis 3, 3, 591–92.

pensable element in the life of Reformed Churches. At least on the regional and national levels all important decisions are generally taken through this instrument. The responsibility of the individual leader is embedded in the shared responsibility of an elected representative college. Every exercise of authority is therefore limited. In contrast to the Roman Catholic Church, the order of the Reformed Churches is basically "democratic" in the sense that it provides opportunities for the participation of the whole community in decision making processes.

II. Is there room in this understanding of the Church for a personal "ministry of unity?"

The answer to this question requires a prior remark. Though Reformed Churches have consistently emphasized the need for synods and councils, their ideas about general or universal councils have remained relatively vague and imprecise. Though their synod practice at regional and national levels is impressive they have not really succeeded in developing a vision of the universal Church. The question remained without answer as to how the universal Church can be made visible and how its witness can effectively be made heard. The debate in the sixteenth century on the calling of a universal council with the mandate to overcome the conflict of the Reformation was from the beginning fraught with difficulties. The demand of the Reformers that such a council should recognize Holy Scriptures as its only authority was not heeded. The Council of Trent which was finally called could not be recognized by the Protestant Churches as a true council because it met under the authority of the pope. They felt unable to participate in debates they judged to be biased in advance. As the conflict continued, the hope for a truly universal council gradually vanished. The ideas which had been developed by Reformed theologians could no longer be put into practice. They only became relevant again in the nineteenth century with the foundation of the World Alliance of Reformed Churches and the rise of the ecumenical movement. At least for part of the Reformed Churches the international assemblies organized to give expression to the growing interchange among the Churches, in the twentieth century, especially the assemblies of the World Council of Churches, were considered by many Reformed Churches as the fulfillment, or at least the beginning of a fulfillment, of their vision of a universal council.

How can these beginnings be further developed? The Reformed Churches are today facing this task. The issue of a "ministry of unity" is only relevant for them if it is dealt with in this perspective. Is there need for such a ministry in order to call and to carry through a council?

Reformed Churches cannot exclude such a possibility. As much as for an individual congregation, persons are required at the level of a synod to serve as focus of unity. Experience shows that a personal ministry of unity can help synods to work more constructively and to reach more effectively the conclusions which are required. Is it therefore not imperative for the Reformed Churches, precisely because they place so much emphasis on councils, to reflect on the nature and the role of a personal ministry? Does not the present stage of the ecumenical movement make the question unavoidable? There is a beautiful phrase in Calvin's Institutes: "Nous savons que la police, selon la diversité des temps, permet, et même requiert, qu'on fasse des mutations diverses."[13] Is it perhaps part of this freedom, to make the instrument of the council more effective through a personal ministry of unity?

This insight is steadily gaining ground in Reformed circles. In many Reformed Churches today more emphasis is placed on personal ministries. Ministries have been created which had no room in Reformed ecclesiology in previous times. Many Churches have introduced the ministry of full-time presidents. The World Alliance of Reformed Churches is led by a general secretary who together with the president and other officers is entitled to speak in public on behalf of the member churches. There are good reasons for the conclusion that the synodal praxis cannot be effective without persons named for promoting and representing the process.

What are the perspectives the Reformed Churches bring into this ecumenical debate? Let me mention three convictions:

1. Reformed Churches believe that God's promise has been given to the Church as a whole. The Spirit will lead it into the whole truth. It is true that the Church goes again and again through dark periods. She falls into error and can be seduced into dubious decisions by the powers and forces of this world. But she will ultimately be led back to the truth of the Gospel by the power of the Spirit. Faithful is God who has called us into communion with his son Jesus Christ (1 Cor 1:3, 11); he will overcome even the darkest failures of his church. Again and again God will raise witnesses who are capable to manifest the true message of Christ. The light of the Gospel will be made to shine primarily through charismatic figures. Peter was not in the first place the bearer of a particular ministry. He was called to be disciple and apostle for Christ and received authority to carry out this calling. Christ's promise did not

---

[13] IV, 7, 15: "We know that church organization admits, nay requires, according to the varying condition of the times, various changes" (McNeill 2, 1134).

simply turn him into a minister. To understand the role he fulfilled it is important to recall that he had prophetic and visionary gifts. It was a vision which, according to Acts 10, was the origin of one of the most far-reaching decisions ever taken by the church. And did the Church, in the course of its long history, not benefit again and again from such Peter figures? Think of the great figures of the missionary movement such as Francis Xavier or Count Zinzendorf, or of the ecumenical movement such as John Mott, William Temple, Patriarch Athenagoras, or Martin Luther King, or also in other perspectives of Mother Teresa or Shanti Solomon, the founder of the Fellowship of the Least Coin. They are the true successors of Peter. The significance of Peter, the apostle, cannot be exhaustively described by the ministry of a bishop and would be decisively reduced if it would be limited to the role of a ministerial service, though, of course, ministerial services are necessary and demanded and supported by the Holy Spirit.

A ministry serving the unity of the Church will need to be subordinated to this charismatic succession.

2. This leads to the second consideration. The vocation of a ministry of unity will consist primarily in serving the action of the Holy Spirit in the Church. Its role will be above all to encourage and promote the constructive forces in the Church. Its tasks demand, in fact, considerable sacrifices. It will need to undertake everything possible to enable decisive encounters, to get the debate going on issues relevant to the common witness of the churches and likely to lead to conflicts, to find ways making possible common or at least agreed statements on pressing themes. This does not mean that the "ministry of unity" would be confined to organizing conversations. Without adopting clear positions the conciliar process will never advance. The role of the ministry includes the task of contradicting erroneous opinions and inappropriate claims of individuals and groups. The fundamental purpose of the ministry, however, must be the promotion of processes towards discerning the truth.

3. Clearly, a ministry serving the unity of the Church at the level of the Church worldwide can only constructively be exercised within the framework of a collegial body. The ministry is to serve the communion of the Church in the power of the Spirit. It is meant to encourage encounter and debate. In order to achieve these purposes the bearer of the ministry must be part of a representative body. A collegial structure is required on the one hand to widen the horizon, and on the other to set limits to the power which inevitably goes with a ministry of such significance. The collegial structure must be made visible. The college

cannot only consist of consultants acting unnamed behind the scenes. The ministry of unity must be represented not simply by a single person but through the college.

III. How is the present papal ministry to be evaluated in this perspective?

In how far does the papal ministry today correspond to this view of a ministry of unity? In how far can the papal ministry in its present form serve the unity and the common witness of the Churches?

The contrast between papacy and the picture of a ministry of unity proposed here is evident. The two images are today, obviously, incompatible. True, the style of the papal ministry has in the last decades undergone many modifications. A significant evolution has taken place. The role of papacy has been adapted to the requirements of the present epoch. The baroque style of the papal court has to a large extent been abandoned. Papacy has no doubt been modernized in the last decades. It has become more efficient. Through the encounter with the expectations of the modern times but surely also in response to the questioning by other Churches, the Roman Catholic Church has been led to adopt far-reaching reforms. The critique of the Reformers, as far as it concerns the style of the ministry, has lost its relevance in more than one respect.

But the claims of the ministry have basically remained unchanged. They are too high to allow even for the thought of recognizing ecumenically the value of a papal service of unity. Will further ecumenical dialogue as proposed and hoped for by the encyclical *Ut unum sint* create a new situation? A sober evaluation of today's situation will rather give rise to doubts. The claims associated with papacy are too deeply rooted in Roman Catholic spirituality and theology as to allow for basic changes within the foreseeable future. This assessment is confirmed by the dialogues on papacy held so far. Several interconfessional dialogues and studies published in connection with these dialogues have sketched a picture of papacy which could possibly lead to an ecumenical breakthrough. Nevertheless the evolution of papacy has not really followed the direction suggested by the dialogues. The dialogue reports which have carefully been worked out remain to a large extent a *pium desiderium*. The conversations provoked by *Ut unum sint* are likely to suffer from the same weakness.

The debate on papacy is different from the ecumenical dialogue on other themes in so far as it does not only deal with a controversial issue of the past which has today lost much of its relevance and can therefore be discussed apart from today's life issues. In this case difference of views concern the present. It does not suffice to propose an ideal picture of papacy which, if it had been practiced in the sixteenth century, would have prevented the split of the Reformation. The issue is in how far the papal ministry in its present form could be accepted *today* as a factor of unity.

I mention four aspects which continue to cause difficulties:

1. The reports of bilateral dialogues dealing with papacy invariably emphasize that the pope is primarily to be considered as the Bishop of Rome; only through and within this function does he exercise the primacy within the communion of other bishops. He is not, we are often reminded, the *episcopus universalis* above the bishops, but his primary task consists in promoting the communion of all bishops. At the same time the reports underline the selfhood, freedom and self-determination of each local church. The general development of the last few decades, however, has clearly gone in the opposite direction. By abandoning the *stabilitas loci* in Rome and by paying pastoral visits to one local church after the other, the popes have, in fact, given themselves in a new way the image of a universal bishop. They have offered themselves to the public as the personified symbol of the Roman Catholic Church. The media readily accepted this claim and contributed to strengthen it. True, the pope is no more a monarch exercising undisputed authority over the Church. But he successfully continues to make a similar claim at the symbolic level. At the same time the role of the papal ministry for the internal unity of the Roman Catholic Church is being reemphasized. After a period of relative freedom of episcopal conferences the authority of the pope over whole Church is being more systematically recalled, primarily through administrative measures.

2. The difficulty is made more serious by the fact that the message the pope is offering today differs in essential points from the message other churches, in particular Reformed churches, are committed to. The proclamation of the pope cannot be accepted as being representative for wide parts of the ecumenical community. But because it is regarded to be universally representative by the media, non-Catholic Churches are placed in an awkward situation. If they wish to maintain their identity they are obliged to distance themselves from the Roman Catholic Church. Again and again they are forced to take a stand on positions which do not represent priorities for them or to point to priorities which seem to be no priorities for the Roman Catholic Church. A few examples may illustrate this difficulty:

a) The addresses of the present pope tend to dwell on the ethical issues regarding the relationship of men and women, marriage and procreation. Though Reformed churches recognize the importance of these themes they do not attribute to them the same weight and urgency as they have for the pope. On the issue of birth control they hold definitely different views. The interventions of the Roman Catholic Church in public, e.g., on the occasion of the U.N. Conference on population in Cairo, constitute therefore an embarrassment. Should they contradict the Roman Catholic or should they—out of ecumenical politeness keep silent?

b) A second example of divergence is the understanding of the position of women in the Church and, in particular the issue of the ordination of women to the ministries of the Church. The difference of understanding among the Churches is evident, a difference which did not exist, at least not in its present form, one hundred years ago. Increasingly the Churches of the Reformation have been led to recognize more fully the role of women in the Church and have also decided to ordain women to all ministries. A process of change has been initiated which is steadily expanding. For many Churches the willingness to ordain women to the ministries has become an *essential* aspect of their ecclesiology. In their eyes the ecumenical debate on the issue has therefore become inescapable. If the ordination of women is not to lead to new divisions it needs to be taken up at the level of the ecumenical movement. Clarification must be achieved. How are the differing positions to be evaluated? What solutions can be envisaged? Is the difference really church dividing? Or can the differing positions co-exist within one and the same Church? It would seem to be part of the tasks of a ministry of unity to contribute to the clarification of such issues.

c) For many Christians the proclamation of the pope is disappointing for its lack of attention to today's ecological crisis. It becomes more and more evident that the model of society the industrialized nations are adopting today can in the long run not be sustained. The claims this society makes on the resources of the earth cannot be fulfilled. Obviously, human beings are in process of transgressing the limits God has set for them within creation. The threats for the present and even more for future generations can no longer be ignored. Humanity is on a suicidal course and engages in risks which may turn out to destroy the quality of life on the planet. The success of the program of a "sustainable development" proposed by the Earth Summit in Rio de Janeiro is far from assured. But the highest authority of the Roman Catholic Church appears to be relatively unimpressed by these perspectives. There are strong papal statements on social justice. For the poor, oppressed and persecuted the pope fulfills no doubt a role of advocacy. Christians of other Churches are grateful for this witness. There is little mention in papal statements, however, of the fact that there is no room in creation for infinite growth. But today this is the decisive point. How can justice continue to be achieved in a world with shrinking resources? Whoever follows the activities of the pope is struck by a strange contradiction. On the one side the pope speaks forcefully of the protection of unborn life, on the other side the quality of life of future generations receives only scant attention.[14]

Can the present economic system be maintained? A debate on this question has taken place at the last General Council of the World Alliance of Reformed Churches. The delegates came finally to the conclusion that the ideology of economic growth and the expansion of human claims on creation which underlie the present development are incompatible with the faith in Jesus Christ. The Gospel demands of the church resistance against the double trend, on the one hand towards more and more social exclusion, and on the other towards more and more exploitation of creation. They were unable to agree on a text because they differed in the interpretation of the present situation. They recognized that further analysis was required before any statement could be issued. But they were agreed that the attitude to the present system represented a challenge to the integrity of Christian faith and witness. They spoke of a process leading towards an act of confession *(processus confessionis)* which needed to be launched, and addressed to the Churches an urgent appeal to participate in it.

3. Every Church is, of course, entitled to offer its own message. There is therefore no problem with the fact that the witness of the Holy

[14] A particularly disturbing illustration is the recent intervention by Archbishop Jean Louis Tauran on behalf of the Holy See on the occasion of the nineteenth Special Session of the General Assembly of the United Nations in New York (June 27, 1997).

See has its own profile. The choices made by the pope need to be respected. At this consultation, however, the issue is the extent to which the papal ministry can be recognized as a ministry of unity by other Churches. Under this aspect the positions promoted by the pope are problematic because they are not submitted to any discussion. The Holy See claims to represent the voice of *the* Church. The fact that there are, besides this one voice, also other Christian voices is not denied but is not taken seriously either. So far no structured dialogue has taken place on the challenges *of our time*. Take the example of the United Nations. Not only at the population conference in Cairo but also at other international conferences, the Roman Catholic Church usually raises its voice as if there were no other churches. No attempts are made to offer a common vision, even contacts and exchanges which could possibly lead to a certain degree of complementarity of the positions are largely inexistent. How can a ministry which decides and acts in isolation serve the unity of the Churches?

Allow me to refer in this context to an aspect which has so far received little attention in ecumenical discussion—the fact that the pope, the highest authority in the Roman Catholic Church, is also the head of a state. Both in Roman Catholic ecclesiology and in ecumenical discussions the fact is rarely referred to and reflected upon. Roman Catholic theologians tend to declare the issue to be non-essential for a proper understanding of papacy. In their eyes the Vatican State is merely an instrument which is at the service of the spiritual vocation of the Holy See. But it cannot be denied that the statehood of the Holy See has considerable consequences for the exercise and style of the papal ministry. True, the Vatican is a very special state. Benito Mussolini was right when he ironically remarked in 1929 that the definition of the precise nature of the new juridical entity will offer "delight" to generations of commentators. But whatever the answer to this question, the statehood offers to the Holy See privileges which no other Church enjoys. What is the value of these privileges? Can they be shared with other Churches? At present the activities of the Holy See at the level of its diplomatic service are carried out in almost hermetic isolation from ecumenical contacts.

4. The fourth difficulty arises from the claim of infallibility. Reformed Christians are bound to reject this claim. The doctrine of infallibility as it was formulated by the First Vatican Council is not the theme of this consultation. The question nevertheless arises in how far a ministry which has the aura of this claim is apt to serve the unity of the Churches. The claim makes it almost impossible to admit that popes

have at times defended errors and taken dubious decisions. The ministry is so to say placed under the obligation to have been right throughout the centuries. The claim of infallibility leads almost inevitably to the institutionalization of being in the truth or more precisely of "always having been in the truth." In the eyes of Reformed Christians, Roman Catholic theologians spend an unproportionate amount of time for providing the evidence that the utterances of the magisterium were, at least in the context of their time, in harmony with the truth of the Gospel, and perhaps even more, that new insights gained by the Churches are not really new but correspond, at least implicitly, to the teaching of all times. It is true that remarkable developments have taken place since the Second Vatican Council. Certain errors and failures have explicitly been recognized and named by the popes. The ministry of unity continues to be characterized, however, by a lack of freedom in this respect. The concern to make manifest the unbroken continuity in the truth often prevents the magisterium from admitting obvious deviations of the past or to engage freely in new departures.

This critique of papacy does not obviously mean that the Reformed Churches hold all the answers. Though they cannot avoid criticizing the papal ministry in its present form, the dialogue with Roman Catholics makes them aware of their own failure. Their main weakness is their understanding of the Church and its unity. In contrast to the Roman Catholic Church their consciousness of the continuity of the church through the centuries is only insufficiently developed. They are in danger of overemphasizing the new beginning which has taken place in the sixteenth century, and often behave as if all that counted was today's Church. They do not see themselves as the heirs of a continuous history from the earliest times to the present. They do not regard the experience accumulated in the course of centuries as a treasure from which they take old and new insights. The Church is for them rather like a house they inhabit but which has many hidden rooms they do not know nor use. In addition, the Reformed Churches are so deeply divided that they are unable to form a universal communion capable of transcending effectively the boundaries of nations. To overcome the present situation the Reformed churches need the encounter and the critique of other churches. Without being challenged from outside they will not be able to make a valuable contribution to the ecumenical movement.

IV. Are there ways leading beyond the present dilemma?

Realistically, a consensus on the significance of the papal ministry is unlikely to be reached in the foreseeable future. What does this mean for the Churches? Do they have to abide with the status quo? Or can steps be imagined which can be undertaken together?

An important presupposition for a fruitful further development is the realistic assessment of the differences. One of the most constructive aspects of the Encyclical *Ut unum sint* consists in openly pointing to the divergence and so making possible a new conversation. For a long time the issues connected with papacy have been avoided in ecumenical dialogues. In the early stages of the dialogues it was considered to be wiser to postpone the debate on papacy to later rounds. By now several dialogues have dealt with papacy and through the encyclical the debate has been legitimized by the pope himself.

But has not the time come to go a step farther and to develop what I would call an ecumenical *transparency which allows also contradiction?* The present ecumenical situation continues to be characterized by a dilemma. The Churches in the ecumenical movement do not dare to contradict one another. They hesitate to criticize the witness other Churches bear. The concern to hurt the other Church and to put at risk the still young and vulnerable relations prevent an open debate. After several decades of ecumenical encounters this concern must begin to recede into the background. Not only the differences inherited from the past but also the differences in their witness must be openly recognized and addressed. Dialogues which circumvent the differences are irresponsible. Lack of transparency is incompatible with a true sense of ecumenical responsibility. Advance can only be achieved through critique and contradiction.

To make possible a constructive exchange of this kind some form of structured communion is required. A forum must come into existence which enables the Churches despite their continuing separation to meet and to exchange, even more which obliges them to face their differences in dialogue and encounter. As long as such a framework is lacking dialogues will not be able to bear fruits. Only as the Churches begin to share their life and witness, the ministry of unity can gradually develop to a form which is acceptable to all.

Let me mention two illustrations. In June 1997, for the second time in the history of the ecumenical movement, a Pan-European Ecumenical Assembly has come together. The gathering in Graz was a moving event. It has shown how far the ecumenical relations in Europe have progressed. Delegates from all European countries were present, almost all Churches were represented. Thousands of lay people participated. An impressive number of spontaneous ecumenical initiatives became visible. For many the assembly was a liberating experience because it was not simply a celebration of unity but an occasion to name the differences which divide the Churches. Will it be possible to continue and deepen this experience? The difficulty is evident. For the implementation of the recommendations which were formulated as well as for sustained work on the remaining differences no framework is yet available. Very easily therefore the communion which has grown can again disintegrate.

My second illustration is the celebration of the year 2000. Only a few years separate us from the transition into the third millennium. But clearly we are not yet really prepared for the event. Various projects are being developed. But could not this transition be the occasion for creating the framework which allows the Churches to bear witness together? Instead of separate statements, a common witness is needed which on the one hand reflects the consensus on the essential affirmations of the Christian faith and on the other does not hide the continuing differences but, on the contrary, seeks to give them a common expression. By openly recognizing differences, the unifying force of the Gospel would become even more evident. The common struggle of the Churches for the truth would become manifest.

The transition into the third millennium inevitably raises the question of the future of humankind. How will future generations evaluate in retrospect the past millennium with its heights and depths? How much understanding will they have for the inertia with which long-standing divisions have been maintained and continued beyond the threshold of the millennium? They will judge the past by evaluating the spiritual forces they will have received to deal with the dangers and the possible destruction they will have to face.

The unity of the Church? A ministry at the service of the universal Church and capable of leading it to an effective common witness? Appropriate answers to these questions are more likely to emerge when the Churches commit themselves even more radically to the task of discerning the core of the Christian message and fulfilling accordingly their vocation in today's world.

10

The Petrine Ministry and the
Unity of the Church:
A Baptist Perspective

Erich Geldbach

It needs to be pointed out at the beginning that what follows is, indeed, *a* Baptist perspective, not *the* perspective. For nobody, not even the president or the secretary general of the Baptist World Alliance (BWA) can speak with authority for all Baptists. The Baptist movement not only gives the individual and his/her assessment a high priority (without necessarily falling into the trap of a rugged individualism); it is also far from being a unified Church. There is no unity among Baptist folk even though we have the BWA. The emphasis on the individual finds its expression in the so-called autonomy of the local church—a principle that is a distinguishing mark of Baptists and is very often misunderstood among themselves.

The Baptist beginnings, as part of the Puritan movement early in the seventeenth century, is characterized by an awareness that Baptists stand in line of others. John Smyth, who is often referred to as the first Baptist theologian, wrote a book in 1608 entitled *Differences of the Churches of the Separation*. In it he argued that a true constitution of the Church is of "absolute necessitie" for the obvious reason that "if the Church be truly constituted & framed, ther is a true Church: the true spowse of Christ." Conversely, if the Church is falsely constituted, there is a false church. Smyth went on to say that the Puritan brethren were right when they "reduced the Church to the true Primitive & Apostolique constitution." This, then, is the area of complete agreement; nothing needs to be added by the Baptists.

Smyth lists three points which are essential for the true constitution of the Church and which reflect the "primitive puritie" of the church of the Apostles. These points are: "1. The true matter which are sayntes only. 2. The true forme which is the vniting of them together in the covenant. 3. The true propertie which is communion in all the holy things, & the powre of the L. Iesus Christ, for the maintayning of that communion."[1]

The true Church, therefore, consists of saints only who have entered into a covenant with one another and who maintain their communion by participating in the sacraments and by being exposed to the power of the Lord. These principles of a true Church were found in the writings of the "brethren of the separation for which help wee alwayes shall honour them in the Lord and in the truth." However, even though these principles constitute a true Church, Antichrist is not yet defeated by them. In fact, Smyth maintains "that in a verie high degree he [= Antichrist] is exalted even in the true constituted Churches."[2]

A true constitution, according to Smyth, is no sufficient ground for exposing and abolishing "Antichristianisme" and for coming out of "spirituall slavery" and "Antichristian captivity." Smyth lists a number of items which make up the differences between the Baptist approach and that of the "brethren of the separation." Thus, reading out of a book cannot be considered "part of spirituall worship." Likewise, when prophesying or singing a psalm, it is unlawful to have a book before the eye. Spiritual worship flows from the heart.

Besides these differences in liturgy, there is also, more significantly, a difference in the concept of presbytery. Smyth and his followers held the position "that the Presbytery of the church is vniforme; & that the triformed Presbyterie consisting of three kinds of Elders viz. Pastors Teachers Rulers is none of Gods Ordinance but mans devise." Also, Smyth and his Baptists maintained "that all the Elders of the Church are Pastors." Finally, Smyth held "that in contributing to the Church Treasurie their ought to bee both a separation from them that are without & a sanctification of the whole action by Prayer & Thanksgiving."[3]

Why is it important to present these quotes? They give evidence that a new Church is in the making. It is not entirely new, as its proponents gratefully make use of insights that brethren of the separation had earlier discovered. Upon this foundation Smyth and his people can continue to build their Church. Or, to put it another way, the quotes help to trace back the origin of the new Church both historically and as far

[1] H. L. McBeth, *A Sourcebook for Baptist History* (Nashville: Broadman, 1990) 14.
[2] *Ibid.*
[3] *Ibid.*, 15.

as content is concerned. The latter is far more important than the historic circumstances. For through the mediation of the "brethren of the separation" Smyth comes to the conclusion that the Church ought to reflect the simplicity of the primitive Church. The present true Church must be identical with the Church of the apostles. Only then can spiritual slavery be abandoned and a true liturgy, a true presbytery, and true financial support be reached.

The point of departure for the new Church is the fact that there were different Churches with competing truth claims, each one advancing the idea that it was the only true Church. Smyth added yet another group with an equally strong claim to the only truth. Two significant consequences are derived from this claim: The first is that it is not only possible but commendable to change one's religious affiliation if one changes from a false to the true religion. There may even be grades or steps from one to the other, as Smyth explains. Thus, if a Turk becomes a Jew, and if he then turns to papism and subsequently to Protestantism, it is all commendable as Protestantism is closer to the truth than papism which in turn surpasses Judaism, and that being superior to Islam. Even though a person may go through those stages within one year or even within only one month, it is properly done, for "to retaine a false Religion is damnable."

The second consequence leads immediately to the heart of Smyth's Baptist thought. For just as it is commendable to turn from papism to Protestantism, so it is to be approved "that we should fal from the profession of Puritanisme to Brownisme, & from Brownisme to true Christian baptisme." Puritanism and the congregational concept of Robert Browne (ca. 1550–ca. 1633) are forerunners of the Baptists, but only the Baptists have advanced far enough in the truth to embrace the apostolic mode of baptism:

> If wee therfor being formerly deceaved in the way of Pedobaptistry, now doe embrace the truth in the true Christian Apostolique baptisme: Then let no man impute this as a fault vnto vs: This therfor is the question: whither the baptisme of infants be lawful, yea or nay: & whither persons baptized being infants must not renounce that false baptisme, & assume the true baptisme of Chr: which is to be administered vppon persons confessing their faith & their sinnes: This being the controversy now betwixt vs, & the Separation commonly called Brownists.
>
> For Smyth there is no doubt that infant baptism is a grave error and that, as baptism is the door to the church, it is the "cheef point of Antichristianisme, & the very essence & constitution of the false Church."[4]

[4] *Ibid.*, 19.

The distinctive mark of the new church that is in the making is not only its true constitution which is reflective of the true, primitive, apostolic Church, but also the true apostolic mode of baptism. This is also the distinction between those that would later be referred to as Congregationalists and the emerging Baptists. Browne and his followers separated themselves from the Church of England, but retained infant baptism. To Smyth this attitude is impossible: "they that do Separate from England as from a false Chu. must of necessity Separate from the baptisme of England, & account the baptisme of England false, & so account the baptisme of infants false baptisme: Therfor the Separation must either goe back to England, or go forward to true baptisme."[5] The new Church, then, is a forward movement which, at the same time, is congruent with the purity of the primitive Church of the apostolic age. The underlying principle of the move forward is a restitutionist theory. The true church can be re-instated or restored if the true constitution, involving also the baptism of confessing Christians only, is set up and put to practice. It follows also that the Congregationalists—"the brethren of the separation"—cannot be looked upon as a true Church. "For we proclaime against them as they proclaime against their owne mother England: That the Separation, the yonges & the fayrest daughter of Rome, is an harlot: For as is the mother so is the daughter."[6]

It is important to note that the Brownists, even though they are very close to the emerging Baptists, are nevertheless subjected to the apocalyptic notion of being a harlot. The category which Brownists had used against the Church of England is taken by Smyth and applied to the Brownists. This serves the purpose of elevating Smyth's cause. It is so much more convincing as Smyth traces the lineage of the Brownists not back to the Church of England, but to Rome. Hardly any reader in England then had doubts that Rome was, indeed, a false Church, the "mother harlot" of all other harlots. To trace Congregationalism, Puritanism and the Church of England in this order back to Rome was to demonstrate the fall of the Church and the desperate need for its restitution.

It also indicates how far removed the Roman Catholic Church was from the Baptist concept. Baptists and Catholics were on the extreme ends; Baptists looked upon the Roman Church as the source of all evil, as "Antichristianisme," and they applied to the pope the traditional title of "Antichrist." If Baptists were convinced, as they were, that the Church of England had a false constitution, a false ministry, a false worship, a

---

[5] *Ibid.*, 19f.
[6] *Ibid.*, 20.

false government and a false baptism so that all is false in it,[7] how much more was all of this so in the Church of Rome! "Popish inventions" had for a long time concealed the truth of believers' baptism,[8] and Christopher Blackwood, a Cambridge graduate and an Anglican priest turned Baptist, wrote a book in 1644 entitled *The Storming of Antichrist, in His Two Last and Strongest Garrisons: of Compulsion of Conscience and Infants Baptisme.* The martial language of the title suggests that two very sensitive issues are under discussion. Antichrist can maintain his empire only by applying coercive, compulsory means; in fact, Blackwood lists as one of the absurdities of infant baptism that it is such a means: "Whereas the Scriptures requires only persons to be baptized who gladly receive the word, Acts 2:41 and desire baptisme, Acts 8:36 by this infant baptisme all are compelled, they and their children to be made Christians whether they will or no."[9]

The storming of the two last and strongest garrisons of Antichrist consisted of nothing less than the introduction of the concept of "soul liberty," "liberty of conscience" or "religious liberty" and believer's baptism. The two go hand in glove. It needs to be emphasized that Baptists not only demanded liberty for themselves, but for all people of all persuasion. The king, Thomas Helwys wrote to James I, is mortal as any human and therefore has no power over immortal souls. Had the king the authority to make spiritual laws and to appoint bishops, he would be an immortal God. "Let them be heretiks, Turcks, Jewes or whatsoever it apperteynes not to the earthly power to punish them in the least measure" in matters of religion. Helwys, as did others after him, defended the rights even of Catholics to enjoy full religious freedom.[10]

The polemical tone that prevailed during the seventeenth century is not surprising, but very common. It shows, however, how far removed the two faith communities were. There was no room for any kind of appreciation for the office of the pope or his Petrine ministry. The pope was identified with the Antichrist and therefore responsible for all the wrong teachings and practices. Church reform that resulted in the restitution of the apostolic Church by necessity involved the demolishing of popedom as a step in the freeing of nations and peoples from the coercive power of an enslaving religion. As all Churches can be

---

[7] See the Letter from Hughe and Anne Bromheade, 1609.

[8] *Ibid.*, 31.

[9] *Ibid.*, 45.

[10] Cf. Thomas Helwys, *A Short Declaration of the Mistery of Iniquity*, 1st printed in 1612 (London: Kingsgate Press, 1935) 69 as cited by H. L. McBeth, *The Baptist Heritage. Four Centuries of Baptist Witness* (Nashville: Broadman Press, 1987) 86 and 103.

traced back to Rome to which they are all chained, the storming of Antichrist would result in a "chain reaction" of freedom.

Baptists are often accused of showing little concern for the unity of the Church. In fact, it is said that they act upon the principle "when in doubt, let's split." That almost all power is vested in the local church helped to create the Baptist problem of divisions among themselves. The autonomy of the local church, however, was originally not intended to function as a catalyst for endless divisions. It was rather introduced to correct what Baptists perceived to have been a wrong development. The bishops had become not only too powerful and too worldly, but also too far removed from the congregations. Besides, the rule by bishops from above stood in sharp contrast to Baptist egalitarianism. They rejected even the threefold Presbyterian system in favor of the priesthood of all believers. This was a new form of church polity, replacing the sacerdotal concept of the Church. Christ, the only high priest, had abandoned all special priestly power. The sacerdotal power exerted by bishops—and subsequently by priests—was rejected in favor of congregational power.

When layman Thomas Helwys (ca. 1570–ca. 1615) put together *A Declaration of Faith* in 1611 as one of the first Baptist confessions of faith, he summed it up in Article 11 as follows:

> That though in respect off CHRIST, the Church bee one, Ephes. 4.4. yet it consisteth off divers particular congregacions, even so manie as there shallbee in the World, every off which congregacion, though they be but two or three, have CHRIST given them, with all the meanes off their salvacion. Mat. 18.20. Roman. 8.32. I.Corin. 3.22. Are the Bodie off CHRIST. I.Cor. 12.27. and a whole Church. I.Cor. 14.23. And therefore may, and ought, when they are come together, to Pray, Prophecie, breake bread, and administer in all the holy ordinances, although as yet they have no Officers, or that their Officers should bee in Prison, sick, or by anie other means hindered from the Church. I: Pet. 4.10 & 2.5.[11]

The Church is to be one, but it is made up of autonomous congregations. When a congregation comes together for worship, even if it may consist of only two or three and has no officer, it is truly the body of Christ and can enjoy all means of salvation, including the sacraments. The unity is thus expressed on the local level. When in 1654 messengers, elders, and brethren of the "Baptized Churches" met "from severall parts of this Nation" in London, they were concerned with the unity on the national level. They came together "to consider how and which way the affairs of the

---

[11] H. L. McBeth, *A Sourcebook* . . . , 40.

Gospell of Christ, so farre as it concerns them, might best be promoted and all divisions and offences contrary thereunto removed or prevented."[12]

There is by this time an awareness that the congregations belong together. The local autonomy has limits which are determined by the missionary task to spread the Gospel of Christ. This endeavor calls for unity of action which is why delegates convened for deliberations on how best to remove or prevent divisions. The authority to do so is conferred by the congregations to the delegates who are aware of their common calling: They sign common statements on behalf of themselves and their "respective Congregations to which they belong."[13]

It is obvious how far removed this grass-root approach to church polity is to the Roman Catholic concept which is organized from the top down. That the Church universal would be represented by a pope, by the bishops and—subsequently—by the priests who through the act of ordination become an ontologically separate legal body through the imparting of an indelible character (= *character indelebilis*) and who alone are thus made eligible to administer the sacrament of the altar and hold the keys to the kingdom is and remains in Baptist thought an impossibility.

Baptist thinking starts with the local church. It is not a fraction of the Church, but, if properly organized, the Church itself. It lacks nothing; all the means of grace are at its disposal. The local congregation has the jurisdiction to admit new members as it alone is best equipped to judge a candidate's qualification. Likewise, the local church has the power to excommunicate a person if he/she fails to live a life in the faith. Also, the local community rather than any kind of superior judicatory has the right to choose its minister. This provision was undoubtedly in reaction to the experience of many Anglican congregations who had unwanted ministers imposed upon them by the bishop. The fact that the ministry belongs to the whole Church—all are called to be witnesses of the Gospel, all are to be of service to their fellow-humans, and all are to take part in the priesthood of the believers—does not mean that anyone may perform ministerial functions. There are special ministers set aside for the ministry; they do not, however, derive any sacerdotal power from the act of ordination or from a human superior. Instead, it is the Lord of the Church who through the Holy Spirit extends an "inward calling" to which the candidate testifies and which is then confirmed by the local church. "The call is by the church, but it is from Christ."[14]

---

[12] *Ibid.*, 56.

[13] *Ibid.*, 57.

[14] W. S. Hudson, *Baptists in Transition. Individualism and Christian Responsibility* (Valley Forge, N.J.: Judson Press, 1979) 54.

These meetings of delegates are indication that the churches, although autonomous, did not live in splendid isolation. They were committed to one another and also knew that in their deliberations they were to discern or to "determine"[15] the mind of Christ through the leading of the Holy Spirit. As the emerging Baptist movement wanted no authoritarian leadership or tyranny of bishops, the delegates had no coercive power or superior jurisdiction over the congregations.

So much did early Baptists believe in the power of the Holy Spirit for direction that neither the pope nor kings or princes are entitled to be called earthly heads or supreme governors of the Church. God had entrusted all the mysteries of the Gospel to his only Son who, in turn, handed them over to the Holy Ghost. No mortal man may use the title *vicarius Christi*; it is reserved only for the Holy Spirit. The Spirit is, therefore, called a "public" spirit, and it is the Spirit who is the exclusive vicar of Christ on earth. To be under the guidance of this Spirit means to be introduced into all truths and to trust in its convincing power, even as a minority. There need not be any burning of books nor any religious warfare. The weapon of the Spirit is the open and informed public debate. Only by following the spiritual directions of the third person of the trinity can "The Bloody Tenet of Persecution for Cause of Conscience" (Roger Williams) be overcome. Civil peace will result.

It may be added, at this point, that a logical result of this approach is the rise of "Democracy or Popular Government." A nineteenth century Baptist minister from Germany put it succinctly in a tract called *Manifesto of Free Primitive Christianity to the German People* of 1848, only a few months after the "Communist Manifesto" had been published, when he said that "any aristocratic and hierarchical element" is alien to the Christian Church and that there were "no natural sympathies for the principles of aristocracy and absolutism."[16] The egalitarian principle in the Church calls for an equally egalitarian approach in the realm of politics. In both cases the "Romisch Hyrarchy" is explicitly and implicitly rejected.

During the nineteenth century Baptists as other faith communities were shocked by the *Syllabus errorum* (1864) of Pope Pius IX which listed as "errors" many of the religious and civil accomplishments of democratically-minded people. It is small wonder that Baptists along with other Protestants became very frightened when millions of Roman Catholic Irish and South as well as South-East Europeans arrived as immigrants in the U.S.A. These "new Americans" came from countries "where tra-

---

[15] Cf. W. S. Hudson, *Baptists in Transition . . .* , 47f.

[16] H. Gieselbusch, ed., *Um die Gemeinde. Ausgewählte Schriften von Julius Köbner* (Berlin: Kulturelle Verlagsgesellschaft, 1927) 165.

ditions and ideals utterly foreign to us prevail." The *Righteous Empire*[17] was shaking as almost all major cities in New England had fallen "under Catholic control." It looked to many Protestants as though, this time, it was the pope and his army with its seemingly unlimited number of peoples who were out to storm the evangelical garrison and make America Catholic. To many American Protestants, a loyal Catholic could not, at the same time, be a loyal supporter of the free American institutions such as freedom of speech, freedom to assemble peacefully, freedom of the press, freedom of conscience, freedom of religion and, as a consequence, the separation of church and state. When the First Vatican Council dogmatically defined that the pope, as successor of Peter, has the judicial primacy over the entire church and may, as occasions arise, make infallible definitions *ex sese*, all fears seemed to have come true that the Roman Church was incorrigibly totalitarian.

In conclusion, it may be said that the aim of this short historical survey was not to indulge in "fruitless polemics,"[18] but to point out that, historically-speaking, Baptists did not follow a prejudice, but reached a clear theological verdict supported by hard evidence that for the Church of Christ to function properly and credibly a papal office was unnecessary. It was contradictory to the simplicity of the apostolic age, and its claim to universal primacy and infallibility was counter-productive both to the Gospel of Christ and freedom-loving humankind.

Early on and long before Vatican II spoke about the "hierarchy of truths," Baptists maintained that some doctrines of the Church are "fundamental," others are "circumstantial."[19] From the foregoing there can be no doubt that for Baptists the dogmatic pronouncements of Vatican I were neither; they were simply a false belief as expressed by a Church with which there was no communication. This changed when "good Pope" John XXIII summoned Vatican II and invited "separated brethren" as observers. Lines of communication were opened for the first time, and an official dialogue between the two communities was held between 1984 and 1988. It lists several areas that needed further exploration.

One such area to which an entire paragraph is devoted deals with the "shape of *koinonia*." For the Baptists, this concept is "expressed principally in local congregations gathered voluntarily under the lordship of Jesus Christ for worship, fellowship, instruction, evangelism and mis-

[17] M. Marty, *The Protestant Experience in America* (New York: Dial Press, 1970).

[18] John Paul II, *Ut unum sint. That They May Be One: On Commitment to Ecumenism* (Washington, D.C.: United States Catholic Conference, 1995) §96 (hereafter cited *Ut unum sint*).

[19] H. L. McBeth, *A Sourcebook* . . . , 86.

sion." In the interdependency of associations, conventions, unions and the BWA they recognize the Spirit's direction. Legally binding structures which would threaten both the individual believer's freedom and that of the local congregations have not been developed or have only in the last few years been introduced in the Southern Baptist Convention as a result of the onslaught of the extreme fundamentalists who were able to seize control of leadership positions. But this is a recent development, and it is hoped by most Baptists around the world that it will be only an episode. It would be very interesting, however, to show how much Fundamentalist and Roman Catholic polity resemble each other. After three-hundred years of existence the Baptist movement, especially where it was able to attract as many people as it did in the Southern United States, is entering its "Catholic" phase (Glen Hinson).

The dialogue says of the Roman Catholic position that "the *koinonia* which the Spirit effects in the local congregation is simultaneously a *koinonia* with the other local congregations in the one universal church. Correspondingly, they recognize the Spirit's activity in the spiritual and institutional bonds which unite congregations into dioceses presided over by bishops and which unite dioceses into the whole church, presided over by the Bishop of Rome." The paragraph concludes: "Vital to future ecumenical progress would be further discussion of the relationship between the Spirit and structures."[20]

These statements clearly reflect the differences. The Roman approach to *koinonia* is hierarchical whereas the Baptists in their egalitarianism insist upon the freedom of the individual and the individual church. What these statements do not reveal, however, are important aspects in both traditions which are of help to find the divergent points of departure for each. With the Baptists it concerns the much too frequent failure to recognize that in their tradition the world-wide Church is not entirely absent. The influential Second London Confession spoke of "the Catholick or universal Church" and defined it as "the whole number of the Elect, that have been, are and shall be gathered into one, under Christ the head thereof . . . All persons throughout the world, professing the faith of the Gospel, and obedience unto it."[21]

Baptists, on the whole, have paid only lip service to the image of the Church as the mystical body of Christ with its implications of intimate organic relationships. When Baptists use the word "body," they all too often refer to "the body of baptized believers," thus again introduc-

---

[20] *1989 Yearbook of the BWA* (manuscript), 54.

[21] Art. XXVI in W.L. Lumpkin, ed., *Baptist Confessions of Faith* (Valley Forge, N.J.: Judson Press, 1974) 285.

ing a local rather than a universal perspective. As the freedom of individuals is so prominent in Baptist thinking and as this emphasis finds its expression in the insistence on voluntary membership through believer's baptism, Baptists tend to use conversionist rather than incarnationalist terminology. To stay clear of any image that would open the floodgates for hierarchical and authoritarian "Churchianity" was of particular concern to Baptists. The image of the body could easily be manipulated insofar as the "head" of the body could be the pope instead of Christ or in the English tradition the king.[22]

The description of the Catholic position in the B-RC dialogue could easily be misunderstood to mean that local churches organize themselves into dioceses which in turn form the world-wide Church. This would be a misconception as both historically and systematically the organizations on all levels are highly centralized and not from the bottom up, but from the top down. A hierarchical structure is essential and part of the *esse* of the Church; no bishop, thus, may be appointed without the approval of the pope, and no person may celebrate the eucharist other than the ordained priests. It is the claim of the Roman Church to have been entrusted with all the means of grace so that the Church of Christ "subsists in the Catholic Church, which is governed by the Successor of Peter and by the Bishops in communion with him."[23] Christ himself endowed Peter as visible head of the college of the apostles, and his successors down to the present are in the same position within the college of the bishops who are the direct successors of the apostles. The Bishop of Rome thus exercises the supreme jurisdiction in the Church of Christ thanks to divine right. In addition, he also is granted the supreme teaching authority and may define matters of faith and morals infallibly.

Even Catholic theologians and church leaders felt that this monarchical approach to *koinonia* needed to be balanced by other elements in the Church. It seems, therefore, that the concept of collegiality of the bishops, as envisioned by the Council Fathers of Vatican II, was to serve as a complementary to the absolute papalism of Vatican I. However, the *nota praevia* by Pope Paul VI specifically reminded the fathers that the decrees of Vatican I needed no corrections or modifications. Thus, the pope can make use of his power of immediate jurisdiction and of his teaching office at his own discretion. He may consult with the bishops, but is under no

---

[22] Cf. Henry VIII, *Only Supreme Head on Earth of the Church of England* as cited in H. Schöffler, *Die Anfänge des Puritanismus. Versuch einer Deutung der englischen Reformation* (Leipzig: Verlag von B. Tauchnitz, 1932) 36.

[23] Second Vatican Council, Dogmatic Decree on the Church *Lumen gentium*, 8.

obligation to do so. The monarchical element of the papacy remained untouched. The infallible decision of Vatican I remained infallible.

The ramifications of the *nota praevia* are far-reaching. If the collegiality of the bishops do not balance the power of the pope, how can anyone else, least of all the laity? In *Lumen gentium* the Council Fathers had presented their view of the Church: it was first a mystery (chapter 1), and secondly, it was defined "synthetically" as the people of God (chapter 2) before the Church as a hierarchical institution (chapter 3) is taken up. In post-Vatican II documents, notably in the Final Report of the Extraordinary Synod of Bishops in 1985 and in the Catechism the concept of the "People of God" as the point of departure for thinking about the Church is not prominent. The Church is not a democratic institution, and the fear seems to be that the unity of the Church would be lost if people would gain some degree of control. On the other hand, Baptists want to invest the power in the people, and the principle of voluntarism is an essential ingredient. Where do we go from here? Are we encountering an impasse which leaves no room to maneuver? Several factors may help to re-assess the situation:

1. Baptist confessions frequently have an introductory note which much like Reformed confessions and contrary to Lutheran thinking states that the confession reflects the present state of recognition of the truth and that the drafters want to be open to future insights. Baptists are open not to new revelations, but to new interpretations of the truth in light of Holy Scripture. Is there room to re-evaluate the papacy?

2. It must be freely admitted that the Baptist ideal as here outlined has not really been faithfully acted upon in the history of the Baptist movement. The fact that delegates from the individual congregations proved unable to keep the unity and that divisions, sometimes over trivial things, happened time and again may demonstrate that the faith in the working of the Holy Spirit in the deliberations lacked direction and supervision.

3. The impression was created that Baptists show very little concern for unity. Even though they maintain regional, national and international agencies (European Baptist Federation, BWA), these do not occupy a prominent place. John Clifford, first president of the BWA, found it "surprising" that the BWA was created in 1905 by "a people delivered over, body and soul, to individualism, and in mortal terror of the slightest invasion of their personal and ecclesiastical independence."[24]

---

[24] H. L. McBeth, *A Sourcebook . . .* , 371.

Yet, he spoke of the BWA as being "really and not factitiously ecumenical," i.e., world-wide, and as being based upon "catholic principles" and bound together by "an indissoluble spiritual union." Baptists need to remind themselves of this heritage for their own benefit and that of the ecumenical movement.

4. Baptists also need to remind themselves that their traumatic fear of the papacy, although not unfounded in the past, must be re-examined. One element in this process could be that the pope's power of infallibility has been made use of only once within the last 125 years. Another could be that hardly any serious student today would point to secret or open activities of the Pope to gain apocalyptic power or would call the Pope the "beast" or the "antichrist" of Revelations. Only fringe groups would resort to this kind of language.

5. Nonetheless, it must be clearly stated that generally speaking Baptists are very reluctant to find a positive value in the papacy. If they are concerned about the papacy at all, they would tend to agree with Pope Paul VI's appraisal that the papal office is the greatest stumbling stone for Christian unity.[25] Even this phrase may be used to indicate that there exists a basic disagreement. For the term "stone of stumbling" is, indeed, a scriptural one; however, the reference is not to the pope, but to Christ.[26] The identification of the pope with Christ as a "stone of stumbling" is a further complication rather than a help. What at first sight appears to be a humble assessment turns out to be a claim that a single person may not raise without intruding into the Lordship of Christ. For Christ is the stone of stumbling, and he alone is the head of the Church Universal.

6. Before Baptists can discuss the issue of a Petrine ministry, they must, as a non-episcopal community, first face the issue whether or not there is "the necessity for an office of superintendency with succession."[27] All indications are that Baptists deny that episcopal succession is a necessity, i.e., is an indispensable part of the being of the church *(esse)*, not its well-being *(bene esse)*. Thus, chances for the acceptance of a Petrine ministry among Baptists are not very favorable. This assessment is further supported by the anxiety that any kind of superintendency might be exercised as a form of control. Baptists would outright reject such a

[25] *Acta Apostolicae Sedis* 59, 4 (1967) 498: "Le Pape, Nous le savons bien, est sans doute l'obstacle le plus grave sur la route de l'œcuménisme."
[26] Cf. Rom 9:32f.
[27] J. L. Garrett, "The Shifting Foci of the Protestant-Roman Catholic Confrontation: Peter, Mary and the Sacraments," *Review and Expositor* 68, 1 (1971) 39.

construct. They would further deny that there is evidence to support the notion that Jesus instituted the papacy and that he wanted Peter to be the first pope and his successors to form a personal, continuous succession on the Roman see.

There is, then, very little space to maneuver. One aspect that would open some room may, perhaps, be the very term "Petrine ministry." It seems to carry not the full weight of the papacy, but only a limited function. The present Pontiff recalls the expression of Pope Gregory the Great that the pope's ministry is that of *servus servorum Dei*.[28] Throughout his recent Encyclical Letter, John Paul II emphasizes the servant aspect of the papacy, and this aspect seems behind the idea of a Petrine ministry. What would be the obligation and the task of the pope in his role as successor of Peter?

Peter's role was that of an authentic witness of the tradition[29] and that of a pastor.[30] Although the New Testament frequently presents Peter in ambiguous terms and situations, it must be assumed that he played a leading role in the early Church, even though he certainly had no monarchical position: James and John are mentioned as being also pillars of the Church along with Cephas,[31] and Paul could follow a rather independent course in his ministry. There can be little doubt that the Petrine functions of witnessing and pastoring were not meant to be exclusively Peter's as these were genuine responsibilities of the early Church leaders. There can equally be little doubt that the centralization of the Petrine functions in one person is the result of a long historical process, culminating in Vatican I. Whether this development can be interpreted as divinely guided by the Spirit, is open to debate for non-Catholics. Baptists, as was shown above, see little reason that this claim can be substantiated, and they would also assume that the decisions of Vatican I were a deformation rather than a correct interpretation of the New Testament tradition.

It follows that a Petrine ministry could only be part of an ecumenical agenda for Baptists if and when the Roman Catholic Church would declare that the pontiff's universal jurisdiction by divine right and his infallibility apply only to its own sphere of influence and that it would respect other Churches' decision to find these pontifical functions theologically irrelevant. Such respect would also imply that different forms of church order are acceptable.

---

[28] *Ut unum sint*, 88.

[29] "rock," Matt 16:17-19.

[30] John 21:15-19 "feed my sheep" and Luke 22:32 "strengthen thy brethren."

[31] Gal 2:9.

A further difficulty for accepting the notion of Petrine ministry is its limited scope even though it is meant to carry universal weight. The limitation follows from the Roman interpretation of Peter's obligation to "strengthen his brethren." Who are Peter's "brethren"? They are his co-apostles, and as the pope is the successor of Peter, so the bishops succeed the apostles. Just as Peter was the head of the College of the Apostles, so now the pope is the head of the College of Bishops. The bishops represent the particular Churches so that if the bishops meet in a council, the entire church is represented, and if the bishops are in communion with the Bishop of Rome, the full and visible unity of the Church universal is expressed.

To Baptists, this whole concept is unacceptable. Not only is the issue of the succession of Peter and the apostles highly questionable, but the total male structure of this church order reflects a petrified historic state of affairs; it is an order shaped by a *Zeitgeist* of the past. The total exclusion of women indicates the most serious *defectus* in the Roman Catholic system, i.e., the exclusion of the people of God. To say that the entire Church is represented when the bishops meet in Council with the Roman pontiff is just as foolish as to say that the secret cabinet meeting under the leadership of a king represents the people. One must not confuse the claim of either actually to represent the people with the reality that they do not.

Given these limitations, there seems only one possible solution for the Petrine ministry to be exercised. It is along the lines of a spokesperson for the world-wide Christian community. However, such a ministry could never be done by one person alone. The World Council of Churches notion of "conciliar fellowship" points in the right direction. The unity of the churches finds its highest expression in a Council. Any decision reached in council must be followed by an intense process of reception: a Petrine ministry could facilitate such a process by respecting and supporting the divergences of Churches and yet keep them in dialogue as a legitimate form and expression of a unity that already exists. The "Petrine minister" would not only be a facilitator of dialogue—in Council and out of Council,—but would also be complemented by the collegiality, not only of bishops, but of representatives of the whole people of God. Collegiality would constitute an indispensable ingredient and a necessary prerequisite for exercising a Petrine ministry. In light of Luke 22:32 this office could be seen as a pastoral ministry towards particular Churches which are weak, poor or oppressed and which need encouragement as well as support and which may need to be protected by all Churches as they face injustice, oppression or persecution by some national leaders hostile to Christianity.

This approach to the Petrine ministry as the spokesperson of world Christianity would, logically considered, not rely solely on the Roman pontiff. The office could be rotating between the archbishop of Canterbury, the ecumenical patriarch of Constantinople, the Bishop of Rome, the secretary general of the World Council of Churches, or even an executive committee of World Christianity.

To limit the Petrine ministry and to limit the pontifical functions in the way as outlined above is incompatible with the Roman concept of unity. To restore the unity that Christ prayed for (John 17) is the highest ecumenical priority of the Roman Church's involvement in the ecumenical movement. It is the claim of the Roman Catholic Church that it alone has kept the unity that God wills for his Church throughout history,[32] and it is equally its claim that the one Church of Christ not only subsists in the Catholic Church,[33] but that it has been entrusted with the fullness of the means of salvation.[34]

In keeping with this quantitative approach to Christian unity, the encyclical letter states that "full communion will have to come about through the acceptance of the whole truth."[35] This invitation to accept the whole truth is directed towards the separated churches whose "elements" of sanctification and truth "possess an inner dynamism towards Catholic unity" anyway.[36] The aim of ecumenical dialogues is to help all churches that "the *full* content and *all* the requirements of the 'heritage handed down by the Apostles'"[37] may be present in them. When all have entered into the fullness "the journey towards the necessary and sufficient visible unity"[38] will have come to an end.

The papacy is one of the elements which is "strictly necessary" for full communion according to Catholic teaching. "Among all the Churches and Ecclesial Communities, the Catholic Church is conscious that she has preserved the ministry of the Successor of the Apostle Peter, the Bishop of Rome, whom God established as her 'perpetual and visible principle and foundation of unity'"[39] "and whom the Spirit sustains in order that he may enable all the others to share in this essential

---

[32] *Ut unum sint,* 11.

[33] *Lumen gentium,* 8.

[34] Second Vatican Council, Decree on Ecumenism *Unitatis redintegratio,* 3; *cf. Ut unum sint,* 86.

[35] *Ut unum sint,* 36.

[36] *Unitatis redintegratio,* 3; *Ut unum sint,* 10.

[37] Quote from *Unitatis redintegratio,* 14.

[38] *Ut unum sint,* 78.

[39] *Lumen gentium,* 23.

good."[40] The Bishop of Rome is "the visible sign and guarantor of unity."[41]

In the strongest possible terms the office of the papacy is presented: God established it, the Spirit sustains it; it is the foundation of the Church's unity and an essential good. The visible unity of the Church universal and the papal office are intimately and indissolubly connected; one cannot be without the other. The "long and arduous pilgrimage of ecumenism" will be successfully concluded only when each ecclesial community will fully accept all that is demanded for unity.[42] The final aim of the ecumenical movement is reached when all churches have undergone their conversion to be aligned with the Bishop of Rome as the focus of unity. In God's plan, this is an essential requirement "of full and visible communion."[43]

Is there a need for such a ministry "which presides in truth and love" so that the ecumenical ship will "reach its haven?"

Even though Baptist history lacks cohesion and direction, it is hard to think that the recognition of a papal office with all its claims and implications will rectify the situation. Such a recognition, especially if it would include the acceptance of the way in which the pontifical office is currently exercised as a reflection of its interpretation of "truth and love," is totally unthinkable. The pope is right when he says that the fraternal dialogue on this subject demands much patience—on both sides.

[40] *Ut unum sint,* 88.
[41] *Ibid.*
[42] Cf. *ibid.,* 82.
[43] *Ibid.,* 99.

11

Trinity, Unity, Primacy on the Trinitarian Nature of Unity and Its Implications for the Question of Primacy[1]

Miroslav Volf

A Papal Invitation

Toward the end of his encyclical letter *Ut unum sint,* John Paul II has offered an invitation. Given "the real but imperfect communion existing between" Christians, he called upon

> Church leaders and their theologians to engage with me in a patient and fraternal dialogue on this subject [i.e. the primacy], a dialogue in which, leaving useless controversies behind, we could listen to one another, keeping before us only the will of Christ for his Church and allowing ourselves to be deeply moved by his plea "that they may all be one . . . so that the world may believe that you have sent me" (John 17:21).[2]

Though I am neither a "church leader" nor a "theologian of a church leader" but a theologian who is nonetheless deeply committed to the Church and its mission in the world, I want to respond to the invitation. I will also try to heed the twofold papal advice as to how the

[1] A paper presented at the symposium "Petrine Ministry and the Unity of the Church," Society of the Atonement, Rome, December 4–6, 1997. I wish to thank Jill Colwell, my research assistant, and the participants of the symposium for their helpful engagement with a previous draft of this text.

[2] John Paul II, *Ut unum sint. That They May Be One: On Commitment to Ecumenism* (Washington, D.C.: United States Catholic Conference, 1995) §96 (hereafter cited *Ut unum sint*).

dialogue on the subject of primacy is to proceed. First, we should leave "useless controversies behind," especially name-calling. Nothing is gained and much is lost when the pope is defamed as "the Antichrist," as Protestants of all stripes have done over the centuries, just as nothing is gained and much is lost when Catholics call Protestant leaders "wild boars" (as Martin Luther was called almost five centuries ago) or "rapacious wolves" (as the leaders of Latin American independent Churches were called more recently). Second, we should let the prayer of Jesus "that they may be one, as we are one" move us deeply, so much that it not only holds the vision of unity before us but shapes our thought about the nature of unity. Only if we pursue the kind of unity for which Jesus prayed, will the unity of the church be a fitting testimony to the engagement of the triune God with the world.

As I see it, the question of primacy is not in the first place about the nature of church government—ecclesial "monarchy" versus ecclesial "oligarchy" or ecclesial "democracy." Rather, as many theologians engaged in dialogues recognize, the question of primacy is above all about the nature of church unity. Echoing the constitution *Pastor aeternus* of Vatican I,[3] the constitution *Lumen gentium* of Vatican II states that the Bishop of Rome is the "perpetual and visible principle and foundation of unity" of the Church.[4] Similarly, *Ut unum sint* sees the Bishop of Rome as "the first servant of unity."[5] When the encyclical speaks of "the power"—including the power to "declare *ex cathedra* that a certain doctrine belongs to the deposit of faith"[6]—it places that "power" partly at the service of unity: "With the power and the authority *without which such an office would be illusory,* the Bishop of Rome must ensure the communion of all churches."[7] Clearly, the issue of papal power is important—so much so that many Churches outside the Catholic Church perceive the way papal power is dogmatically defined and ecclesiastically practiced in the Catholic Church as one of the main stumbling blocks to unity. Yet the importance of papal power derives from the nature of the church unity it is designed

---

[3] Cf. Vatican I, First Dogmatic Constitution on the Church of Christ, *Pastor aeternus,* in N. P. Tanner, ed., *Decrees of the Ecumenical Councils,* vol II: *Trent to Vatican II* (London/Washington, D.C.: Sheed & Ward/Georgetown University Press, 1990) 812, lines 4f, hereafter cited Tanner followed by page and line number [=H. Denzinger and A. Schönmetzer, eds., *Enchiridion Symbolorum. Definitionum et declarationum de rebus et fidei et morum,* 36th ed. (Freiburg/Rome/Barcelona: Herder, 1976) no. 3051, hereafter cited *DS* followed by the paragraph number].

[4] Vatican II, Dogmatic Constitution on the Church, *Lumen gentium,* 23.

[5] *Ut unum sint,* 94.

[6] *Ibid.*

[7] *Ibid.,* italics added.

to serve. Though some cynically-minded theologians may disagree, the order of entailment clearly goes from a given conception of ecclesial unity to a given "office" of unity, and not the other way around.

This paper addresses the fundamental question of the nature of ecclesial unity itself and the appropriateness of conceiving "primacy" as a way of serving that kind of unity. The backdrop for my reflection is a consensus that has emerged over the past three decades among many theologians engaged in ecumenical dialogues to the effect that a properly understood primacy is either, as Alexander Schmemann puts it, "a necessary expression of the unity in faith and life of all local Churches,"[8] or, as the documents of the Lutheran-Catholic dialogues suggest, the desirable form which the ministry of unity in the church should take.[9] In the following I want to explore the extent to which this consensus is theologically persuasive. I will leave aside the important but subsequent question of how primacy ought to be exercised, "as a matter of law and rights" or "as founded on grace,"[10] as if it existed above the community or as an integral dimension of the community.[11]

The Fate of a Conjunction

Consider the following text from *Pastor aeternus*, important in its theological grounding of the primacy and, even after Vatican II, non-controversial for all but opponents of the papacy:

> The eternal shepherd and guardian *(episcopus)* of our souls (1 Pet 2:25), in order to render permanent the saving work of redemption, determined to build a church in which, as in the house of the living God, all the faithful should be linked by the bond of one faith and charity. Therefore, before he was glorified, he besought his Father, not for the apostles only, but also for those who were to believe in him through their word, that they all might be one as the Son himself and the Father are one (John 17:20f). So then, just as he sent

[8] A. Schmemann, "The Idea of Primacy in Orthodox Ecclesiology," in J. Meyendorff, ed., *The Primacy of Peter in the Orthodox Church*, 1st edition 1963 (Crestwood, N.Y.: St. Vladimir's Seminary Press, 1992) 165.

[9] See J.M.R. Tillard, *The Bishop of Rome*, trans. J. de Satgé, Theology and Life 5 (Wilmington/London: Michael Glazier/S.P.C.K., 1983) 11 who cites P. C. Empie and T. A. Murphy, eds., *Papal Primacy and the Universal Church*, Lutherans and Catholics in Dialogue 5 (Minneapolis: Augsburg Publishing House, 1974) no. 32.

[10] N. Afanassieff, "The Church Which Presides in Love," in J. Meyendorff, ed., *The Primacy . . .* , 141.

[11] See J. D. Zizioulas, *Being as Communion. Studies in Personhood and the Church*, Contemporary Greek Theologians 4 (Crestwood: St. Vladimir's Seminary Press, 1985).

apostles, whom he chose out of the world (see John 15:19), even as
he had been sent by the Father (see John 20:21), in like manner it
was his will that in his church there should be shepherds and teachers until the end of time (Matt 28:20). In order, then, that the episcopal office should be one and undivided and that, by the union of
the clergy, the whole multitude of believers should be held together
in the unity of faith and communion, he set blessed Peter over the
rest of the apostles and instituted in him the permanent principle of
both unities and their visible foundation.[12]

Notice two features of this text which rotates around the quotation from
the high priestly prayer of Jesus about the unity of the disciples. First,
the *formal* grounding of unity. The oneness of believers, expressed in a
single faith and single love, requires "one and undivided" episcopate,
and the one and undivided episcopate demands the single person of
Peter as "a lasting principle and visible foundation" of its unity. The one
pope is here the precondition of the unity of bishops, just as the one
bishop is the precondition of the unity of the priests, and ultimately, of
the faithful. Communal unity is a function of personal singularity. Second, the *material* grounding of unity. The line of thought is consistently
christological. The one eternal shepherd sent the apostles into the world
and, to ensure that they would be "one and undivided," placed "blessed
Peter" and his successors at their head. The one temporal shepherd is
willed by and corresponds to the one eternal shepherd. Everything in
the above passage from *Pastor aeternus* rests on these two complementary
ways of grounding the primacy—the one person is necessary to guarantee the unity of many persons and the one earthly shepherd corresponds
to the one heavenly shepherd.[13]

Notice, however, what these two ways of grounding the unity do to
John 17:20-22—the New Testament text about ecclesial unity whose vision they are meant to express and secure. The text reads: "I ask not
only on behalf of these, but also on behalf of those who will believe in
me through their word, that they may all be one. As you, Father, are in
me and I am in you, may they also be in us, so that the world may believe that you have sent me. The glory that you have given me I have
given them, so that they may be one, as we are one." The critical word

---

[12] Tanner 811, 29–812, 5 [=*DS* 3050–51].

[13] The notion that the singleness of the one is the precondition of the unity of many
is by no means unique to the theological grounding of papacy in the Catholic tradition.
Most ecclesiologies, especially those in the episcopal tradition, tend to operate with it.
Collegiality, they argue explicitly or implicitly, presupposes "primacy"—if not of the pope,
then of the patriarch or bishop.

in this text is not so much the adjective "one" ("that they may be one") but the conjunction "as" ("as we are one") which qualifies it. "As" underscores that the fact that the unity of the divine "we," lived out as the mutual interiority of the Father and the Son, provides the model for the unity of the ecclesial "we." The nature of ecclesial unity for which Jesus prayed is trinitarian. How does the twofold grounding of unity in the singleness of its earthly shepherd operative in *Pastor aeternus* fit the trinitarian character of ecclesial unity? I suggest there is a rift between the principle of unity as advocated in the ecclesiastical document and the nature of unity as understood in the biblical text. The principle of unity in this document is monistic—in a qualified sense, Christomonistic—but the nature of unity should be trinitarian.

The disjunction between the nature of unity and the principle of unity is most glaring in the thought of theologians who explicitly argue for understanding the church as the image of the Trinity. Take, for example, the ecclesiology of Joseph Cardinal Ratzinger, a person who is, in his own way, deeply sensitive to the trinitarian character of the Church. After noting that "to become a believer means stepping out of one's isolation to become part of the 'we' of the children of God," he claims that the deepest reason for Christianity having this "we" character is shown to be the fact that God himself is a we: the God confessed by the Christian creed is not thought thinking itself in solitude, is not an absolute and indivisible ego shut in on itself, but unity in the trinitarian relationship of I-you-we, so that being we as the fundamental form of God precedes all earthly forms of this relationship.[14]

For Ratzinger, the nature of the ecclesial unity is clearly trinitarian. But how about the principle of unity? He notes explicitly that the correspondence of the Church to the Trinity points away from "the exercise of the primacy by a single human being"[15] and toward something like "communal primacy." He entertains the idea of communal primacy long enough to ask hypothetically whether the idea may represent "the reconciliation of collegiality and primacy" and provide the way of "squaring the ecumenical circle in such a way that the papacy, the chief obstacle of non-Catholic Christians, would have to become the definitive vehicle for the unity of all Christians."[16] Quickly, however, he brushes the idea of communal primacy aside with the double explanation that it represents "a distortion of the doctrine of the trinity and an

---

[14] J. Ratzinger, *Church, Ecumenism, and Politics. New Essays in Ecclesiology*, trans. R. Nowell (New York/Slough: Crossroad/St. Paul, 1988) 31.

[15] *Ibid.*, 31.

[16] *Ibid.*, 32.

intolerably simplified form of combining confessing one's faith and Church politics."[17] Instead, he seeks to ground primacy in a twofold way: first in "the God who has a name," to whom a responsible human personality corresponds,[18] and second in Jesus Christ, the witness, to whom "the witnesses" correspond and "because they are witnesses, vouch for him by name."[19] And so the trinitarian character of ecclesial unity notwithstanding, "Christians' unity as 'we' . . . is held together by persons responsible for this unity and is represented once again in a personalized form in Peter."[20]

Ratzinger senses an apparent tension between this grounding of the single principle of unity with the trinitarian nature of ecclesial unity.[21] He insists, however, that the principle of "one responsible person" is "anchored fast in the trinitarian belief in God itself, since the trinity becomes meaningful and in fact recognizable for us through the fact that in his Son as man God himself has become witness to himself."[22] Though the suggestion properly underscores that the coming of Jesus Christ is a part of a trinitarian history, it does not go far enough. To ground primacy christologically is not *ipso facto* to ground it in a trinitarian way, just as to ground the primacy twice (or even thrice) in the one God is not yet to ground it in the triune God. Ratzinger offers a monist grounding of the primacy: one human person who "holds together" the unity of Christians corresponds to the one person of God and the one witness, Jesus Christ. His proposal is a variation on what is in *Pastor aeternus:* the one God and the one Christ ground the one pope as the principle of ecclesial unity, claimed to be modeled on the Trinity. So again, a split opens between the nature of unity which is trinitarian and the proposed principle of unity which is monist. The intention to let ecclesiology be informed by the high priestly prayer of Jesus "that they may be one, as we are one" is internally subverted because the proposed

---

[17] *Ibid.*

[18] *Ibid.*, 33.

[19] *Ibid.*, 34.

[20] *Ibid.*, 36.

[21] As I have tried to show elsewhere, in an important sense the monist grounding of primacy does correspond to the concrete shape of Ratzinger's doctrine of the Trinity. If persons are *pure relations* and if *no* person possesses *anything* of its own, as Ratzinger explicitly argues, then they can hardly be distinguished from one another and from the divine substance sustaining them. With such a notion of persons and their unity, it is only consistent that Ratzinger conceive of ecclesial structures by way of the one substance of God, see M. Volf, *After Our Likeness: The Church as the Image of the Trinity* (Grand Rapids: Eerdmans, 1998) 67–72.

[22] *Ibid.*, 34.

means of expressing and securing unity are at odds with the character of unity. The all important conjunction "as" in that prayer– "so that they may be one, *as* we are one" –has been disregarded.

In the remainder of this paper I want to argue that the visible principle of ecclesial unity ought to correspond to the nature of unity; the principle of unity should be trinitarian as the nature of unity itself is trinitarian. I also want to argue that the demand for a trinitarian principle of unity does not entail a distortion of the doctrine of the Trinity but flows from its proper understanding, just as that demand does not represent an inadmissible politicizing of one's faith but constitutes an expression of its best spiritual insights. The confines of this paper require only a sketchy and suggestive insight. I will first explore the nature of trinitarian unity and then, after briefly addressing the nature of ecclesial unity, raise the question of the viability of conceiving of a single person as the visible principle of ecclesial unity.[23]

Trinitarian Unity

The two central and interrelated issues in the debate about the nature of trinitarian unity as it relates to ecclesial unity emerge with clarity when we ask the following two questions: (1) Should the doctrine of the Trinity be understood in hierarchical terms? (2) What is the nature of trinitarian love? I will briefly explore the first question and then concentrate more on the second.

In recent years theologians have devoted a great deal of attention to the debate about hierarchical versus egalitarian understandings of the Trinity. During most of the doctrine's history, hierarchy was uncontested in the Trinity—as uncontested as it was in human communities. The primacy of the one person seemed a necessary precondition both of the unity of the three[24] and of their distinction.[25] Egalitarian con-

---

[23] I repeat, summarize and expand aspects of arguments that I have made in the books *Exclusion and Embrace. A Theological Exploration of Identity, Otherness, and Reconciliation* (Nashville: Abingdon, 1996) and *After Our Likeness . . .* and in the essay "'The Trinity is Our Social Program.' The Doctrine of the Trinity and the Shape of Social Engagement," *Modern Theology* 14, 3 (1998).

[24] W. Pannenberg, *Systematic Theology I*, trans. G. W. Bromiley (Grand Rapids: Eerdmans, 1991) 325 and J. D. Zizioulas, "The Teaching of the 2nd Ecumenical Council on the Holy Spirit in Historical and Ecumenical Perspective," in *Credo in Spiritum Sanctum. Atti del congresso teologico internazionale di pneumatologia in occasione del 1600° anniversario del I Concilio di Costantinopoli e del 1550° anniversario del Concilio di Efeso. Roma, 22–26 marzo 1982*, Teologia e filosofia 6 (Vatican: Libreria Editrice Vaticana, 1983) vol. I, 45.

[25] J. D. Zizioulas, *Being as Communion . . .* , 44f, note 40.

structions of the Trinity appear from this perspective as projections onto God of the shallow democratic sentiments which emerged when modern, functionally-differentiated societies replaced traditional, hierarchically-segmented societies. The denials of hierarchy in the Trinity, so the argument, seem to be fueled more by the falsely egalitarian spirit of the age than shaped by the revelation of the character of God.

Recently, however, voices have emerged contesting hierarchical constructions of the doctrine of the Trinity and advocating trinitarian egalitarianism.[26] Joining this growing group of theologians, I have suggested elsewhere that hierarchy is not necessary either to guard the divine unity or to secure the distinctions between divine persons.[27] Here I want to add that in a community of perfect love between persons who share all divine attributes, a notion of hierarchy is unintelligible. Arguments in favor of divine hierarchy must make a distinction of the kind Wolfhart Pannenberg expresses with the categories of "ontological equality" and "moral subordination" —the Son, though not being ontologically inferior, is morally subordinate to the Father.[28] This makes sense at the level of the economic Trinity. But at that level subordination is not disputed. At the level of the immanent Trinity, however, the distinction is unintelligible because it is impossible to specify what "moral" subordination of a person with all the attributes of the divinity to another person with the exact same attributes ("ontological equality") could mean. The absence of hierarchy seems a consequence of the perfection of the divine persons. Hierarchical constructions of the trinitarian relations appear from this perspective as projections of the fascination with earthly hierarchies onto the heavenly community. On the surface biblical justification notwithstanding, they seem to be less inspired by a vision of the triune God than driven either by a nostalgia for a bygone world or by fears that chaos may invade human communities if hierarchies are leveled.

As I see it, the equality of divine persons is but the formal side of perfect love between them. But how should this love itself be understood? It consists in the "practice" of self-donation. The self gives something of itself, of its own space, so to speak, in a movement in which it contracts itself in order to be expanded by the other and in which it at the same time enters the contracted other in order to increase the other's plenitude. This giving of the self which coalesces with receiving the

[26] J. Moltmann, *The Trinity and the Kingdom of God: The Doctrine of God*, trans. M. Kohl (San Francisco/London: Harper Collins/SCM Press, 1981).

[27] M. Volf, *After Our Likeness . . .* , 215–17.

[28] W. Pannenberg, *Systematic . . .* , 324–25.

other is nothing but the circular movement of the eternal divine love—a form of exchange of gifts in which the other does not emerge as a debtor because she has already given by having joyfully received and because even before the gift has reached her she was already engaged in a movement of advance reciprocation. If we adjusted the famous statement of John, "We love because God first loved us" (1 John 4:19) to fit the cycle of exchange between perfect lovers, we would have to say that *each* always both loves first and loves because he is loved. Put less paradoxically, the perfect cycle of self-donations must start moving simultaneously at all points. This is why only God is love properly speaking (1 John 4:8)—God conceived as a communion of perfect lovers.[29]

Ultimately, it is this perfect divine love between equal divine persons that provides the model for the relations between the members of the church. Ultimately, I say, because the correspondence of the church to the divine communion can be realized only in the perfect world to come, not in the sinful world we inhabit. Even God cannot repeat the acts of self-donation in a world of sin. The engagement with such a world entails a process of complex and difficult *translation*. Sent by God in the power of the Spirit, the Word became "the Lamb of God who takes away the sin of the world" (John 1:29). In the labor of "taking away the sin," the delight of love is transmuted into the agony of love—the agony of opposition to non-love, the agony of suffering at the hand of non-love, and the agony of sympathy with non-love's victims. Hence the cross of Christ. It is the face of the perfect divine love turned toward the world of sin.

From the cruciform nature of divine love in the world follow important consequences for conceptualizing Christ's relation to ecclesial unity. Christ unites people into the one people of God, not simply by virtue of the singleness of his person ("one leader—one community") or by virtue of the singleness of his vision ("one principle or law—one community"), but above all through his self-donation. True, the apostle Paul writes: "Because there is one bread we who are many are one body, for we all partake of the one bread" (1 Cor 10:17). On the surface, the singleness of the bread seems to ground the unity of the body. And yet the one bread stands for the *crucified* body of Jesus Christ, the body that has refused to remain a self-enclosed singularity, but has opened itself up so that others can freely partake of it. The single personal will and the single impersonal principle or law—two variations of the transcendent

---

[29] R. Swinburne, *The Christian God* (Oxford: Clarendon Press, 1994) 170–91.

"one"—enforce unity by suppressing and subsuming the difference; the crucified Messiah creates unity by giving his own self.

If it is true that what divides people is not so much "difference" but enmity, then the solution to divisions cannot be found in "the one." Neither the imposition of a single will nor the rule of a single law removes the enmity. Hostility can be "put to death" only through self-giving. Peaceful unity is achieved "through the cross" and "by the blood" (Eph 2:13-17). Hence, to see Jesus Christ as the foundation of unity is to see the perfect cycle of trinitarian self-donations turned toward the world of sin as the foundation of unity.

Ecclesial Unity and Communal Primacy

If my argument about the place of the "one" in the Trinity and about the nature of trinitarian love—two issues that are in fact but formal and material aspects of a single issue—is cogent, the implications for the nature of ecclesial unity and for the question of primacy are immense. Since the ecclesial unity is modeled on the trinitarian unity, we can expect the unity of the Church not to be grounded in the preeminence of the one, but in the self-giving love of the many. In the remainder of the paper I want to argue that (1) this is exactly what we find in the New Testament and that therefore (2) this is how we ought to theologically understand and institutionally configure "primacy."

As I have suggested above, the high-priestly prayer of Jesus brings all who believe in Jesus Christ into correspondence with the unity of the triune God, which is grounded in the self-giving love of three equally divine persons. Do we have traces of such an understanding of ecclesial unity elsewhere in the New Testament? The apostle Paul, it would seem, argues from a trinitarian perspective—or rather, from a proto-trinitarian perspective—when he admonishes the Corinthian congregation to unity (1 Cor 12:4-7; cf. Eph 4:3-6). He writes: "Now there are varieties of gifts, but the same Spirit; and there are varieties of services, but the same Lord; and there are varieties of activities, but it is the same God who activates all of them in everyone. To each is given a manifestation of the Spirit for the common good." The various gifts, services, and activities that all Christians have correspond to the divine multiplicity. Just as the one deity exists as "God," "Lord," and "the Spirit," so also do these different divine persons distribute different gifts to all members of the church. That these gifts are distributed for the *benefit of all*, however, corresponds to the divine unity; *the same* Spirit, *the same* Lord, and *the same* God, are active in these various gifts. A symmetrical reciprocity of the relations of the trinitarian persons finds its correspondence in the image of the church in which *all* members serve one another with their specific gifts in imitation of the Lord and through the power of the Father. Like the divine persons, they all stand in a relation of mutual giving and receiving.

At the trinitarian level, unity does not presuppose the unifying one, rather it is constituted through perfect love, which is the very nature of God. By contrast, since ecclesial unity is a unity of human beings who are by nature imperfect, ecclesial unity is inconceivable without the one. This one cannot be part of the ecclesial communion, however. With respect to papacy, the reason typically given in Protestant and some Orthodox polemics for such a claim is that the church cannot have a visible head because Christ is its invisible head. But, as Alexander Schmemann rightly notes, the alternative of this kind between visible and invisible is "theological nonsense."[30] Rather, the reason why the "one" which grounds unity cannot be part of the ecclesial community itself is that this would contradict the analogy to the structure of trinitarian relations. The principle of ecclesial unity could then not reflect the character of trinitarian unity.

It is significant that in the New Testament we find no particular office of unity. Not until the letters of Ignatius does the preservation of unity become a specific task of the bishop. Here the "council of the bishop" corresponds to the "unity of God" (*Phil.* 8:1). The bishop is thereby in a position to preside within the church "in the place of God" (*Magn.* 6:1) and thus to ensure its unity. In the New Testament the unity of the church seems to come about through the indwelling of the *one Spirit* (and with the Spirit, of the entire Trinity) *in every person*. In analogy to the Trinity, *every person* as a bearer of the Spirit participates in the constitution of the unity. This is also commensurate with the Pauline admonitions to foster unity, which are as a rule directed to all members of the congregation and never specifically to the leadership of the church (see 1 Cor 1:10-17; Eph 4:3). It would be, however, inaccurate to claim that the ordained ministry has no responsibility whatsoever for the unity of the Church. Insofar as the activity of ordained ministers always relates to a congregation as a whole, in exercise of their office the ministers have to attend to the unity of the whole. But the service of the unity is but one dimension of their ministry, not its main focus. The responsibility for the unity lies with the people of God themselves.

The dual argument about ecclesial unity–the argument from the nature of the Trinity and from New Testament ecclesiology–has impor-

---

[30] A. Schmemann, "The Idea . . . ," 151.

tant consequences for the question of primacy. Partly on the basis of a somewhat differently developed doctrine of the Trinity than the one I proposed above, Heribert Mühlen has suggested in *Entsakralisierung* that since a single person cannot correspond to a relational network, the office in the church should be exercised collegially. He applied the same argument to the question of primacy and proposed a "trinitarization" of the papal office—adding, however, wisely that in his mind the trinitarization of the primacy "does not necessarily mean that the latter must consist in establishment of a triumvirate."[31] From my perspective, this proposal to free the exercise of the ecclesiastical offices from the clutches of singularity is exactly right. In the New Testament the office is consistently exercised in a collegial way (Phil 1:1 and 1 Thes 5:12). If one follows the arguments of Gordon Fee, even the Pastoral Epistles do not seem to form an exception.[32] To fit the predominant New Testament conception of ministry and to correspond to the nature of the Trinity, the highest level of church leadership should be theologically understood, institutionally configured, and practically exercised in a communal way.

It could be argued that a communal exercise of primacy is unrealistic. In fact, the argument for preeminence of the "one" is sometimes defended precisely for this reason. Consider Alexander Schmemann's argument in his excellent article on the "Idea of Primacy in the Orthodox Ecclesiology." He writes,

> The primate *can* speak for all because the Church is one and because the power he exercises is the power of each bishop and of all bishops. And he *must* speak for all because this very unity and agreement require, in order to be efficient, a special organ of expression, a mouth, a voice. Primacy is thus a necessity because therein is the expression and manifestation of the unity of churches as being the unity of *the* Church.[33]

Schmemann grounds the necessity of the primacy negatively in the difficulty of having *efficient* unity and agreement without the "first" who speaks for all. Given the propensities of human beings, it may well be that a communal primacy would be inefficient. In the absence of clarity about who is "the first," in communal decision-making, decisions are al-

---

[31] H. Mühlen, *Entsakralisierung: Ein epochales Schlagwort in seiner Bedeutung für die Zukunft der christlichen Kirchen* (Paderborn: F. Schöningh, 1971) 257.

[32] G. D. Fee, *1 and 2 Timothy, Titus*, New International Biblical Commentary 13 (Peabody: Hendrickson, 1988) 20ff.

[33] A. Schmemann, "The Idea . . . ," 165.

ways being made not only about issues at stake but also about preeminence among the members of the group. But on this line of reasoning the necessity of the "one temporal shepherd" rests not so much in the admirable correspondence to the "one eternal shepherd," but in the competitiveness of the temporal shepherds. The Church then needs the "one" because it is *not* what it ought to be. Far from being simply the visible principle and ground of unity, the one then in fact *manifests* the lack of unity. More precisely, the one is able to overcome disunity only by underscoring the permanence of disunity at the same time!

For those who remain unpersuaded by the argument from efficiency and instead seek to ground primacy in a trinitarian way (as I am inclined to do), it is essential not to conceive of "communal primacy" in a purely formal way—instead of one there should be three or more who decide. If one were to stop at this formal level, the proposal would serve merely to introduce democratic checks and balances at the highest level of church leadership. The issue of primacy would be reduced to the question of the distribution of ecclesial power and the protection from its abuse. Without denying the importance of social power in the Church and without denigrating the importance of communal decision-making at the bottom as well as at the top, I want to suggest that if the proposal about "communal primacy" remained at this formal level, it would fail to bring into correspondence the visible expression of ecclesial unity with the trinitarian nature of that unity. Ecclesial unity will be trinitarian only if the formal condition of the communal exercise of primacy is accompanied by a consistent practice of self-donation which is at the very heart of the Trinity's life. More concretely, since the exercise of primacy must take place in a world of sin, it should be modeled on the love of the triune God turned toward the world of sin. Primacy must be modeled on the life of Christ that led him to the cross. *Ut unum sint* puts it well: the ministry of primacy is "a ministry of mercy, born of an act of Christ's own mercy."[34]

Have I argued for a trinitarian principle of ecclesial unity only to end up with a Christological one? No, because in my account, the Christological grounding of unity does not function as a monist replacement of the trinitarian grounding; rather, the narrative of the self-giving of Christ provides the material content for the visible principle of unity that is formally structured in a trinitarian way. The communal nature of primacy and its exercise as a practice of self-donation must combine to make the visible service of unity correspond to the nature of the unity

---

[34] *Ut unum sint*, 93.

which is trinitarian. To the extent that the primacy is located in the singleness of a person and exercised in virtue of formal power received, it will fail to correspond to the Trinity and may even generate disunity rather than serve unity. To the extent that primacy is understood, structured, and exercised communally and takes the form of self-giving service to the community, however, it will not only correspond to the Trinity but also function as a wellspring of unity.

Does this alternative with which I conclude my remarks entail a misunderstanding of the doctrine of the Trinity and an illicit politicizing of the Christian faith? I hope not. I would like to believe that the alternative springs from the deepest theological and spiritual resources of our faith.

12

The Ecumenical Kairos and the Primacy

Jean-Marie R. Tillard, O.P.

If I have understood rightly, the aim of this important symposium was to give an opportunity to theologians acquainted with the ecumenical situation, to define the position of their respective confessional traditions with regard to the delicate problem of the Roman primacy. What has been called "John Paul II's unexpected invitation" to speak fraternally on this matter should make it possible for each one to do so with clarity and constructive intention.

So far the meeting has achieved its aim. After listening to everything, it is now for me to show the overall perspectives emerging from this series of presentations. It has to be done, as it were, on the moment, without any possibility of critical withdrawal, or returning (for reflection and evaluation) to the many sources of which the speakers have made use. I am asked to forget as far as possible my personal opinions on the matter and to be no more than a theological mirror of the discussions. Very irenical discussions, it must be said at the outset. It seems that this is no longer the time for partisan disputes. Anyone who tries will be burnt in the process.

I. 1. One first fact has to be noted. It is of the greatest importance. It is agreed that from Peter, head of the apostolic community, to the bishop presiding today over the see of Rome, there is continuity. But a continuity that follows the different, and at times tortuous, paths of human history. Along these paths, in a way that has become evident, it mingles with the socio-cultural and religious fabric of the times and places, while the tangled threads are often difficult to take apart. Like the whole Church, the papacy exists within history. At several levels, it is even subject to history, for better and for worse. The needs, the responses demanded by concrete situations, modify the outward aspect of the primacy. The need of the whole Church, faced with the crises of Christological and Trinitarian faith; the need for one who will defend the *Libertas Ecclesiae*; the need for a point of confessional identity at a time when the internal unity of the West is broken; the need for an anchor in the storms of modernity; all these needs—and others again,—lead the papacy to give new expression to its function, its *munus*. For many of the traditions represented here, some of these new features present a problem and have made the Roman primacy unacceptable. Today it is a question of trying, together and in all honesty to determine whether, on the one hand, these features are fully in harmony with the Gospel and with the spirit of Christ transmitted by the Gospel, and whether, on the other hand, they are so deeply theological that, with the passing of the emergency for which they had been introduced, they should be made a constitutive element of the primacy on a permanent basis. For instance, is the role of the papacy in the Councils held after the break with the East and the Reformation an emergency role, or does it respond to a function required as such by the nature of the Church? This simple, but enlightening example shows the need to distinguish between contingent historical forms and what is essential.

2. A. The guiding principle that binds permanently together all these various forms of the function of primacy and that justifies them in the eyes of those who shape them, is no doubt the watch that is kept (*episkopē*) over the ecclesial community in the *koinōnia* of faith and charity. That is what the encyclical *Ut unum sint* calls presiding in truth and love, so that the boat will not be shattered in the storms and can reach harbor whole and entire. At the same time it must be strongly affirmed that this primacy is only authentic insofar as it is exercised under the authority of the one Head of the Church, Christ; and furthermore, that its object is *visible communion,* since God alone is master of the secrets of the human heart which He can justify at will drawing it into the trinitarian *koinōnia*.

It seems to me that—although with different evaluations—almost all the confessions represented here agree that the present evolution is promising. But it is clear that all the elements and aspects of the primacy, including what seems to be emerging today, have to be evaluated or judged with reference to the two great evangelical norms: on the one hand, submission to the ἐξουσία of the one Head of the Church, Christ;[1] on the other hand, communion in truth and *Agapē*.[2] In this ref-

---

[1] Matt 28:18; John 17:2; cf. John 3:35; 13:3.
[2] Eph 4:15; 2 John 1:1-3.

erence to Truth and *Agapē* are, obviously, included the insistence of the Lutheran and Reformed traditions on the rectitude of faith,[3] especially the stress on the primacy of the Gospel with its essential reference to the gratuitousness of salvation.

B. Allow me to underline the agreement here with the great principle of discernment that, at least since Robert Grosseteste, bishop of Lincoln (around 1250), and Thomas Aquinas, is found throughout the West: the primacy only exists *ad aedificationem, non ad destructionem Ecclesiae*. Reiterated by Wycliffe, and then by John Hus (in 1413), this principle will inform Reformation theology, and will reemerge at Vatican I from the lips of Zinelli.[4] I underline also that, in a text often overlooked, *Pastor aeternus* indicates "union (communion) of faith and charity"[5] as an essential characteristic of the Church willed by God.

The criteria for judgement are therefore the same. But, whereas (Roman) Catholic tradition tends to apply them mainly in particular cases, to judge the authenticity of one or another decision, the value of one or another Pontificate—think of the verdict of Cardinal Gasparo Contadini in the *Consilium de emendanda Ecclesia* (around 1536) or the more aggressive verdict of Jerome Savonarola—the Reformation uses them to judge, at one and the same time, the forms taken by the primacy and the primacy *as such*. Clearly, under present circumstances, even for Rome it is no longer merely a matter of the particular cases for which John Paul II, after Paul VI, is asking forgiveness.[6] Here again, the perspectives are the same.

II. 1. The primacy, as we said, always threads its way through the fabric of the times and places. It is inseparable from history. If, in this

---

[3] Weimar Edition of Luther's Works: Weimarer Ausgabe, *D. Martin Luthers Werke. Kritische Gesamtausgabe* (Weimar: Hermann Böhlaus Nachfolger, 1883ff) 40/I, 357 and 50, 270–71 (hereafter cited *WA*).

[4] J. D. Mansi, *Sacrorum conciliorum nova et amplissima collectio*, new ed., L. Petit and J.-B. Martin. Reprint [1st ed. 1759–1798] (Graz, 1960–61) vol. 52, 1105 C–D (hereafter cited Mansi).

[5] Vatican I, First Dogmatic Constitution on the Church of Christ *Pastor aeternus*, in N. P. Tanner, ed., *Decrees of the Ecumenical Councils*, vol. II: *Trent to Vatican II* (London/Washington, D.C.: Sheed & Ward/Georgetown University Press, 1990) 812, lines 6–14 (hereafter cited Tanner followed by page and line number) [=H. Denzinger and A. Schönmetzer, eds., *Enchiridion Symbolorum. Definitionum et declarationun de rebus et fidei et morum*, 36th ed. (Freiburg/Rome/Barcelona: Herder, 1976, no. 3052), hereafter cited *DS* followed by the paragraph number], Tanner 813, 25–37 [=*DS* 3059], Tanner 815, 5–10 [=*DS* 3065].

[6] John Paul II, *Ut unum sint. That They May Be One: On Commitment to Ecumenism* (Washington, D.C.: United States Catholic Conference, 1995) §88 (hereafter cited *Ut unum sint*).

light, we reread right through *Ut unum sint*, we soon realize that John Paul
II is situating his reflection in a very precise and characterized historical
context. A context over which the (Roman) Catholic Church has not entire control.

A. This context, wholly new and entirely in the hands of *divina
Providentia*, is that created by the ecumenical movement.[7] To be sure as I
pointed out recently in my contribution to the *Essays in honor of Paul Crow*—
the (Roman) Catholic Church has never acquiesced in the division.[8] But,
clearly, the progress of the last decades and the turning point of Vatican
II would have been impossible without what has been coming to matu-
rity since 1910 (the World Missionary Conference in Edinburgh), 1927
(the World Conference of Faith and Order), 1948 (the founding of the
World Council in Amsterdam). But—largely because of her concept of
the primacy—Rome had deliberately chosen to remain dissociated from
these events.[9] It must even be said that Vatican II would not have been
what it was without this ecumenical context. And that not only because
of the part played by the Observers from other confessions, but also because of the seeds sown by the ecumenical movement, in particular
through *Faith and Order*. It was the—perhaps unsuspected—"reception" of
many subjects mentioned in the World Conferences of Lausanne, Lund,
Edinburgh, Montreal, and remaining present in the Christian conscience
as such, that allowed a number of central points of the Conciliar documents to be gradually defined: the value of the one baptism, the relation
between Scripture, Tradition and traditions, the supreme freedom of the
act of faith, conciliarity or *sobornost*, and above all, the whole idea of communion, of *koinōnia*. This last was brought into the discussion ever since
the encyclical Letter of the patriarch of Constantinople (1919) and the
Conference of Lausanne. After Vatican II, ARCIC and the other bilateral dialogues were to make it explicit, develop it and let it become the
central theological theme at the World Conference of Faith and Order in
Santiago de Compostela (1993). With reference to this history John Paul

---

[7] Let us think of the influence of a name too often forgotten, R. H. Gardiner (see O.
Rousseau, "Le grand voyage œcuménique des fondateurs de Foi et Constitution," *Irénikon*
43, 3 (1970) 325–61); and of John Mott, Nathan Söderblom, George Bell, Germanos. . . .

[8] See J.M.R. Tillard, "The Roman Catholic Church and Ecumenism," in T. F. Best
and T. J. Nottingham, eds., *The Vision of Christian Unity. Essays in Honor of Paul A. Crow, Jr.*
(Indianapolis: Oikoumene Publications, 1997) 179–97.

[9] Benedict XV had at first gladly welcomed the announcement of the Conference of
Lausanne. His final refusal can be explained by the influence of Card. Merry del Val, an
intransigent. It was the Cardinal who again played a key role in the publication of *Mor-
talium animos* under Pius XI in 1928.

II made *koinōnia* the basis of his reminder of *Ut unum sint* and his question concerning the primacy.

B. It is certainly not accidental that it was above all the ecumenical dialogue, in its multiform research on *koinōnia*, that came to recognize the urgent necessity of a fresh look at the primacy. The historical *dossier* must be revisited for an evaluation according to the principles mentioned above. Both the bilateral dialogues, with their attention to the nature of ecclesial *koinōnia*, and the multiconfessional dialogue of Faith and Order, came to the conclusion that it would not be possible to reach the goal of authentic visible *koinōnia* without accepting to reread this crucial *dossier*. But, in all these dialogues the Catholic Church is a full participant. She shares this conviction. So it is significant that John Paul II explicitly places himself within this context:[10] the context, precisely, of a new stage in ecclesial history, encompassed on all sides by ecumenical concern. There is a need felt by the Catholic Church herself—often ill at ease in face of decisions or ways of acting that seem to be going back from the positions of Vatican II—a need that is taken up into a larger and decisive dynamism, coming from Christendom as a whole, under the urging of the Holy Spirit towards visible *communion*. We have here a completely new situation—*this stage* of the history of the Church, in a world that is torn apart and in search of unity—and we need to take the measure of its value and importance. The Catholic Church no longer agrees to settle *by herself* this question that is central, for her as for the others. For once, it seems right to me to use the term *kairos*. The Catholic Church is pulled out of her isolation.

2. A. If there is readiness at this stage to "receive" the call of the Spirit, there is a twofold task incumbent on the Catholic Church, for to her also the call of *Ut unum sint* is addressed. The first task, in face of the universal desire for visible *koinōnia*, is to bring to light the reasons why the other Christian confessions have, in conscience, broken their link with the Roman *sedes* and have thought that they could live without her, "as long as she was what she was." The task of the Catholic Church, faced with this vast *dossier*, is also to ask herself what the Spirit expects from her so that the Roman primacy may be able to respond to the desire of everyone, including Catholics themselves: a primacy which has been from the beginning inseparable from her ecclesial existence and which, she is deeply convinced, is an instrument willed by God for this visible *koinōnia*. What is the visage of the primacy required for our ecumenical era?

---

[10] *Ut unum sint,* 96.

B. a. As to the *how,* the Catholic Church, in her own theological research and in ecumenical dialogues, has acquired or has better understood certainties, several of which have, happily, been recalled during
this symposium. The first, and the one that has been most stressed
within her own life for some years past, is respect for all the dimensions
of episcopal collegiality and *affectus collegialis* as spelled out in *Lumen gentium.* The word *collegium,* coming from Roman law and given by Cyprian
to Western ecclesiology, is the juridical translation of the beautiful biblical concept of ἀδελφότης, that is, the apostolic fraternity of the ministers
of the Gospel. The Bishop of Rome is a brother among brothers who
are *sacramentally all equal in the episcopate,* and each one of whom—in his
own Church, from which he is inseparable—is responsible, as firmly expressed by *Lumen gentium,* for the Church of God, and "in God's stead."[11]
The primacy is primacy *in a fraternal* college, responsible for the Church,
and not *over this collegium.* The *sub* inseparable from the *cum.* The authors
of *Haec Sancta,* at Constance, were keenly aware of this. The primacy is
set within the collegial fraternity, which is itself at the service of the synodality of all the sister-Churches as they move together along the paths
of Christ the Lord. If the primate happens to cut himself off from the
episcopal college, he is no longer primate; he is no more than a solitary
pastor. Whence the importance of the Councils and synodal dynamism.
It is in the Council that the ἀδελφότης manifests itself and is fully realized. The pope alone could not have accomplished what was done by
Vatican II! John XXIII was well aware of this when he convened this
general council.

Every decision faithful to this fraternal solidarity therefore requires
that the ἀδελφότης be always taken into account, even when it occurs
that the Primate has to speak alone. His word can only be that of the
fraternal *consensus,* as expression of his own *affectus collegialis,* which also
for him, and not only for the other bishops, is the norm of episcopal action. Once he forgets this *affectus,* he cuts himself off from the *collegium*
and can no longer speak as its head. The exercise of the authority and
the ἐξουσία that the Spirit gives him (so that this authority may not be
merely a title) can never abstract from the *una cum fratribus* that Paul VI
so happily restored in the promulgation of the documents of Vatican II.
The primate can never, by virtue of his *munus,* declare a truth unless he
has the certainty *before God* (*soli Deo devinctus*) that what he is saying expresses the faith of his brother bishops. His primatial authority is inseparable from collegiality and synodality. The primate's *affectus collegialis*

[11] Second Vatican Council, Dogmatic Decree on the Church *Lumen gentium,* 20.

is for him the guarantee of presidency in the *communion* of *Agapē ad aedificationem et non ad destructionem* of the Church founded on the apostles.

We can guess the ecumenical importance of this fact that has been recalled during these days. Whatever the name given to those who are or will be or would be recognized as authentic *vicarii Apostolorum* once visible communion had been restored, it is clear that their relation to the Primate should then be understood within this collegial ἀδελφότης, in ways to be defined. Communion with the Roman *sedes* is not renunciation (someone wrote *redditio!*) of true ἐξουσία, but is entering into a fraternal solidarity of which the Bishop of Rome is called to be the cement (after the Spirit and the Eucharist, whose servant, whose minister he is), and the guardian. It is fortunate that the non-Catholics insist on this point, obliging the Catholic Church to question herself.

b. Communion of *Agapē* and communion of Truth are indispensable. It has been said again during these days—and many other documents of the Churches of West and East could have been added to those mentioned—that Peter brings us back to the faith of the apostolic community, to the solidity (ἀσφάλεια) of the acceptance of God's Word as revealed in Jesus Christ. The words from Luke: "I have prayed for you that your faith may not fail; and when you have turned again, strengthen (στήρισον) your brethren,"[12] are like the reverse side of the confession of Caesarea.[13] Now, this responsibility with regard to the ἀσφάλεια of the faith is wholly measured and conditioned by three absolutes from the New Testament. The first is, obviously, the total sufficiency of what has been said in Jesus Christ and transmitted by the apostolic witness. Whence the necessity of putting all teaching under the judgement of "the Gospel of the grace of God." Adding nothing to it, but also taking nothing away; and this, we should note, includes the indications of *all* the canonical books on the διακονία of the ministers of the community. The Church of God must be kept within the "memory" of what God has *truly* said and meant in Jesus Christ; a Word which comes from elsewhere, and only from the *elsewhere* of God.

The second absolute, regarding truth, refers to the mission of the Spirit in all its entirety. The Pauline *corpus* and the Johannine writings assure us that every baptized person and every community of the baptized are instructed by the Spirit. Whether the Spirit is presented as the anointing that "is true and is no lie,"[14] that teaches you about every-

---

[12] Luke 22:32.
[13] Matt 16:13-20.
[14] 1 John 2:27.

thing,[15] or whether the Spirit is seen as the One who inspires faith and responds to it,[16] it is the Spirit of Truth at work in what Paul calls the Body of Christ *as such*. The particular and specific service that the "Vicar of Peter"–according to the most ancient title, supplanted only with Innocent III in the XIII century, by that of "Vicar of Christ"–has the mission to accomplish, is a service in this Body of Christ, where the Spirit precedes him by arousing what is called the *sensus fidelium*. Whence the necessity for "listening" on a wide scale to this *sensus,* with the help of the *cathedra* of theologians (not excluding those of other Christian traditions and without refusing a priori certain schools which have their titles of nobility), while resisting pressures and avoiding short-circuits in reflection through over-hasty decisions; the necessary intellectual space must be left for expertise. The experience, already long, of the bilateral and multilateral dialogues has taught us how much patience is needed for this listening to the *sensus fidei*. But it has also taught us methods. We would not be at a loss if we accepted to widen the field of discernment. I am surprised that so little has been said about this *sensus fidelium* during these days.

The third absolute in this field of the primatial service of Truth brings us back to what we know about synodality and collegiality. It is to the apostolic group *as such*[17] that the task of "teaching (διδάσκειν) to observe (τηρεῖν)" the evangelical Word is entrusted. This is shown, in its way, by the meeting of Paul and Barnabas with the "pillars" of the apostolic community.[18] The word of the Primate neither replaces nor relativizes that of his brother bishops. It also is an act of *affectus collegialis,* an act within the *collegium*. Paul VI, in his address for the promulgation of *Lumen gentium,* said: "We are not afraid of seeing our authority diminished or disparaged when we affirm and celebrate your authority, for we know that each one of you is seeking the same goal". This, implies that, within the episcopal fraternity, in the search for truth which is the common task of the *collegium as such,* the Primate's seeking cannot be separated from the discernment of his brother bishops nor imposed on them as from outside. Especially because the grace of the Episcopate gives them the *prudentia* (in the Thomistic sense) which enables them to measure the relation between necessities and concrete situations, between what is desirable and what is possible. In face of these three absolutes, in this ecumenical phase, the Catholic Church must, obviously, accept the exercise of the fraternal

---

[15] Cf. John 14:16-17; 16:7, 13-15.
[16] 1 Thess 1:5; 4:8; Gal 3:2; 1 Cor 12:3.
[17] Matt 28:16-20.
[18] Gal 2:1-10.

judgement of the other Churches; but she must also not hesitate to challenge them when she deems it to be necessary. The service of Truth takes precedence over excesses of diplomatic courtesy.

C. I think that as regards this *how* we can speak of overall agreement. During this symposium I have noted many signs of convergence which authorize us to think so. If I am right, this is a considerable step forward, and all its implications must be weighed, taking into account the fine shades of the different positions.

There remains the *why* and the necessity of the primacy: its importance in *God's plan* for *God's Church*. Everything here is less clear. That is why I have chosen to speak of it only at the end of my presentation and now I speak in my own name.

a. May I remind you that a clear judgement on this point, in the ecumenical context of our rereading of the primacy—treated at length above, and purposely so—must take into account both the tradition of the East and the tradition of the West. This requires that those who speak should know both traditions. How, for instance, can we judge the West without a serious reading of its principal representatives while being content with repeating trenchant and unverified judgements? In Augustine there are a thousand more shades of meaning than in what has been said about him on the basis of *Roma locuta est causa finita est*, taken out of its context. Moreover, his vision of Catholicity does not correspond to what is said when relying only on his reactions to Donatism. Our ecumenical ethos demands mutual respect for the two traditions. It excludes all *a priori* contempt, all lazy selectiveness, all concession to easy slogans.

Having said this, I confess that the more I search through this *dossier*, with one eye on the East and one on the West, the more light is thrown on the *why* of the primacy and its place in God's plan. The symposium has contributed to this, in its own way, through the frankness of certain speakers.

b. Why the primacy? I repeat one of my statements which was very much misunderstood: "The primacy is necessary because, as *catholic* and as a *communion* of local Churches, the Church is necessarily plural in the diversity of many aspects of her life. But between diversity and division the frontier is quickly crossed. With Augustine, the father of the Latin ecclesiology of *communion,* we even have to say that the Eucharist, the supreme sacrament of communion is wounded when the ministers presiding over it in *communion* with their people, are not themselves in fraternal *communion,* canonical *communion.* This is the *summum* of scandal."

In God's plan, the primacy represents, within the ecclesial ministry, an instrument of *divina Providentia* to enable the local Churches entrusted to the fraternity (ἀδελφότης) of the episcopal college (the ministerial college) to live authentically as sister-Churches in the *communion* of Truth and *Agapē*. A Church of God that is torn cannot correspond to its nature and mission. Here we are all convinced of this. Division, in particular, contradicts the vocation of witnessing to the reconciliation that comes from God. But the difference of cultures, histories, ethnic roots, even political differences and, at times, the violent clashes between the nations to which they belong or, at least, their conflicting interests all these are challenges to the *koinōnia* of Churches that are deeply rooted in their people. The temptation then appears of provincialism, of closing in upon local concerns. The role of the primacy, rightly understood, always in relation to the *affectus collegialis* (in the rich sense of the Latin *affectus*)—is to widen the outlook, to open up the horizon, always to recall the *common good* of the Church of God in its visible reality. What is at stake is what prevents the local Churches from turning in upon themselves so as to be out of harmony with the full scope of reconciliation, content with living reconciliation within their own segment of humanity. The primacy has the mission of being guardian for this *common good* that characterizes God's Church in a humanity where individualistic withdrawals constantly provoke ruptures. That is where its ἐξουσία comes in.

We have been told again during these days how powerful, in the different confessions, are the dynamisms working towards internal *communion* at the worldwide level. This includes all primacy and at its level, the Roman primacy, which is, inseparably, that of the local Church of Rome. This local Church is convinced that it has kept, in its "soil" and its "place"—together with the trophies of Peter and Paul—the abscissa and the ordinate of this *common good* (one linking it with the night of its origin in Israel, the other opening it up to the universality of the world), entrusted to the bishop of this *sedes*. No need to stress this here. Allow me, for what it is worth, a personal observation. When I look at the motley array of the Catholic dioceses, and at the intolerance of some of the movements of which they are composed, I often wonder whether it is not because they are all in *communion* with Rome that they are able to stay together, accepting one another in certain tasks. Objectively, in any case, one thing is sure: Without Rome, the Catholic Church would not have taken the steps she has towards social justice and, above all, the ecumenical plunge whose importance has been shown by this symposium. "If it were not for the pope . . . a Croatian would never embrace a Serb," one Croatian wrote to me. "That is something beyond the duty of charity!" There are few church leaders today who speak as often as the Bishop of Rome about the need for ecumenism.

I sum all that up by saying—and this is a reading of the *jus divinum* that, if God wills the Unity of the Church, this implies a primacy at the service of Unity. A Unity that is not uniformity but a *communion* of Churches deeply rooted in their human soil; a primacy that is precisely at the evangelical service of the ministries sent into this human diversity, that the Spirit wants to inscribe at the heart of the universal reconciliation that comes from God and from God alone. Primacy is a gift of God, for the *communion* brought about by the only One who, on his Cross, broke down the walls of hatred, and which only the Spirit can make effective there where humanity is capable of receiving it. But this is not the only gift of God for *koinōnia!*. . . under the Spirit and the Word. It must be placed within the vast field of the οἰκονομία.

D. In conclusion, I will be content with quoting Augustine (*Sermo* 295):

> It is right that after the Resurrection the Lord entrusts to Peter in person the task of feeding his sheep. He is not, indeed, the only one to have this merit of feeding the Lord's sheep. But, if Christ speaks only to one, it is to stress unity.

It seems to me that, in the particular context in which we are trying to reread the question of primacy, these words of Augustine are of great value. We were saying that the visage of the primacy has changed in the course of history, according to the different contexts. We are in an ecumenical context, a unique, providential context. There are features which the majority of the baptized want to see assumed by the primacy— a desire from which the Spirit is not absent—and for which, at many levels, they are preparing, if the primacy is capable of "receiving" them: The Roman primacy is called, in fact, to become for all, and in the first place for Catholics themselves, what *Lumen gentium* considered to be its mission: the servant of *koinōnia* in Truth and *Agapē,* under the authority of Jesus Christ and of his Word. Is that, perhaps, the grace of this ecumenical kairos? Let us hope for it . . . in patience.

To prevent this hope from being extinguished, the great service that the Roman *sedes* could *already* render to all the Churches of all confessions would, perhaps, be to continue, without fail, in her commitment, so that whatever has already been achieved by way of visible *communion* may be deepened, may not be frittered away, may not sink into banality. We know the Lund principle, often badly translated! Our ecumenical attempts want to have a future . . . at the very least, a clear witness to Christ, rendered *really in common* by all Christians. Am I too triumphalistic if I repeat something Archbishop Runcie said (after Assisi) to the whole of his Church: Probably, within Christianity, only the Bishop of Rome has enough ἐξουσία to gather all the confessions. On the condition that this is done in genuine dialogue. This would already be a giant step, a glimpse of "primacy" in faith and *Agapē,* under the sole authority of the Father and the Lord Jesus Christ; a step that would also call for deepening, a gain that must not be frittered away. If I have sinned by triumphalism, forgive me . . . but I do not have perfect contrition! I think, however, that many Orthodox, Anglicans, Lutherans, Methodists, and others are ready to give me absolution. I understood this from certain discreet, but sincere remarks I heard during these days.

Afterword

James F. Puglisi, S.A.

The great diversity and richness of the presentations of the symposium can be seen in their full array in the body of this book. This fact, however, should not prevent us from trying to keep some of the more critical observations and constructive suggestions for the dialogue on papal primacy more in the foreground as we move to the next step in our conversations on this subject. We will not attempt to summarize what has already been written in these papers but rather indicate some of the more salient points which need to be further dealt with in the dialogue. Some of the points which we will indicate were brought up in the discussion following each of the presentations and merit to be recorded here to complete the picture of the dynamic of the symposium.

One of the first observations which needs to be made concerns the seriousness with which the Vatican has taken this special event which took place in Rome. While the Pope himself could not be present at these deliberations due to the extraordinary synod of the Americas which was taking place at the same time as the symposium, the people whom he has entrusted the delicate task of bringing forward the different dialogues were present during the whole symposium. The Secretary of the Pontifical Council for Promoting Christian Unity, Bishop Pierre Duprey, was present at almost every encounter as were other members who were responsible for the Anglican and Methodist dialogues and the dialogues with the Orthodox and the Oriental Orthodox. His Eminence Edward Cardinal Cassidy brought the symposium to a close with the greetings of John Paul II who was concerned whether or not anything had actually happened with the invitation he made in *Ut unum sint* for a dialogue on this subject.

Another aspect of the symposium was the atmosphere within which this dialogue took place. Many of the participants commented on the deep mutual respect shown by the speakers for one another as well as their profound knowledge and mature reflection on this complicated and sensitive subject. All of the speakers were chosen for their experience in the bilateral and multilateral dialogues as well as their knowledge of the dossier on the question of the primacy and their ability to express their own ecclesial tradition's view on this issue.

Let us turn to some of the points which were made that could be important for furthering and deepening the discussion on the issue of primacy. Obviously these might be considered altogether subjective on my part. I will, however, try to represent what some of the participants felt were points that needed further development or questions which were raised on matters that were insufficiently covered in the presentations. From the historical presentation of Klaus Schatz, reflections on the method of dealing with the question of papacy arose. One of the more important aspects to be kept in mind is the fact that the institution of the papacy took its shape in response to concrete historical situations both theological and political and therefore should never be considered as something static but rather as a response to the exigencies of particular situations. This factor complicates matters of sorting through what are the core or essential elements of the divine institution from those which are not necessary or can change from epoch to epoch.

One of the questions put to Schatz after his talk dealt with the fact that reference to the New Testament was absent from his lecture. In spite of the fact that we would like to find the solution to our queries of today on such issues as the primacy and the papacy in the New Testament, the fact is that the New Testament alone cannot provide the answer to many of the issues which touch upon the papacy and the primacy of the Petrine ministry. There was an evolution which took place with the first communities of Christians as they took their place in the contemporary world and had to live and carry on the mission entrusted to them. Another dimension of the problem which Schatz pointed out is the fact that later theology and history do not sufficiently take into consideration that the Roman *sedes* was actually the see of Peter and Paul. Why has the place of Paul in historical and theological reflection been omitted or played down? This is an important issue for the Catholic tradition to deal with in further discussion on the issues of authority, primacy, and papacy.

The Lutheran position on the subject has reflected on the issues and the positions taken by Luther and the first generation of Lutheran reformers. As with many issues which touch the Lutheran position, key to the discussion is the role and prominence that is given to the Word of God. In fact much of the reaction to the medieval papacy was in terms of the perceived abuses based on the subjugation of the Word of God to the will of one man, the pope. In this context then the pope was seen as the antiChrist where his positions were in opposition to those of Christ as presented in the Scriptures. At the heart, then, of a possible Lutheran position on the papacy would be the desire to see it at the service of the Gospel. The question of the necessity of the papacy is raised in the context of the need for such an institution for the well-being of the Church or simply for the good order in the Church. It should be remembered that Luther and Melanchthon differed on the basis of the power and authority of the pope (*ius humanum* versus *ius divinum*).

Harding Meyer showed that even if Lutherans, in the period following the Reformation, might have been open to a Petrine office, with the publication of Vatican I's teaching on infallibility in *Pastor aeternus*, an open attitude toward it became more difficult to maintain. The question of the subversion of Christian freedom became a central issue. With this dogmatic definition, it became increasingly more difficult for Lutherans to see how the apostolic scriptures of the biblical canon remain the supreme norm in the definition of apostolic truth. Meyer noted how, behind all of the issues which have been and are now being discussed in the dialogues, the question of papal authority still remains the central issue to be dealt with in the end.

Most characteristic of an Anglican ecclesiology is the concept of "bishop-in-synod." This position lends itself to a balance of personal authority exercised in a collegial way in the context of the whole body of the local church. This position is not that different from the Eastern position of the episcopal-synodical system. Bishop John Hind attempted to illustrate how the Anglican position toward the papacy historically either regarded the institution as reformable even though it obviously had been corrupted or that there was no way of saving the institution since it was flawed in its inception.

Some of the most recent Anglican thinking on the relationship between primacy and collegiality is to be found in the *Virginia Report*. This report seeks to link the personal, collegial, and communal elements of the exercise of oversight. Parallels have even been drawn during the Lambeth Conference (1998) to the role of the archbishop of Canterbury and to that of patriarchs. The position of Anglicans on this issue of universal primacy is linked inseparably to the question of provincial primacy and diocesan episcopacy as is seen in the archbishop of Canterbury's role as primate of all England and metropolitan. His authority however is a moral authority and not a jurisdictional one. Given this position some Anglicans at the Lambeth Conference of 1998 desired to see a universal ministry of unity having greater canonical authority attributed to the archbishop of Canterbury. Some of the elements in the Anglican position for a ministry of universal primacy would necessarily include the safeguarding of both unity and diversity, the strengthening of the brethren, and the collegial care for the life of the Church. These elements, taken together with the need for the visibility inherent to the unity of Christians, are necessary if the Church is to be a credible sign of the unity that God wills for the whole of creation.

The bilateral dialogues with Methodists have moved through various stages and at different times have studied the topics of pastoral and doctrinal authority as well as the offices of oversight as Geoffrey Wainwright noted in his lecture. Scriptural categories of unity in truth and love have a clear place in Methodist vocabulary; in Methodist practice one can find structures of oversight doctrine and discipline. These tend to be more collegial in form (for example, the connexional system or the itinerant superintendency or a corporate *episkopē* of the Conference). In spite of this fact, Wainwright has pointed out that more work still remains to be done before Catholics and Methodists could agree on a notion of a unitive superintendency or a universal presidency. Moreover, even though there is a difference in vocabulary there is some similarity in practice especially when considering that the Petrine ministry is principally about service of truth and love in the Church as a whole.

After a systematic study of the Methodist-Catholic dialogues on the topics related to the Petrine office, Wainwright concluded his presentation with a personal suggestion which should be kept in the foreground as the dialogue on the primacy goes forward. It has to do with the link between the unity of Christians and the mission entrusted to them by Christ to proclaim the Gospel to the ends of the earth. The suggestion is that the pope invite those Christian communities that he regards as being in communion (even if imperfect) with the Catholic Church to name representatives to cooperate with him in formulating a statement expressive of the Gospel to be preached to the world today. In the light of the constant emphasis that John Paul II has placed on evangelization this proposal would seem to be very attractive and also demonstrate concrete ways that our real, existing communion might be made visible in the world today.

The presentations given by the representatives from the Oriental Orthodox and the Orthodox Churches focused attention on canonical problems and difficulties in the understanding of the exercise of a universal jurisdiction of primacy. All recognized the positive contributions which the Second Vatican Council made to the healing of relationships between the Churches of the East and the Latin Church. Several concepts in the discussions with the East kept recurring: the meaning of a primacy of honor, the concepts of universal jurisdiction over all churches, of conciliarity, collegiality and synodality.

Archbishop Mesrob Krikorian concluded his presentation with four points for serious reflection. First, the "primacy or the preeminent position of the Bishop of Rome as successor of Peter is a fact. . . ." Second, the question is what kind of preeminence should the primacy of the pope be. Third, in a united church it should be the "privilege of the pope, as the first among equals *(primus inter pares)*, to convoke ecumenical councils and to preside over the assembly, alone or together will other patriarchs. However, the decisions are valid only when the majority of bishops express their agreement and endorse them. . . ." Fourth, "in the light of these considerations, the primacy of the Bishop of Rome is an office of admonishing in the service of unity of the apostolic faith of the church(es), to be exercised in charity and love, without jurisdictional power and authority."

In the presentations of both Metropolitan John of Pergamon and Nicolas Lossky, the relationship of local church to universal Church was highlighted especially in connection with the concepts of conciliarity and synodality. For Metropolitan John it is the eucharistic celebration where we can see the true nature of the communion of the Church expressed. It is here that the theological nature of the problem of primacy is clearly grasped. The ecclesial dignity of each local church must fully be respected. For the Orthodox, the bishop said, primacy is not a matter of jurisdiction and the prerogative of an individual but must be exercised in a synodical context. In the context of pentarchy, papal primacy as universal primacy must be justified for Orthodox to accept it. The "universal primacy of the Church of Rome" means the office of the bishop of Rome be exercised in communion with other churches, namely in collaboration with all of the ecclesial elements (Patriarch, bishops, clergy, and laity).

Lossky in his presentation stressed some of the same points but further articulated the dangers (speaking from the Russian experience) of the autonomy of the local church since local churches do not live in isolation but need one another to be recognized as truly apostolic. To support his argument he cited the thirty-fourth canon of the collection known as the "Apostolic Canons." For Lossky this canon serves as the model of all primacy whereby all bishops of a region must recognize their first one as their head and do nothing without him, while he should equally do nothing without them.

Turning once again to the positions of the reformed traditions, Lukas Vischer underscored the fact that the opinion of the Churches following the Reform of Calvin (who held that the papacy was incompatible with the spirit of the New Testament) excludes a ministry of universal, personal oversight. The basic order of reformed Churches is democratic since it provides for the participation of the whole community in the decision making processes. This is perceived as being in opposition to the order of the Catholic Church. One could feel the reformed tradition's great discomfort with a highly personal model of ministry rather than a participatory, collegial model. The exercise of the ministry of John Paul II as he travels throughout the world only serves to reinforce this uneasiness. The style of the Pope's travels has served to leave the impression that he is the bishop of every local church especially since, on the occasion of these visits, all the signs and symbols of the bishop of these churches is replaced with the bishop of Rome's episcopal coat of arms and motto.

The reformed Churches today have to face the question of whether or not there is a place for a ministry of unity or of a central authority especially in the face of the tendency of these churches to splinter and even to become tight enclaves within a nation or a region. If a ministry of unity of the Church on the worldwide level were to be feasible it would have to be exercised within the context of a collegial body. A constant concern here is the fact that the style of the exercise of this ministry of unity has been, all too often, unilateral. The example of the use of the political style and power of the Holy See was pointed out. Could not other churches be involved in the formulation of statements which touch upon such issues as population growth, the world debt, ecological issues? The perceived misuse of this political power by the popes and the Holy See has only led to a further mistrust of a universal type of primacy within the Church. Vischer suggests that what is needed for the future is some kind of form of structured communion—a forum that would enable the Churches, despite their continuing separation, to meet and exchange views and face their differences.

Erich Geldbach expressed some of the same fears from a Baptist perspective where the overarching concern is the issue of control and the fear of the loss of religious freedom. In some respects he pointed out many of the same dangers that Lossky did in speaking about autonomous congregations. Geldbach indicated the limits of local autonomy "which are determined by the missionary task to spread the Gospel of Christ." "Baptist egalitarianism and congregational power" indicate that unity and any ministry of unity resides in the local church, for which the Holy Spirit, and no individual person, is *vicarius Christi*. Baptists could see the "universal jurisdiction by divine right if it applies only to its own sphere of reference." They might be able to accept the Petrine ministry along the lines of it acting as a spokesperson for the Christian community but this could never be done in isolation, by one person alone. Again the collegial nature of how such a ministry needs to be exercised was emphasized. Another difficult issue arises when one begins to talk about the infallibility of papal statements and declarations which tend to make the ecumenical journey all the more arduous for Baptist participants. Even though there is "very little space to maneuver," Geldbach told his listeners that Baptists need to re-examine their traumatic fear of the papacy. Some space is created by the use of the term "Petrine ministry" rather than papacy because it opens itself to the interpretation of Gregory the Great who saw the ministry as that of service *(servus servorum Dei)*.

Several keen theological insights come from the last Protestant contribution to this symposium offered by Miroslav Volf. At the heart of his reflections lies the fundamental philosophical question of the relationship between the "one" and the "many," a theme particularly dear to metropolitan John. Theologically this gets played out in the formulation of the Trinity and the interrelationship between ecclesial unity and the question of primacy. Let us recall what his thesis is in this regard:

> Since the ecclesial unity is modeled on the trinitarian unity, we can expect the unity of the Church not to be grounded in the preeminence of the one, but in the self-giving love of the many . . . . (1) this is exactly what we find in the New Testament and therefore (2) this is how we ought to theologically understand and institutionally configure "primacy" (180).

This is spelled out as one looks to the New Testament and the manifestation of the Spirit with services and gifts for the common good and the benefit of all. It is the *same* Spirit, the *same* Lord, the *same* God who is active in all, for the benefit of all. Volf argues that in the New Testament we find no particular office of unity (which only appears in the letters of Ignatius of Antioch) as the specific task of the bishop. In the New Testament, it is the Holy Spirit that is the principle of unity (see 1 Cor 1:10-17; Eph 4:3). Volf carefully notes that this fact does not exclude the responsibility of the ordained minister for the unity of the

Church but rather roots it more firmly in the community. The minister is not above the community but is given to the community to "equip the saints" for their particular task of ministry in the world (in this regard see chapter 4 of the Letter to the Ephesians). To apply this then to primacy, Volf states, "the highest level of church leadership should be theologically understood, institutionally configured, and practically exercised in a communal way" (182). When primacy is understood and practiced in this way "it will not only correspond to the Trinity but also function as a wellspring of unity" (184).

Let us bring to a close these reflections "after-the-fact" of the symposium by pointing out what might be the most important element of Jean Tillard's presentation. It serves as a reminder to all Catholics that if we expect to be a credible dialogue partner we need to really examine how we have received the teaching of Vatican II and put it into practice in the day-to-day existence of the Church. He acknowledged the context of the Council's teaching on primacy is that of collegiality. What was left undone by the Council was the further spelling this out in the context of a synodical structure which allowed all elements of the Church to participate fully in the decisions made for the life and mission of the Church in the world.

The Holy Spirit is moving the Churches towards full communion in a world that is seeking unity. The *koinōnia* of Churches is rooted and perceivable in its people, their homes, their local churches. Primacy is the guardian of the common good of the *koinōnia*. Primacy is a gift of God for communion; but primacy is not the only gift for *koinōnia.* In the plan of God primacy is an "instrument . . . for sister churches living in a communion of *agapē* and truth" (194). Referring to *Lumen gentium,* Tillard stated that there must be "respect for all dimensions of episcopal collegiality" in this communion, in which the *"sub"* must not be separated from the *"cum" Petro.* That means, according to Tillard, the "pope's word can only be the word of fraternal consensus *una cum fratribus,* a presidency in the communion of *agapē* and truth. Recalling the words of Gregory the Great, quoted in *Pastor aeternus,* Tillard invited symposium participants to consider the petrine ministry as that office holding the authority (ἐξουσία) it takes to affirm, confirm, strengthen and defend the authority of his brothers with whom he shares responsibility for the *koinōnia.* In this regard he signals three absolutes: the total sufficiency of what has been said in Jesus Christ and transmitted by the apostolic witness; regarding the truth, the mission of the Spirit in all of its entirety and the task of teaching to observe the evangelical Word is entrusted to the apostolic group *as such* (cf. Matt 28:16-20, p. 191f.).

It is my hope that these pages will stimulate further reflection on the complex questions and issues that have been raised in the twelve presentations of the symposium on the "Petrine Ministry and the Unity of the Church" and contained in this volume of essays. For many years the Centro Pro Unione has sought to promote an atmosphere in which serious, open and fraternal dialogue can take place and it has been our honor to have been able to initiate this most important dialogue on the occasion of the centenary of the foundation of the Society of the Atonement (1898–1998).

Index of Names